HAVE YOU
TRULY BEEN
BORN AGAIN
OF WATER AND
THE SPIRIT ?

Dear Readers of This Book:

*W*orldwide websites of

 The New Life Mission

Please find your vernacular websites below.
You can download Christian e-books and request Christian books for free.
Feel free to visit our websites below right now!

A www.nlmafghanistan.com
www.nlmafrikaans.com
www.nlmalbania.com
www.nlmamharic.com
www.nlmangola.com
www.nlmarabemirates.com
www.nlmarabic.com
www.nlmargentina.com
www.nlmarmenia.com
www.nlmaruba.com
www.nlmaustralia.com
www.nlmaustria.com
B www.nlmbahamas.com
www.nlmbahrain.com
www.nlmbangladesh.com
www.nlmbelarus.com
www.nlmbelgium.com
www.nlmbengali.com
www.nlmbenin.com
www.nlmbhutan.com
www.nlmbolivia.com
www.nlmbotswana.com
www.nlmbrasil.com
www.nlmbriton.com
www.nlmbrunei.com
www.nlmbulgalia.com
www.nlmburkinafaso.com
www.nlmburundi.com
C www.nlmcameroon.com
www.nlmcanada.com
www.nlmcebuano.com
www.nlmchichewa.com
www.nlmchile.com
www.nlmchin.com

www.nlmchina.com
www.nlmcolombia.com
www.nlmcongo.com
www.nlmcostarica.com
www.nlmcotedivoire.com
www.nlmcroatia.com
www.nlmczech.com
D www.nlmdenmark.com
www.nlmdioula.com
www.nlmdominica.com
www.nlmdutch.com
E www.nlmecuador.com
www.nlmegypt.com
www.nlmelsalvador.com
www.nlmequatorialguinea.com
www.nlmethiopia.com
F www.nlmfinland.com
www.nlmfrance.com
www.nlmfrench.com
G www.nlmgabon.com
www.nlmgeorgian.com
www.nlmgerman.com
www.nlmgermany.com
www.nlmghana.com
www.nlmgreek.com
www.nlmgrenada.com
www.nlmguatemala.com
www.nlmgujarati.com
H www.nlmhaiti.com
www.nlmhindi.com
www.nlmholland.com
www.nlmhonduras.com
www.nlmhungary.com

Turn over ➤

© Some of these websites may not work because they are still under construction.

Worldwide websites of
🚢 The New Life Mission

I	www.nlm-india.com		www.nlmportugal.com
	www.nlmindonesia.com		www.nlmportuguese.com
	www.nlmiran.com		www.nlmprcongo.com
	www.nlmiraq.com	**Q**	www.nlmqatar.com
	www.nlmisrael.com	**R**	www.nlmromania.com
	www.nlmitaly.com		www.nlmrussia.com
J	www.nlmjamaica.com	**S**	www.nlmsaudiarabia.com
	www.nlmjapan.com		www.nlmserbian.com
	www.nlmjavanese.com		www.nlmshona.com
K	www.nlmkannada.com		www.nlmsingapore.com
	www.nlmkazakhstan.com		www.nlmslovakia.com
	www.nlmkenya.com		www.nlmslovene.com
	www.nlmkhmer.com		www.nlmsolomon.com
	www.nlmkirghiz.com		www.nlmsouthafrica.com
	www.nlmkirundi.com		www.nlmspain.com
	www.nlmkorea.com		www.nlmspanish.com
L	www.nlmlatvia.com		www.nlmsrilanka.com
	www.nlmluganda.com		www.nlmsuriname.com
	www.nlmluo.com		www.nlmswahili.com
M	www.nlmmadi.com		www.nlmswaziland.com
	www.nlmmalagasy.com		www.nlmsweden.com
	www.nlmmalayalam.com		www.nlmswiss.com
	www.nlmmalaysia.com	**T**	www.nlmtagalog.com
	www.nlmmarathi.com		www.nlmtaiwan.com
	www.nlmmauritius.com		www.nlmtamil.com
	www.nlmmexico.com		www.nlmtanzania.com
	www.nlmmindat.com		www.nlmtelugu.com
	www.nlmmizo.com		www.nlmthailand.com
	www.nlmmoldova.com		www.nlmtogo.com
	www.nlmmongolia.com		www.nlmtonga.com
	www.nlmmyanmar.com		www.nlmturkey.com
N	www.nlmnepal.com	**U**	www.nlmuganda.com
	www.nlmnewzealand.com		www.nlmukraine.com
	www.nlmnigeria.com		www.nlmurdu.com
	www.nlmnorthkorea.com		www.nlmusa.com
	www.nlmnorway.com	**V**	www.nlmvenezuela.com
P	www.nlmpakistan.com		www.nlmvietnam.com
	www.nlmpanama.com	**Z**	www.nlmzambia.com
	www.nlmperu.com		www.nlmzimbabwe.com
	www.nlmphilippines.com		www.nlmzou.com
	www.nlmpoland.com		

HAVE YOU TRULY BEEN BORN AGAIN OF WATER AND THE SPIRIT ?

Revised Edition

PAUL C. JONG

Hephzibah Publishing House

A Division of THE NEW LIFE MISSION

SEOUL, KOREA

Have you truly been born again of water and the Spirit?
Copyright © 1999, 2002 by Hephzibah Publishing House
First Published 1999 (Reprinted twelve times)
Revised Edition 2002

Scripture quotations used in this book are from the New *King James Version.*

ISBN 89-8314-035-6
Design by Min-soo Kim
Illustration by Young-ae Kim
Printed in Korea

Hephzibah Publishing House

A Ministry of THE NEW LIFE MISSION
P.O.Box 18 Yang-Cheon Post Office
Yang-Cheon Gu, Seoul, Korea

♠ Website: http://www.nlmission.com
　　　　　http://www.bjnewlife.org
　　　　　http://www.nlmbookcafe.com
♠ E-mail: newlife@bjnewlife.org

Hephzibah Publishing House is a ministry of THE NEW LIFE MISSION founded by Rev. Paul C. Jong in 1991.

THE NEW LIFE MISSION is a non-denominational, nonprofit organization whose main purpose is to preach the words of God to every one. It aims to train disciples of Jesus to spread the gospel of being born again of water and the Spirit.

It has built mission-oriented churches worldwide and published dozens of spiritual books and tapes in many languages.

For more information please call 82-11-1788-2954 or browse its website http://www.nlmission.com, http://www.bjnewlife.org

Thanks

We would like to offer a prayer of thanks to the Lord for giving us the words of salvation and blessing us with the gospel of being born again of water and the Spirit.

Thanks also to all the servants of God, including Rev. Samuel J. Kim and Rev. John K. Shin, who provided invaluable services in the publication of this book; to Mrs. Jungpil Sul for translating it; to brothers and sisters in the Hephzibah Publishing House; and to Elaine Dawe of Kangwon National University and Ross Wallace of THE KOREA TIMES. They have all worked hard on this book. Thank you all again.

I hope and pray that this book and the tapes accompanying it will help many souls to be born again, and I want to give real thanks again to all of those who worked so hard with us.

I sincerely wish that our Lord will permit us to spread the gospel of being born again of water and the Spirit all over the world through those who believe in Jesus.

With undying faith, I thank the Lord.

PAUL C. JONG

Preface

We Must Be Born Again of Water and the Spirit

God, when He created the heavens and the earth in the beginning, also created the eternal worlds, Heaven and hell. He created mankind in His own image, but, since the first man, Adam, sinned before God, all people have to die once. *"And as it is appointed for men to die once, but after this the judgment"* *(Hebrews 9:27).*

The death of our flesh is the passageway to eternal life. Those who are without sin shall enter the eternal world of Heaven and everlastingly enjoy being the children of God, while sinners will be thrown into *"the lake of fire and brimstone" (Revelation 20:10)* and be tormented day and night for all eternity.

Therefore, all of humankind must be born again. We have to be born again through our faiths, be redeemed from all our sins and become righteous. For only then can we enter the eternal Kingdom of Heaven. The Bible says, *"Unless one is born of water and the Spirit, he cannot enter the kingdom of God" (John 3:5).* "To be born again of water and the Spirit" is the only way we can enter the eternal Kingdom of God.

What, then, is this 'water' and 'the Spirit' that allows us to be born again? The 'water' in the Bible refers to 'the baptism of Jesus.'

Why was Jesus, who is God, baptized by John the Baptist? Was it to show His humility? Was it to proclaim Himself the Messiah? No, it wasn't.

When Jesus was baptized by John the Baptist by means of

'the laying on of hands' (Leviticus 16:21), it was *'one Man's righteous act' (Romans 5:18),* which took away all the sins of humankind.

In the Old Testament, God gave Israel the merciful law of redemption. This was so that on the Day of Atonement, all the sins of Israel for that year could be expiated through the High Priest, Aaron, by laying his hands on the head of the 'scapegoat' and passing all the sins onto that scapegoat.

These were the words of revelation, which foretold the sacrifice of eternal atonement. It revealed the truth that all the sins of humanity would be passed onto Jesus all at once, who came in the flesh of a man, according to the will of the Father. And He was baptized by John the Baptist who was the descendant of Aaron and the representative of all humankind.

When Jesus was baptized, He said to John, *"Permit it to be so now, for thus it is fitting for us to fulfill all righteousness" (Matthew 3:15).*

Here, *'for thus'* means 'by the laying on of hands,' in order to pass all the sins of the world onto Jesus, so that all righteousness might be fulfilled for all of us. The word 'righteousness' is *'dikaiosune'* in Greek, and its meaning is "the fairest state" or "to be just in character or deeds with the implication of being righteous or fitting."

Jesus had fulfilled all righteousness for all people through His baptism in a just and fitting manner. Because Jesus took on all the sins of people through His baptism, the next day, John the Baptist testified, *"Behold! The Lamb of God who takes away the sin of the world!" (John 1:29)*

With all the sins of humankind on His shoulders, Jesus walked toward the Cross. He vicariously took the judgment for all the sins He had taken on Himself through His baptism. He died on the Cross, saying, *"It is finished" (John 19:30).* He took all our sins onto Himself and received the complete judgment for them in our place.

The Water, Which Means the Baptism of Jesus, Is the Antitype of Salvation

Therefore, without having 'the faith in the baptism of Jesus,' we cannot be saved. That is why the Apostle Peter declared the water, which means the baptism of Jesus, to be *"an antitype which now saves us" (1 Peter 3:21).*

Today, most people who believe in Jesus do not believe in the baptism of Jesus, the 'water,' but only believe in His death on the Cross. But will this kind of faith save sinners? Can we be redeemed from all our sins by believing only in the blood of Jesus? Can it give us salvation?

No. We cannot be redeemed before God just by believing in Jesus' death on the Cross.

When the people of Israel offered the sacrifice of atonement at the time of the Old Testament, it would not have been correct to kill the sacrificial animal without first laying hands on the head of the animal and passing their sins onto it. Thus, it would be wrong and lawless to believe only in the Cross of Jesus without believing in His baptism.

Therefore, the Apostle Peter said, *"There is an antitype which now saves us, namely baptism, through the resurrection of Jesus Christ" (1 Peter 3:21).*

Just as the people who didn't believe in the great 'water' (the flood) during the time of Noah were destroyed, those who do not believe in the 'water,' the 'baptism of Jesus' now will surely be ruined.

The complete faith that leads us to true salvation is the

faith in Jesus Christ, *"who came by water and blood—Jesus Christ" (1 John 5:6).* We ought to believe in both the baptism and the Cross of Jesus Christ.

The Apostle John said that the correct faith is to believe in *"the witness of the Spirit, the water, and the blood" (1 John 5:8).*

What constitutes true faith is to believe like this. "Jesus is God Himself and He came in the flesh of a man by the Spirit through the body of the Virgin Mary, and He took away all the sins of the world by being baptized at the Jordan by John the Baptist, the representative of all humankind. And Jesus went to the Cross bearing all the sins of the world, and received the vicarious judgment for all of us." Therefore, the gospel cannot be complete without 'the baptism of Jesus,' the 'water,' and no matter how well we believe in Jesus, we can never reach eternal salvation without believing in it.

The Historical Background by Which the True Gospel Was Lost to the Church

Why is it that nowadays, the true 'gospel of the water and the Spirit' has become so rare and the false gospels have instead spread widely throughout the world?

After Jesus was resurrected and ascended to Heaven, the Apostles preached this 'gospel of the water and the blood.' If we read the New Testament carefully, we can see that not only did the writers of the Bible, including Paul, Peter and John, but all the Apostles and the workers of the Early Church, had clearly preached 'the gospel of the water and the Spirit.'

Meanwhile, the devil had been contriving to alter the gospel incrementally and to take away the power of life from the Church. Thus, from the time of the Edict of Milan of 313 A.D., the Christian Church was caught up in a carefully laid trap of the devil. The political powers of the Roman Empire, in exchange for recognizing Christianity as the state religion, were able to attain political stability.

By specifying that "Baptize anyone who entered the church," the Roman Empire maintained its unity over the diversity of its many colonies.

It was the result of these circumstances that caused the recitation of the Apostles' Creed to be substituted as the basis of religious training. Because of that, 'the gospel in strict accordance with the Bible,' in other words, 'the gospel of the water and the Spirit'—which gives us *"the Power, the Holy Spirit and much assurance" (1 Thessalonians 1:5)*—came to be substituted by the false gospel. Just as Satan had planned, the false gospel, allowing no one to be born again, came to prosper throughout the world.

For over a thousand years after the Milan Edict, the Dark Ages of Christianity stifled the whole European world. Although a series of new reformation movements had arisen in many countries, urging people back to 'the Word, Grace and Faith,' none of them had found the true gospel, 'the gospel of the water and the blood.'

This true gospel has been kept alive in the hands of a few who followed the words since the age of the Apostles. Just like a stream that has disappeared into the ground, which springs up again in the lower plains, it surfaced again in the Last Days to be proclaimed throughout the world.

This Is the First Book in This Age to Preach the Gospel of the Baptism of Jesus As It Is Written in the Bible

This is the first book in this age to preach the gospel of the baptism and the blood of Jesus as it is written in the Scriptures. The true gospel clearly tells us that He took away all our sins through His baptism and took over judgment for all our sins on the Cross. I am sure that there is no other book that preaches 'the gospel of the water and the blood' more clearly and faithfully than this one.

In today's world, where the Internet is a valuable tool for the research and discovery of knowledge, I have tried to find some coworkers who know the secret of the baptism of Jesus, and are preaching the true gospel, as it is written in the Bible, who know and preach the secret of the baptism of Jesus by faith. But I have failed so far. Therefore, I have decided to publish this book in English.

When the flood covers the whole world, the water may flow all over the world, but none will be safe to drink. In the same way, there are many so-called 'servants of God' who preach a pseudo-gospel, but there is none who can give us the true life.

The Samaritan woman who drank from the well of Jacob everyday couldn't quench her spiritual thirst, but when she drank the water of life from Jesus, she earned salvation and thus, quenched her thirst immediately and forever.

The water of life in Jesus is flowing in every nook and cranny of this book. Whoever drinks from it will be saved from sin forever. The person will never be bound by sin again, but rather, the living water will flow from him/her and quench the thirst of other souls around him/her.

Let Us Become the Workers of God, the Repairers of the Breach

We are living in an age close to the end of the world. This is the time when the sins of humankind have reached its full measure, and the righteous judgment of God is immanent. Some scientists succeeded to genetically reproduce a sheep, 'Dolly,' and people are almost ready to accept genetically reproduced human beings.

Today, we are building another tower of Babel. The last time when humankind attempted such things, God scattered them all over the earth by confusing their languages. Now is the time when the Great Tribulations, the righteous wraths of God, will soon be poured all over those lost souls who have not yet been born again.

Therefore, I request you to pursue this book carefully. I pray that you may 'be born again of water and the Spirit.' This book preaches the gospel precisely as it is written in the Bible. Therefore, as it is said:

I am sure anyone who peruses this book will not fail to be precisely born again. Jesus our Lord says, *"If you abide in My word, you are my disciples indeed. And you shall know the truth, and the truth shall make you free" (John 8:31-32).* May you get to know the words of truth through this book and be freed from sin and death! May you be redeemed and earn everlasting life in Him!

Let us do the work of the Father together to save the lost souls by preaching 'the gospel of the water and the blood.' I sincerely hope that the true gospel will shine all over the world again. I am sure the true gospel will make you repair the breaches of today's Christian faith with the words of truth.

"Those from among you shall build the old waste places;

you shall raise up the foundations of many generations; and you shall be called the Repairer of the Breach, the Restorer of Streets to Dwell In" (Isaiah 58:12).

Many of you are surely not familiar with the gospel of being born again of the water and the Spirit. So, I have attempted to lay great emphasis on the gospel of the baptism of Jesus and His Cross in every sermon.

If there had been no baptism of Jesus, His death on the Cross would have been meaningless to all of us. These are the reasons why I have stressed His baptism repeatedly.

My purpose is to make it clear to you. Until you are all blessed with the gospel of the water (the baptism of Jesus) and the Spirit, I would like to repeat it for you.

I eagerly expect that all of you come to believe in the gospel of His baptism and the blood in order to be saved from sin. I am sure this book will lead you to be born again of water and the Spirit. ✉

CONTENTS

Part One—Sermons

Part Two—Appendix

SERMON 1

We Must First Know about
Our Sins to Be Redeemed

We Must First Know about Our Sins to Be Redeemed

< Mark 7:8-9 >

"'For laying aside the commandment of God, you hold the tradition of men—the washing of pitchers and cups, and many other such things you do.' And He said to them, 'All too well you reject the commandment of God, that you may keep your tradition.'"

< Mark 7:20-23 >

"And He said, 'What comes out of a man, that defiles a man. For from within, out of the heart of men, proceed evil thoughts, adulteries, fornications, murders, thefts, covetousness, wickedness, deceit, licentiousness, an evil eye, blasphemy, pride, foolishness. All these evil things come from within and defile a man.'"

First, I would like to define what sin is. There are sins defined by God and there are sins defined by man. The word sin, *'hamartia'* in ancient Greek, means to 'miss the mark.' In other words, it is to do something wrong. It is a sin to disobey God's orders. Let's initially observe the human viewpoint of sin.

What is sin?

It is to disobey God's orders.

We recognize sin according through our consciences. However, the human standard of it varies according to one's social background, mental state, given circumstances and conscience.

Thus, the definition of sin varies among different individuals. The same action may or may not be considered sinful depending on each person's own standards. That is why God has given us 613 articles of the Law to be used as the absolute standard of sin.

The diagram below illustrates the sins of humankind.

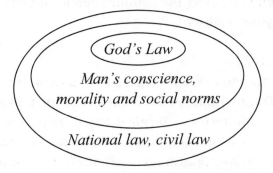

We should never set the standards of sin upon our own consciences based on social norms.

The sins of our consciences are not in accord with what God has defined as sin. Therefore, we should not listen to our consciences, but rather base the standards of sin on God's commandments.

Each of us has our own idea of what sin is. Some consider it to be their shortcomings while others deem it to be based on distorted behavior.

For example, in Korea, people cover their parents' graves with grass and take it upon themselves to care for them until they die. But in one of the primitive tribes in Papua New Guinea, they honor their dead parents by feasting on the body with family members. (I'm not sure if they cook the carcass before eating it.) I believe they want to prevent the body from being eaten by worms. These customs illustrate that the human concept of sin widely varies.

A virtuous deed in one society may be considered barbaric in another society. However, the Bible tells us that it is a sin to disobey God's orders. *"'For laying aside the commandment of God, you hold the tradition of men—the washing of pitchers and cups, and many other such things you do.' And He said to them, 'All too well you reject the commandment of God, that you may keep your tradition'"* (Mark 7:8-9). Our physical appearances are of no importance to God because He looks into the core of our hearts.

One's Own Criterion Is a Sin before God

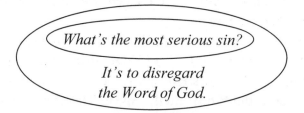

What's the most serious sin?

It's to disregard the Word of God.

To fail to live by His will is a sin before God. It is the same as not believing in His Word. God said that it was a sin to live as the Pharisees, who rejected God's commandments and put more importance on their own traditional teachings. Jesus considered the Pharisees to be hypocrites.

"Which God do you believe in? Do you really revere and exalt Me? You boast about My name, but do you really honor Me?" People only look at outer appearances and disregard His Word. The most serious sin is to disregard His Word. Are you aware of this?

The lawless deeds that originated from our weaknesses are mere iniquities. The mistakes we make and the wrongs we commit due to our imperfections are not fundamental sins, but faults. God distinguishes sins from iniquities. Those who disregard His Word are sinners, even if they have no faults. They are great sinners before God. That is why Jesus scolded the Pharisees.

In the Pentateuch, from Genesis to Deuteronomy, there are commandments that tell us what to do and what not to do. They are the Word of God, His commandments. We may not be able to keep them 100%, but we should recognize them as His commandments. He has given them to us from the beginning and we must accept them as God's Word.

"In the beginning was the Word, and the Word was with God, and the Word was God." Then He said, *"Let there be light, and there was light."* He created everything. Afterwards, He established the Law.

"And the Word became flesh and dwelt among us, and He is the Word" (John 1:1, 14). How, then, does God show Himself to us? He shows Himself through His commandments because God is the Word and the Spirit. Therefore, what do we call the Bible? We call it the word of God.

It is said here, *"For laying aside the commandment of God, you hold the tradition of men."* There are 613 articles in His Law. Do this but don't do that, honor your parents...etc. In Leviticus, it states how men and women should act and what to do when a domestic animal falls into a ditch.... There are 613 such articles in His Law.

Since they are not the words of humans, we should think about them again and again. Though we are unable to keep all of His Law, we should at least acknowledge them and obey

God.

Is there a single passage in God's Word that is not right? The Pharisees laid aside the commandments of God and held the traditions of men over His commandments. The words of their elders carried more weight than the words of God. When Jesus was on earth, this was what He witnessed, and what pained Him the most was that people ignored God's Word.

God has given the 613 articles of the Law to make us realize our sins and to show that He is the Truth, our holy God. Since we are all sinners before Him, we should live by faith and believe in Jesus, who was sent to us from God because of His love for us.

People who lay aside His Word and do not believe in it are sinners. Those who are unable to keep His Word are also sinners, but laying aside His Word is a more serious sin. Those who commit such a severe sin will end up in hell. Not believing in His Word is the gravest sin before Him.

The Reason Why God Gave Us the Law

Why did God give us the Law?

To make us realize our sins and the punishment for them

What was the reason that God gave us the Law? It was to make us realize our sins and return to Him. He gave us the 613 articles of the Law so that we could recognize our sins and be redeemed through Jesus Christ. That's why God gave us the Law.

Romans 3:20 states, *"By the law is the knowledge of sin."* Therefore, we know that God's reason for giving us the Law was not to force us to live by it.

Then, what is the knowledge we gain from the Law? It is that we are too weak to completely obey the Law in its entirety and that we are grave sinners before Him. What do we realize from the 613 articles of His Law? We realize our shortcomings and inability to live by His Law. We recognize that we, the creations of God, are impotent beings, as well as grave sinners before Him. We should all end up in hell according to His Law.

When we realize our sins and the inability to live by His Law, then what do we do? Do we try to become complete beings? No. We must admit that we are sinners, believe in Jesus, be redeemed through His salvation of the water and the Spirit and thank Him.

The reason He gave us the Law was to make us acknowledge our sins and know the punishments for those sins. Hence, we would recognize the impossibility of being saved from hell without Jesus. If we believe in Jesus as our Savior, we will be redeemed. He gave us the Law to lead us to the Savior Jesus.

God created the Law to make us realize how completely sinful we are and to save our souls from such sin. He gave us the Law and sent His only begotten Son, Jesus, to save us by taking all our sins through His baptism. Believing in Him can save us.

We are hopeless sinners who must believe in Jesus to be freed from sin, become His children and return all the glory to God.

We should understand, think and judge through His Word because everything originates from Him. We must also comprehend the truth of redemption through His Word. This is the right and true faith.

What's in the Heart of a Human Being?

What should we do before God?

We should admit our sins and ask God to save us.

Faith should start with God's Word and we should believe in Him through His Word. If not, we will fall into error. That would be the wrong and untrue faith.

When the Pharisees and the scribes saw Jesus' disciples eating bread with dirty hands, they couldn't have reproved them if they had looked at it from the viewpoint of God's Word. The Word tells us that whatever enters a person from the outside cannot defile him/her because it goes through the stomach and exits the body, not affecting heart.

As it is said in Mark 7:20-23, *"And He said, 'What comes out of a man, that defiles a man. For from within, out of the heart of men, proceed evil thoughts, adulteries, fornications, murders, thefts, covetousness, wickedness, deceit, licentiousness, an evil eye, blasphemy, pride, foolishness. All these evil things come from within and defile a man.'"* Jesus said that people are sinners because they are born with sin.

Do you understand what this means? We are born as sinners because we are all Adam's descendants. But we cannot see the truth because we neither accept nor believe in all of His Words. Then, what is inside a human heart?

The above passage states, *"For from within, out of the heart of men, proceed evil thoughts, adulteries, fornications, murders, thefts, covetousness, wickedness, deceit, licentiousness, an evil eye, blasphemy, pride, foolishness."* All kinds of evils come out of people's hearts and defile them.

It is recorded in Psalms, *"When I consider Your heavens, the work of Your fingers, the moon and the stars, which You have ordained, What is man that You are mindful of him, and the son of man that You visit him?"* (Psalms 8:3-4)

Why does God Himself visit us? He visits us because He loves us, created us and took pity on us sinners. He blotted out all our sins and made us His people. *"O Lord, our Lord, How excellent is Your name in all the earth, Heavens!"* King David sang this psalm in the Old Testament when he realized that God would become the Savior of sinners.

In the New Testament, the Apostle Paul repeated the same psalm. It is such an amazing thing that we, God's creations, can become the children of the Creator. It is done only through His compassion for us. This is the love of God.

We should recognize that trying to completely live by the Law of God is an audacious challenge to Him. It is also an arrogant orientation that comes out of our ignorance. It is not right to live outside His love while struggling to keep the Law for oneself and pray desperately for such a life. It is God's will that we should realize ourselves as sinners under the Law and believe in the redemption of the water and the blood of Jesus.

His Word is written in Mark 7:20-23, *"What comes out of a man, that defiles a man. For from within out of the heart of men, proceed evil thoughts, adulteries, fornications, murders, thefts, covetousness, wickedness, deceit, licentiousness, an evil eye, blasphemy, pride, foolishness. All these evil things come from within and defile a man."*

Jesus said that what comes out of a human being, the sins within, defiles him/her. Even the unclean food that God gives cannot defile us. All creations are clean, but only the things that come out of human beings, that is, the sins, defile us. We are all born descendants of Adam. So, with what are we born? We are born with twelve kinds of sins. Is this not right?

Then, can we live without committing sins? We will continue to sin for we are born with sin. Can we stop sinning just because we know the Law? Can we live by the commandments? No.

The more we try to live by the Law, the harder it becomes. We should realize our limitations and give up our past orientations. Then, with humble minds, we can accept the baptism and blood of Jesus, which save us.

All 613 articles of the Law are good and just. But people are sinners from the time they are conceived in their mothers' wombs. When we realize that the Law of God is right, but that we are born as sinners who can never become righteous by ourselves, we come to realize that we need the merciful compassion of God and the redemption of Jesus in the gospel of the water, the blood and the Spirit. When we realize our limitations—that we cannot become righteous by ourselves and we will go to hell for our sins—we cannot but rely on the redemption of Jesus.

We can be delivered. We should know that we are unable to be right or good before God by ourselves. Therefore, we should admit before God that we are sinners who are destined to hell and we can pray for His compassion, "God, please save me from my sins and take pity on me." Then, God will surely meet us in His Word. In this way, we can be delivered.

Let's see the prayer of David. *"That You may be found just when You speak, And blameless when You judge"* (Psalms

51:4).

David knew that he was a mass of sin that was evil enough to be thrown into hell, but he admitted before God, "Lord, if You call me a sinner, I am a sinner. If You call me righteous, I am righteous. If You save me, I will be saved; and if You send me to hell, I will end up in hell."

This is the correct faith and the way to be saved. This is how we should be if we hope to believe in the redemption of Jesus.

We Should Know Exactly What Our Sins Are

Since we are all descendants of Adam, we all have lusts in our hearts. However, what does God tell us? He tells us not to commit adultery even though we have adultery in our hearts. We have murder in our hearts, but what does God tell us? He tells us not to kill. We all defy our parents in our hearts, but He tells us to honor them. We should realize that His Word is right and good, but we all have sin in our hearts.

Is this correct or not? It is absolutely correct. Therefore, what must we do before God? We have to admit that we all are masses of sin and hopeless sinners. It is not right to think that we were righteous yesterday because we did not sin yesterday, but are sinners today because we have committed sins today. We are born as sinners. Whatever we do, we will still be sinners. This is why we should be redeemed through faith in the baptism of Jesus.

We are not sinners because of our deeds: such as committing adultery, murder, theft, adultery...but we are sinners because we were born as sinners. We were born with twelve kinds of sins and since we are born as sinners in the eyes of God, we can never become good by our own efforts. We can only pretend to be good.

We are born with sinful minds, so how can we be righteous even if we don't actually commit these sins? We can never be righteous before God by ourselves. If we claim to be righteous, it is hypocrisy. Jesus called the Pharisees and the scribes *'the hypocritical Pharisees and scribes.'* Humans are born as sinners and they sin before God throughout all their lives.

Anyone claiming that he/she has neither fought nor hit anyone or stolen even a needle from anyone in all his/her life is lying because humans are born as sinners. That person is a liar, a sinner and a hypocrite. This is how God sees him/her.

Every one is a sinner from his/her birth. Even if you don't commit a single sinful act, you are destined for hell. Even if you have kept most of the Law and commandments, you are still a sinner destined to go to hell.

Then, what should we do with such destinies? We must ask for God's compassion and depend on Him to be saved from our sins. If He doesn't save us, then we will go to hell. That is our destiny.

Only those who accept God's Word admit that they were indeed sinners. They also know that they become righteous by faith. So, they know that ignoring and laying aside His Word without recognizing it is the most serious sin. Those who accept His Word are righteous, even though they were previously sinners. They were born again of His Word in His grace and are the most blessed.

Those Who Try to Be Redeemed through Their Works Are Still Sinners

Who are still sinners even after their believing in Jesus?

Those who try to be redeemed through their works

Let's read Galatians 3:10 and 11. *"For as many as are of the works of the law are under the curse; for it is written: 'Cursed is everyone who does not continue in all things which are written in the book of the law, to do them.' But that no one is justified by the law in the sight of God is evident, for 'The Just shall live by faith.'"*

It is said, *"...everyone who does not continue in all things that are written in the book of the law is cursed."* Those who think they believe in Jesus, yet try to be justified by their works are cursed. Where are those who try to be justified by their works? They are under the curse of God.

Why did God give us the Law? He gave us the Law so that we may realize our sins (Romans 3:20). He also wanted us to know that we are complete sinners who are destined for hell.

Believe in the baptism of Jesus, the Son of God, and be born again of water and the Spirit. Then, you will be saved from your sins, become righteous, have eternal life and go to heaven. Have faith in your hearts.

The Most Arrogant Sin in the World

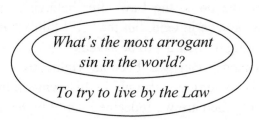

*What's the most arrogant
sin in the world?*

To try to live by the Law

We are blessed by having faith in His blessing. God saves those who have faith in His Word.

But today, among believers, there are many Christians who try to live by His Law. It is commendable that they try to live by the Law, but how is it possible?

We must realize how foolish it is to try to live up to His Law. The more we try, the harder it becomes. He said, *"Faith comes by hearing, and hearing by the word of God."* We need to cast off our arrogance in order to be saved.

We Have to Give Up Our Own Standards to Be Saved

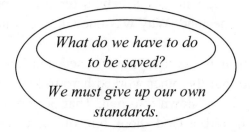

*What do we have to do
to be saved?*

*We must give up our own
standards.*

How can a person be saved? It is possible only when he/she recognizes himself/herself to be a sinner. There are many who have not yet been redeemed because they cannot give up their wrong beliefs and efforts.

God says that those who clench onto the Law are cursed.

Those who believe that they may gradually become righteous by trying to live up to the Law after believing in Jesus are cursed. They believe in God, but they still think that they have to live according to the Law to be saved.

Dear friends, can we become righteous through our works? We become righteous only by believing in the Word of Jesus; and only then are we redeemed. Only by having faith in the baptism of Jesus, His blood, and His Godhead, are we redeemed.

That is why God has prepared the law of faith for us as a way to become righteous. The redemption of the water and the Spirit does not lie in the works of people, but in the faith in the Word of God. God delivered us through faith and that is how God planned and completed our salvation.

Why were those who believed in Jesus not redeemed? Because they did not accept the word of the redemption of the water and the Spirit. But we, who are as imperfect as they were, have been redeemed through our faiths in the Word of God.

If two people were to work on a grindstone, the one left behind would keep on working, even after the other person is taken up. The one who is left behind represents one who has not yet been redeemed. Why was one taken and the other left behind?

The reason is because one listened and believed in the Word of God, but the other worked hard to keep the Law and was eventually cast down into hell. That person was trying to crawl up to God, but God shook him off, as if he/she were a bug crawling up His leg. If a person tries to crawl up to God by trying to keep the Law, he/she will surely be thrown into hell.

That is why we have to be redeemed by faith in the water and the Spirit.

"For as many as are of the works of the law are under the

curse; for it is written, 'Cursed is everyone who does not continue in all things which are written in the book of the law, to do them,'" "But that no one is justified by the law in the sight of God is evident, for 'The just shall live by faith'" (Galatians 3:10-11, Romans 1:17).

Not believing in the Word of God is a sin before Him. In addition, it is also a sin to lay aside God's Word according to one's own standards. We human beings cannot live by His Law because we are all born as sinners and continue to sin all our lives. We sin a little here, a little there, and everywhere we go. We have to realize that we are of the flesh and cannot help but to sin.

A human being is like a big bucket of manure. If we try to carry it around, it will splatter all along the way. We are like that. We keep spilling sin everywhere we go. Can you picture it?

Would you still pretend that you were holy? If you were clearly aware of yourself, you would give up trying in vain to be holy and believe in the water and the blood of Jesus.

Those who are not yet born again need to cast off their stubbornness and admit that they are grave sinners before God. Then, they must return to His Word and discover how He saved them with the water and the Spirit. ✉

SERMON 2

Human Beings Are Born
Sinners

Human Beings Are Born Sinners

< Mark 7:20-23 >
"And He said, 'What comes out of a man, that defiles a man. For from within, out of the heart of men, proceed evil thoughts, adulteries, fornications, murders, thefts, covetousness, wickedness, deceit, licentiousness, an evil eye, blasphemy, pride, foolishness. All these evil things come from within and defile a man.'"

People Are Confused and Live under Their Own Illusions

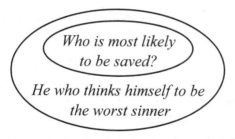

Who is most likely to be saved?

He who thinks himself to be the worst sinner

First of all, I would like to ask you a question. How do you see yourself? Do you think you are good or bad? What do you think?

All people live under their own illusions. You may not be as bad as you think, nor quite as good as you think.

Who, then, do you think will lead a better life of faith? Will it be one who thinks of himself/herself as good? Or one who thinks of himself/herself as bad?

It is the latter. Let me ask you another question. Who is more likely to be redeemed—the one who has committed more sins or the one who has committed only a few sins? The one who admits that he/she has committed countless sins is more likely to be redeemed because the person accepts that he/she is a grave sinner. Such a person can better accept the Word of redemption prepared for him/her by Jesus.

When we really look at ourselves, it is evident that we are merely masses of sin. What are human beings? A person is only *'a seed of evildoers.'* In Isaiah 59, it states that there are all kinds of iniquities in the hearts of people. Therefore, it is clear that people are masses. of sin. However, if we define humankind as a mass of sin, many will disagree. But, defining a person as *'a seed of evildoers'* is the correct definition. If we honestly look at ourselves, it is clearly obvious that we are evil beings. Those who are honest with themselves must arrive at this very same conclusion.

But, it seems that most people refuse to admit that they are indeed masses of sin. Many live comfortably because they do not consider themselves as sinners. Since we are evildoers, we have created a sinful civilization. If it were not true, we would be too ashamed to sin. However, many of us do not feel ashamed while committing sins.

Nevertheless, their consciences know. Everyone has a conscience that tells him/her, "It is shameful." Adam and Eve hid themselves among the trees after they had sinned. Today, many sinners hide themselves behind our vile culture—our culture of sin. They hide themselves among their fellow sinners to avoid the judgment of God.

People are deceived by their own illusions. They think themselves to be more virtuous than others. So, when they hear about some bad news, they cry out in rage, "How can a person do such things? How can a man do that? How can a son do that to his own parents?" They themselves believe that they would not do such things.

Dear friends, it is so hard for you to know yourselves. In order to truly know ourselves, we must first receive the remission of sins. It takes a long time for us to obtain the correct knowledge on our human nature, and there are so many of us who will never find this out until the day they die.

Know Yourself

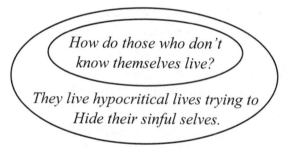

How do those who don't know themselves live?

They live hypocritical lives trying to Hide their sinful selves.

Sometimes we come to encounter such people who really don't know themselves. Socrates said, "Know yourself." However, most of us do not know what is in our hearts: murders, thefts, covetousness, wickedness, deceit, licentiousness, an evil eye....

One who doesn't know oneself has the venom of a serpent on his/her lips but speaks of goodness. The reason for this is because the person doesn't know that he/she was born as an inevitable sinner.

There are so many in this world who do not know their true natures. They have deceived themselves and end up living their lives completely wrapped up in their own deceptions. They do not understand that they are throwing themselves into hell because of their self–deceptions.

People Spill Sin Continuously All Their Lives

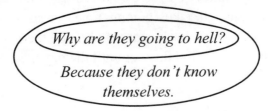

Why are they going to hell?

Because they don't know themselves.

Let's look at Mark 7:21-23. *"For from within, out of the heart of men, proceed evil thoughts, adulteries, fornications, murders, thefts, covetousness, wickedness, deceit, licentiousness, an evil eye, blasphemy, pride, foolishness. All these evil things come from within and defile a man."* The hearts of people are filled with evil thoughts from the day they are conceived.

Let us just imagine that a person's heart is made of glass and filled to the brim with some filthy liquid, namely, our sins. What would happen if this person moved back and forth? The filthy liquid (sin) would of course spill everywhere. As the person moves about, sin would repeatedly spill all over the place.

We, who are but masses of sin, live out our lives just like that. We spill sin wherever we go. We will sin throughout our lives because we are masses of sin.

The problem is that we do not realize that we are masses of sin, or in other words, the seeds of sin. We are masses of sin and have sin in our hearts from the day of our births.

The masses of sin are ready to overflow. However, people do not believe that they are, in fact, inherently sinful. They think that others lead them into sin and therefore, they aren't the ones who are bad.

Even while committing sins, people think that the only requirement needed to wash themselves clean again is for sin to be expunged. They keep wiping up after themselves every time they sin, telling themselves that it is not their own faults. Just because we clean up after ourselves, does it mean that it's okay to keep on spilling? We would have to continually wipe up over and over again.

When a glass is full of sin, it will keep on spilling. There is no use in wiping up the outside. No matter how often we wipe the outside with our virtuous deeds, it is useless, as long as the glass full of sin.

We are born with so much sin that our hearts will never become empty; no matter how much sin we spill along the way. Therefore, we commit sins throughout our lives.

When someone does not realize that he/she is indeed just a mass of sin, he/she continues to hide his/her sinful nature. Sin is in the hearts of all people and it does not go away by wiping the surface clean. When we spill a little sin, we wipe it up with cloth and when we spill again, we wipe it up with a mop...a towel and then a rug.... We keep hoping that if we just keep wiping up the mess over and over again, it will be clean, but it simply spills again and again.

How long do you think this will go on? It goes on until the day a person dies. People act sinfully until their dying days. This is why we have to believe in Jesus to be redeemed. To be redeemed, we need to first know ourselves.

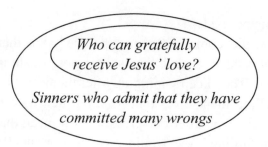

Who can gratefully receive Jesus' love?

Sinners who admit that they have committed many wrongs

Let us say there are two men who can be compared to two glasses full of filthy liquid. Both glasses are full of sin. One looks at himself and says, "Oh, I am such a sinful person." Then, he gives up and goes to find someone who can help him.

But the other one thinks that he is not really evil. He cannot see the mass of sin within himself and thinks that he isn't so sinful. All his life, he keeps on wiping up the spills. He wipes up one side, and then the other side...quickly moving over to the other side....

There are so many who carefully live their lives, trying to have as little sin as possible to avoid spilling it over. But since they still have sin in their hearts, what good does it do? Being careful will not lead them any closer to Heaven. 'Being careful' puts them on the road to hell instead.

Dear friends, 'being careful' only leads to hell. We should take this lesson to heart. When people are careful, their sins may not spill over as much, but they are still sinners.

What is in the heart of humanity? Sin? Immorality? Yes! Evil thoughts? Yes! Is there theft? Yes! Arrogance? Yes!

We cannot help but admit to the fact that we are masses of sin, especially when we see ourselves act sinfully and wickedly, without being taught to do so.

It may not be as evident when we are young. But how is it, as we get older? As we go to high school, college, and so on, we come to realize that all that we have inside us is sin. Is this not true? Honestly speaking, it is impossible to hide our sinful natures. Correct? We cannot help but to spill sin. We then regret, "I shouldn't do this." However, we find it impossible to truly change. Why is that so? Because each of us is born as a mass of sin.

We do not become clean simply by being careful. What we need to know is that we are born as masses of sin in order to be completely redeemed. Only sinners who gratefully accept the redemption prepared by Jesus can be saved,

Those who think, "I haven't done much wrong or sinned very much," do not believe that Jesus took away all their sins and that they are destined for hell. We have to know that each of us has this mass of sin within us because we were all born with it.

If one thought, "I have not done much wrong if only I could be redeemed for this little sin," then would he/she be free of sin afterwards? This can never be the case.

One who can be redeemed knows that he/she is a mass of sin. He/she truly believes that Jesus took away all our sins by being baptized in the Jordan River and that He paid the wages of sins when He died for us.

Whether we are redeemed or not, we all are prone to live in an illusion. We are masses of sin. That is what we are. We can only be redeemed when we believe that Jesus took away all our sins.

God Didn't Redeem Those Who Have 'a Bit of Sin'

Who is the one who deceives the Lord?

The one who asks for forgiveness of daily sins

God doesn't redeem those with only 'a bit of sin.' God does not even glance at those who say, "God, I have only a little bit of sin." The ones He shows pity for are those who say, "God, I am a mass of sin. I am going to hell. Please save me." The complete sinners who say, "God, I would be saved if only You saved me. I cannot pray for repentance anymore because I know I cannot help but to repeatedly sin. Please save me."

God saves those who depend on Him completely. I myself tried to offer daily prayers of repentance too, but prayers of repentance never freed me from sin. So, I knelt down before God and prayed, "God, please take pity on me and save me from all my sins." The ones who pray like this will be saved. They come to believe in the redemption of God and the baptism of Jesus by John the Baptist. They will be saved.

God only delivers those who know themselves to be masses of sin, a brood of evildoers. The ones who say, "I have only committed this tiny sin. Please forgive me for it," are still sinners and God cannot save them. God only saves those who admit to themselves that they are complete masses of sin.

In Isaiah 59:1-2, it is written, *"Behold the Lord's hand is not shortened, that it cannot save; nor His ear heavy, that it cannot hear. But your iniquities have separated you from your God; and your sins have hidden His face from you, so that He will not hear."*

Because we are born as masses of sin, God cannot look upon us fondly. It is not because His hand is shortened, His ear is heavy, or that He cannot hear us asking for His forgiveness.

God tells us, *"Your iniquities have separated you from Me; and your sins have hidden My face from you, so that I will not hear."* Because we have so much sin in our hearts, we cannot enter Heaven, even if the doors are wide open.

If we, who are but masses of sin, asked for forgiveness every time we sinned, God would have to repeatedly kill His Son. God does not want to do this. He says, "Do not come to Me everyday with your sins. I sent you My Son to redeem you from all your sins. All you have to do is understand how He took away your sins and accept that it is the truth. Then, believe in the gospel of the water and the Spirit to be saved. This is the greatest love I have given you, my creations."

This is what He tells us. "Believe in My Son and receive the remission of your sins. I, your God, sent My own Son to atone for all your sins and iniquities. Believe in My Son and be saved."

Those who do not know themselves to be masses of sin ask His forgiveness for their every little sin. They go before Him without knowing the terrible weight of their sins and just pray, "Please forgive this tiny bit of sin. I will never do it again."

They also try to deceive Him with such prayers. We do not commit sin just once, but do so continually until we die. We would have to keep asking for forgiveness until the very last day of our lives, because we cannot stop sinning and our flesh serves the law of sin until we die.

Being forgiven for one little sin cannot solve the problem of sin because we commit countless sins every day. So, the only way we can be free of sin is by passing all our sins onto

Jesus.

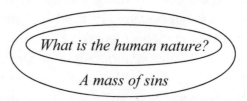

The Bible enumerates the sins of human beings: *"For your hands are defiled with blood, and your fingers with iniquity; your lips have spoken lies, your tongue has muttered perversity. No one calls for justice, nor does any plead for truth. They trust in empty words and speak lies; they conceive evil and bring forth iniquity. They hatch vipers' eggs and weave the spider's web; he who eats of their eggs dies, and from that which is crushed a viper breaks out. Their webs will not become garments, nor will they cover themselves with their works; their works are works of iniquity, and the act of violence is in their hands. Their feet run to evil, and they make haste to shed innocent blood; their thoughts are thoughts of iniquity; wasting and destruction are in their paths. The way of peace they have not known, and there is no justice in their ways; they have made themselves crooked paths; whoever takes that way shall not know peace"* (Isaiah 59:3-8).

People's fingers are defiled with iniquity and all they do throughout their lives is sinful. Everything they do is evil. And our tongues *'have spoken lies.'* All the things that come out of our mouths are lies.

"When a devil speaks a lie, he speaks from his own resources" (John 8:44). Those who are not born again like to say, "I am telling you the truth.... I am really telling you. What I am saying is the truth...." However, everything that they say is nevertheless a lie. It is as it is written. *"When a devil speaks a lie, he speaks from his own resources."*

People put their trust in empty words and speak lies. People conceive evils and bring forth iniquities. They hatch vipers' eggs and weave spiders' webs. God says, *"He who eats of their eggs dies, and from that which is crushed a viper breaks out."* He says that there are vipers' eggs in your heart. Vipers' eggs! There is evil in your heart. That's why we have to be redeemed by believing in the gospel of the water and the blood.

Whenever I begin to talk about God, there are those who say, "Oh, dear! Please don't talk to me about God. Every time I try to do something, sin spills out of me. It just floods out. I can't even take a step without spilling sin all over the place. I can't help it. I am too full of sin. I am quite hopeless. So don't even talk to me about the holy God."

This person knows for sure that he/she is just a mass of sin, but does not know that God has saved him/her completely through the gospel of His love. Only those who know themselves to be masses of sin can be saved.

In fact, everyone is like that. Everyone continuously spills sin everywhere he/she goes. Sin just overflows because all people are masses of sin. The only way for us to be saved from such an existence is through the power of God. Is it not simply amazing? Those who spill sin whenever they are upset, happy, or even comfortable can be saved only through our Lord Jesus Christ. Jesus came to save us.

He has completely blotted out all your sins. Admit that you are a mass of sin and be saved. ✉

SERMON 3

If We Do Things by the
Law, Can It Save Us?

If We Do Things by the Law, Can It Save Us?

< Luke 10:25-30 >

"And behold, a certain lawyer stood up and tested Him, saying, 'Teacher, what shall I do to inherit eternal life?' He said to him, 'What is written in the law? What is your reading of it?' So he answered and said, 'You shall love the Lord your God with all your heart, with all your soul, with all your strength, and with all your mind, and your neighbor as yourself.' And He said to him, 'You have answered rightly; do this and you will live.' But he, wanting to justify himself, said to Jesus, 'And who is my neighbor?' Then Jesus answered and said: 'A certain man went down from Jerusalem to Jericho, and fell among thieves, who stripped him of his clothing, wounded him, and departed, leaving him half dead.'"

What's human's biggest problem?

They live with many mistaken illusions.

Luke 10:28, *"Do this and you will live."*

People live with many mistaken illusions. It seems that they are especially vulnerable in this respect. They seem to be intelligent but are easily deceived and remain unaware of their evil sides. We are born without knowing ourselves, but we still live as if we do. Since people do not know themselves, the Bible repeatedly tells us that we are sinners.

People talk about the existence of their own sins. It seems that people are incapable of doing good, however, they are inclined to characterize themselves as good. They boast of their good works and show off, though they say they are sinners with their lips.

They don't know that they neither have good in them nor the ability to do good, so they try to deceive others and sometimes even deceive themselves. "Come on, we can't be completely evil. There's got to be some good inside of us."

Consequently, they look at others and tell themselves, "Gosh, I wish he hadn't done that. It would have been better for him if he hadn't. He would have been much better off if he talked like this. I think it is better for him to preach the gospel in such and such a way. He was redeemed before me, so I think he should act more like one who has been redeemed. I was redeemed just recently, but if I learn more, I will do much better than he does."

They sharpen the knives in their hearts whenever they are hurt. "You just wait. You will see that I am unlike you. You may think that you are ahead of me now, but just you wait. It is written in the Bible that those who come last will be first. I know it applies to me. Wait and I will show you." People deceive themselves.

Even though he would react the same way if he were in the other person's place, he still judges him. When he stands at the pulpit, he suddenly finds himself stuttering helplessly because he is over conscious of his attire. When asked if people have the ability to do good, most people say by their lips that they don't. But in their hearts, they are under the illusion that they themselves have the ability. So, they try hard to be virtuous until they die.

They think that they have 'goodness' in their hearts and that they have the ability to do good. They also believe that they themselves are good enough. Regardless of how long they have been religious, especially among those who have achieved greater progress in the service of God, they think, 'I can do this and that for the Lord.'

But if we take the Lord out of our lives, can we really do good? Is there good in humanity? Can we really live doing good works? Human beings do not have the ability to do good. Whenever they try to do things on their own, they commit sin. Some push Jesus aside after believing in Him and try to be good on their own. There's nothing but evil in all of us, so we can only practice evil. By ourselves (even those who have been saved), we can only sin. It is the reality of our flesh.

In our praise book, *'Praise the Name of Jesus,'* there is a song that goes like this, *"♪Without Jesus we only stumble. We are as worthless as a ship that crosses the sea without the sail♪."* Without Jesus, we can only sin because we are evil beings. We have the ability to do righteous works only after being saved.

The Apostle Paul said, *"For the good that I will to do, I do not do; but the evil I will not to do, that I practice" (Romans 7:19).* If a person is with Jesus, it doesn't matter, but when he/she has nothing to do with Him, he/she tries to do good deeds before God. However, the more the person tries, the more he/she practices evil.

Even King David had the same innate nature. When his country was peaceful and prosperous, one evening, he went up to the roof for a stroll. There, he saw a tempting picture and fell for sensual pleasure. What was he like when he had forgotten the Lord? He was truly evil. He committed adultery with Bathsheba and killed Uriah, her husband, but he couldn't see the evil in himself. He made excuses for his actions instead.

Then one day, the prophet Nathan came to him and said, *"There were two men in one city, one rich and the other poor. The rich man had numerous flocks and herds. But the poor man had nothing except one little lamb. And a traveler came to the rich man, who refused to take from his own flock and from his own herd but took the poor man's lamb and prepared it for the man who had come to him"* (2 Samuel 12:1-4).

David said, *"The man who has done this shall surely die!"* His anger was greatly aroused, so he said, "He has so many of his own; he could surely take one of them. But instead, he took the poor man's only lamb to prepare food for his guest. He should die!" Then, Nathan told him, *"You are the man."* If we do not follow Jesus and be with Him, even the born-again can do such evil things.

It is the same for all people, even the faithful. We always stumble and practice evil without Jesus. So we are thankful again today that Jesus saved us, regardless of the evil in us. *"♪I want to rest under the shade of the Cross♪"* Our hearts rest under the shade of the redemption of Christ, but if we leave the shade and look at ourselves, we can never rest.

God Gave Us the Righteousness of Faith before the Law

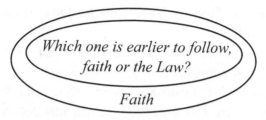

Which one is earlier to follow, faith or the Law?

Faith

The Apostle Paul said that God gave us the righteousness of faith from the beginning. He gave it to Adam and Eve, Cain and Abel, Seth and Enoch, Noah, Abraham, Isaac and finally to Jacob and his twelve sons. Even without the Law, they became righteous before God through the righteousness that came from the faith in His Word. They were blessed and given rest through the faith in His Word.

Time passed and Jacob's descendants lived in Egypt as slaves for 400 years because of Joseph. Then, God led them out through Moses into the land of Canaan. However, during the 400 years of slavery, they had forgotten the righteousness of faith.

So God let them cross the Red Sea through His miracle and led them into the wilderness. When they reached the wilderness of Sin, He gave them the Law at Mount Sinai. He gave them the Law, which contained the Ten Commandments and the 613 detailed articles. God declared, *"I am the Lord your God, the God of Abraham, the God of Isaac, the God of Jacob. Let Moses come up to Mount Sinai, and I will give you the law."* Then, He gave Israel the Law.

He gave them the Law so that they would *'have knowledge of sin' (Romans 3:20)*. It was to inform them about what He liked and disliked and to reveal His righteousness and holiness.

All the people of Israel who had been enslaved in Egypt for 400 years crossed the Red Sea. They had never met the God of Abraham, the God of Isaac and the God of Jacob. They didn't know Him.

While they were living as slaves for those 400 years, they had forgotten the righteousness of God. At that time, they didn't have a leader. Jacob and Joseph were their leaders, but they had passed away long ago. It seems that Joseph failed to pass the faith onto his sons, Manasseh and Ephraim.

Therefore, they needed to find their God again and meet Him because they had forgotten His righteousness. We have to bear in mind that God gave them the righteousness of faith first and then gave them the Law, after they had forgotten the faith. He gave them the Law to return them to Him.

To save Israel and to make them His people, He told them to be circumcised.

His purpose in calling them was to let them know that He existed by establishing the Law and secondly, to let them know that they were sinners before Him. God wanted them to come before Him and become His people by being redeemed through the sacrificial system that He had given them. And He made them His people.

The people of Israel were redeemed through the sacrificial system of the Law by believing in the Messiah who was to come. But the sacrificial system had also faded away with time. Let's see when that was.

In Luke 10:25, a certain lawyer who tested Jesus is mentioned. The lawyer was a Pharisee. The Pharisees were extreme conservatives who tried to live up to God's Word. They tried to protect the country first and then live by God's Law. Then, there were also the Zealots, who were very impetuous and tended to resort to violence in order to achieve their vision, the independence of Israel from Rome.

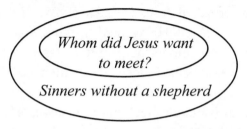

Whom did Jesus want to meet?

Sinners without a shepherd

There are some religious figures like them even today. They lead social movements with slogans like 'save the oppressed people of the world.' They believe that Jesus came to save the poor and oppressed. So, after learning theology in seminaries, they take part in politics, and try to 'deliver the deprived' in every field of society.

They are the ones who insist, "Let us all live by the holy and merciful Law...live up to the Law, by His Words." But they don't realize the actual meaning of the Law. They try to live by the letter of the Law while not recognizing the divine revelation of the Law.

Therefore, we can say that there were no prophets, servants of God, in Israel for about 400 years before Christ. Because of this, they became a flock of sheep without a shepherd.

They neither had the Law nor a true leader. God didn't reveal Himself through the hypocritical religious leaders of that time. The country had become a colony of the Roman Empire. So, Jesus said to those people of Israel who followed Him into the wilderness that He would not send them away hungry. He took pity on the flock without a shepherd because there were many who were suffering at that time.

The lawyers and others in such positions were essentially the ones who had vested privileges; the Pharisees were of the orthodox lineage of Judaism. They were very proud.

This lawyer asked Jesus in Luke 10:25, *"What shall I do to inherit eternal life?"* He seemed to think that there was no one better than him among the people of Israel. So this lawyer (one who had not been redeemed) challenged Him, saying, *"What shall I do to inherit eternal life?"*

The lawyer is but a reflection of ourselves. He asked Jesus, *"What shall I do to inherit eternal life?"* Jesus replied, *"What is written in the law? What is your reading of it?"*

So he answered, *"You shall love the Lord your God with all your heart, with all your soul, with all your strength, and with all your mind,"* and *"love your neighbor as yourself."*

And He said to him, *"You have answered rightly; do this and you will live."* Jesus told him, *"You have answered rightly; do this and you will live."*

He challenged Jesus while not knowing himself to be evil, a lump of sin who could never do good. So Jesus asked him, *"What is written in the law? What is your reading of it?"*

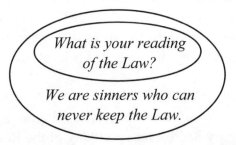

"What is your reading of it?" With this passage, Jesus asks how one, including you and me, knows and understands the Law.

As many people do nowadays, this lawyer also thought that God gave him the Law for him to keep. So he answered, *"Love the Lord your God with all your heart, with all your soul, with all your strength, and with all your mind, and your neighbor as yourself."*

The Law was without fault. He gave us the perfect Law. He told us to love the Lord with all our hearts and souls, with all our strength and minds and to love our neighbors as ourselves. It is right for us to love our God with all our hearts and strength, but it is a holy commandment that can never be kept.

"What is your reading of it?" means that the Law is right and correct, but how do you understand it? The lawyer thought that God gave it for him to obey. However, the Law of God was given to us so that we might realize our shortcomings, by completely exposing our iniquities. "You have sinned. You killed when I told you not to kill. Why did you disobey Me?"

The Law exposes the sins in people's hearts. Let's suppose that on my way here, I saw some ripe melons in the field. God warned me by the Law, "Don't pick those melons to eat. It will shame Me if you do." "Yes, Father." "The field belongs to Mr. so and so, therefore, you should never pick them." "Yes, Father."

The moment we hear that we should never pick them, we feel an inclination to pick them. If we push down a spring, it bounces back up in reaction. The sins of people are just like that.

God told us to never do evil deeds. God can say that because He is holy, complete and has the ability to do so. On the other hand, we can 'never' not sin and 'never' be purely good. We 'never' have good in our hearts. The Law is stipulated with the word 'never'. Why? Because people have lusts in their hearts. We cannot help but to act on our lusts. We commit adultery because we have adultery in our hearts.

We should read the Bible carefully. When I first tried, I analyzed the Word to the letter. I read that Jesus died on the

Cross for me and couldn't stop the tears from flowing. I was such an evil person and He died on the Cross for me.... My heart ached so terribly that I believed in Him. Then I thought, 'If I'm going to believe, then I'm going to believe according to the Word.'

When I read Exodus 20, it said, *"You shall have no other gods before Me."* I prayed in repentance according to this commandment. I searched my memory to recall if I had ever had other gods before Him, called His name in vain, or if I had ever bowed before other gods. I realized that I had bowed to other gods many times during the rituals in honor of my ancestors. I had committed the sin of having other gods.

So I prayed in repentance, "Lord, I have worshiped idols. I have to be judged for it. Please forgive my sins. I shall never do it again." Afterwards, one sin seemed to be taken care of.

I then tried to recollect if I had ever called His name in vain. Then, I remembered that when I first started to believe in God, I smoked. My friends told me, "Aren't you bringing shame to God by smoking? How can a Christian smoke?"

That's the same thing as calling His name in vain, isn't it? So I prayed again, "Lord, I called Your name in vain. Please forgive me. I'll quit smoking." So I tried to quit smoking but continued to light up, on and off for a year. It was really hard, almost impossible to quit smoking. But at last, I managed to quit smoking completely. I felt that another sin had been dealt with.

The next one was *"Keep the Sabbath day holy."* This meant that I shouldn't do other things on Sundays; work or earn money.... So I stopped that too.

Then there was "Honor your father and your mother." I could honor them when I was away, but there was a source of heartache when I was near. "Oh my goodness, I have sinned before God. Please forgive me, Lord." I prayed in repentance.

But I couldn't honor my parents anymore because they were both dead by then. What could I do? "Lord, please forgive this worthless sinner. You died on the Cross for me." How thankful I was!

This way, I thought that I had dealt with my sins one by one. There were other laws such as not to kill, not to commit adultery, not to covet.... Until the day I realized I hadn't kept even a single one, I prayed all night every night. But you know, praying in repentance is not really enjoyable. Let's talk about it.

When I thought about Jesus' crucifixion, I was able to sympathize how painful it was. And He died for us who could not live up to His words. I cried all night thinking how He loved me and thanked Him for giving me real pleasure.

My first year of attending church was generally quite easy but for the next couple of years it became more and more difficult for me to cry in repentance because I had to think much harder for the tears to flow since I did it so often.

When the tears still did not come, often I went to pray in the mountains and fasted for 3 days. Then, the tears came back. I was soaked in my tears, came back to society, and cried in the church.

People around me said, "You have become so much holier with your prayers in the mountains." But the tears inevitably dried up again. It became really hard the third year. I would think of the wrongs I had done to my friends and fellow Christians and cry again. After 4 years of this, the tears dried up again. There were tear glands in my eyes, but they no longer worked.

After 5 years, I couldn't cry, no matter how hard I tried. My nose started to run. After a couple of more years of this, I became disgusted with myself, so God made me turn to the

Bible again.

The Law Is for the Knowledge of Sin

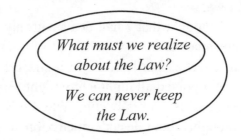

What must we realize about the Law?

We can never keep the Law.

In Romans 3:20, we read, *"By the law is the knowledge of sin."* At first, I considered this verse to be merely a personal message to the Apostle Paul and only tried to believe in the words that I preferred. But after my tears dried up, I couldn't continue my religious life of faith.

So, I sinned repeatedly and found out that I had sin in my heart and that it was impossible to live by the Law. I couldn't bear it, but I also couldn't discard the Law because I believed that it was given to be obeyed. In the end, I became a lawyer, like those mentioned in the Scripture. It became so difficult for me to continue a life of faith.

I had so much sin that, while reading the Law, I began to realize those sins whenever I violated each of the Ten Commandments in my heart. Sinning in the heart is also committing sin, and I had unwittingly become a believer in the Law.

When I kept the Law, I was happy. But when I couldn't keep the Law, I became miserable, irritated and sad. Eventually, I became desperate over it all. How smooth it could've been if I were taught from the beginning the very true knowledge of the Law like this, "No, no. There's another meaning to the Law. It shows you that you are a lump of sin; you have love for money, the opposite sex and for things that are beautiful to look at. You have things that you love more than God. You want to follow the things of the world. The Law has been given to you, not to keep, but to recognize yourself as a sinner with evil in your heart."

If only someone had taught me the truth then, I would not have had to suffer for 10 years. Thus, I had lived under the Law for 10 years before I came to this realization.

The fourth commandment is *"Remember the Sabbath day, to keep it holy."* That means that we should not work on the Sabbath. They teach that we should walk, not ride if we are traveling far distances on Sunday. I thought that it was more appropriate and honorable to walk to the place where I was to preach. After all, I was about to preach the Law. Thus, I felt that I had to practice what I preached. It was so difficult that I was about to give up.

As it is recorded here, *"What is your reading of it?"* I didn't understand this question and suffered for 10 years. The lawyer misunderstood it as well. He thought that if he obeyed the Law and lived carefully, he would be blessed before God.

But Jesus told him, *"What is your reading of it?"* The man answered according to his legalistic faith. And then He said to the man, "Yes, you answered right; you are taking it as it is written. Try and keep it. You will live if you do, but die if you don't. The wages of sin is death. You will die if you don't." (The opposite of life is death, isn't it?)

But the lawyer still didn't understand. This lawyer is like every one of us, you and me. I studied theology for 10 years. I tried everything, read everything and did everything: fasting, having illusions, speaking in tongues.... I read the Bible for 10 years and expected to accomplish something. But spiritually, I was still a blind man.

That is why a sinner must meet someone who can open his/her eyes, and that someone is our Lord Jesus. Then, one can realize that "Aha! We can never keep the Law. No matter how hard we may try to keep the Law, we will only die while desperately trying. But Jesus came to save us with the water and the Spirit! Hallelujah!" The water and the Spirit can redeem us. It is the grace, the gift of God. So we praise the Lord.

I was lucky enough to graduate from the hopeless line of legalism, but some spend their whole lives studying theology in vain and never realize the truth until the day they die. Some people believe for decades or from generation to generation, but are never born again.

We graduate from being a sinner when we realize that we can never keep the Law, then stand before Jesus and listen to the gospel of the water and the Spirit. When we meet Jesus, we graduate from all judgments and damnation. We are the worst sinners, but we become righteous because He saved us by the water and the blood.

Jesus told us that we could never live in His will. He told this to the lawyer, but he did not understand. So Jesus told him a story to help him understand.

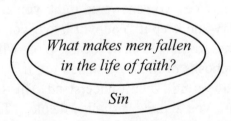

"A certain man went down from Jerusalem to Jericho, and fell among thieves, who stripped him of his clothing,

wounded him, and departed, leaving him half dead" (Luke 10:30). Jesus told the lawyer this parable to awaken him from the fact that he suffered all his life, just as this man was beaten by thieves and almost died.

A man went down from Jerusalem to Jericho. Jericho represents the secular world while Jerusalem represents the city of religion; the city of faith, populated with the boasters of the law. This story tells us that if we believe in Christ in just a religious way, we will be ruined.

"A certain man went down from Jerusalem to Jericho, and fell among thieves, who stripped him of his clothing, wounded him, and departed, leaving him half dead." Jerusalem was a big city with a large population. There was a high priest, a host of priests, Levites and many outstanding men of religion there. There were many who knew the Law well. There, they tried to live up to the Law, but eventually failed and headed for Jericho. They kept falling into the world (Jericho) and could not avoid meeting thieves.

The man also met thieves on the way from Jerusalem to Jericho and was stripped of his clothes. *'To be stripped of his clothes'* means that he lost his righteousness. It is impossible for us to live by the Law, to live up to the Law. The Apostle Paul said in Romans 7:19-20, *"For the good that I will to do, I do not do; but the evil I will not to do, that I practice. Now if I do what I will not to do, it is no longer I who do it, but sin that dwells in me."*

I wish I could do good and live in His words. But in the heart of a man are evil thoughts, adulteries, fornications, murder, thefts, covetousness, wickedness, deceit, licentiousness, an evil eye, blasphemy, pride, and foolishness (Mark 7:21-23).

Because they are in our hearts and come out now and then, we do what we will not to do and we do not do what we should do. We keep repeating those evils in our hearts. What the devil has to do is to give us only a small stimulus to sin.

The Sins within the Heart of All Humankind

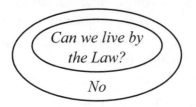

It is said in Mark 7, *"There is nothing that enters a man from outside which can defile him; but the things which come out of him those are the things that defile a man."*

Jesus is telling us that there are evil thoughts, adulteries, fornications, murder, thefts, covetousness, wickedness, deceit, licentiousness, and an evil eye, blasphemy, pride, and foolishness in the heart of a man.

We all have murder in our hearts. There is no one who does not murder. Mothers yell at their children, "No. Don't do that. I told you not to do that, damn you. I told you over and over not to do that. I'm going to kill you if you do that again. I said don't do that." That is murder. You might have killed your children in your mind with your thoughtless words.

Our children must be alive because they run away from us so swiftly; but if we had let out all our anger on them, we may have killed them. Sometimes we scare ourselves. "Oh my God! Why did I do that?" We look at the bruises after hitting our children and think that we must have been crazy to do that. We cannot but act that way because we have murder in our hearts.

So, *'I do what I will not to do'* means that we do evil because we are evil. It is so easy for Satan to tempt us to sin.

Let's say that a man who has not been redeemed sat in a hut for 10 years, facing a wall and meditating like Sungchol, the late great Korean monk. It is fine while he is sitting with his face to the wall, but someone has to bring him food and take away his excrement.

He has to have contact with someone. It would not be a problem if it was a man, but let's suppose it was a beautiful woman. If he happened to see her by chance, all of the time he spent sitting would have been in vain. He may think, "I should not commit adultery; I have it in my heart, but I have to blot it away. I have to drive it out. No! Get out of my mind!"

But his determination is evaporated the moment he sees her. After the woman leaves, he looks into his heart. 5 years of his ascetic exercises turns into nothing, all for naught.

It is so simple for Satan to take away a person's righteousness. All that Satan has to do is give him/her a little push. When a person struggles not to sin without being redeemed, he/she keeps falling into sin instead. That person may pay the tithe faithfully every Sunday, fast for 40 days, offer 100 days of dawn prayers...but Satan tempts and deceives him/her with the seemingly good things in life.

"I would like to give you an important position in the company, but you are a Christian and you cannot work on Sundays, can you? It is such a great position. Maybe you could work 3 Sundays and go to church just once a month. Then, you would enjoy such high prestige and have a big fat paycheck. How about it?" At this, probably 100 out of 100 people would be bought.

If that doesn't work, Satan plays another trick on people who are easily trapped in lust for women. Satan puts a woman in front of him and he falls head over heels in love, forgetting God in an instant. That is how the righteousness of man is stripped.

If we try to live by the Law, all we have in the end are the wounds of sin, pain and spiritual poverty; we lose all righteousness. *"Went down from Jerusalem to Jericho, and fell among thieves, who stripped him of his clothing, wounded him, and departed, leaving him half dead."*

This means that though we may try to stay in Jerusalem by living by the will of Holy God, we will stumble time after time because of our weaknesses and will eventually be ruined.

You may still pray in repentance before God. "Lord, I have sinned. Please forgive me; I shall never do it again. I promise you that this will really be the last time. I beg and implore you to forgive me just this once."

But it never lasts. People cannot live in this world without sinning. They may be able to avoid it a couple of times, but it would be impossible not to sin again. So, we cannot help but to repeatedly commit sins. "Lord, please forgive me." If this goes on, they will drift away from the church and their religious lives. They drift away from God because of their sins and eventually end up in hell.

To travel to Jericho means to fall into the secular world; getting closer to the world and farther away from Jerusalem. In the beginning, Jerusalem is still closer, but as the cycle of sinning and repenting is repeated, we find ourselves standing in the downtown of Jericho; fallen deeply into the world.

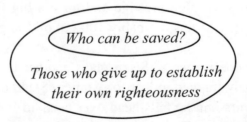

Who did the man meet on his way to Jericho? He met

thieves. One who doesn't even know and live by the Law lives a life similar to an abandoned dog. He/she drinks, falls asleep anywhere and urines anywhere. This dog wakes up the next day and drinks again. An abandoned dog would eat its own excretion. That's why such a person is called a dog. He/she knows not to drink, yet does so and repents the next morning, repeating the process over and over again.

It is like the man who met thieves on the way to Jericho. He is left behind, wounded and almost dead. It means that there's only sin in his heart. This is what a human is.

People believe in Jesus while trying to live by the Law in Jerusalem, the religious community, but are left behind with only sin in their hearts. All they have to show for their religious lives are the wounds of sin. Those with sin in their hearts are thrown into hell in the end. They know it, but don't know what to do. Haven't you and I been in a similarly religious city too? Yes. We were there all the same.

The lawyer who misunderstood the law of God would struggle all his life, but end up in hell, wounded. He is one of us, you and me.

Only Jesus can save us. There are so many intelligent people around us and they constantly brag about what they know. They all pretend to live by the Law of God and aren't honest with themselves. They cannot call a spade a spade, but are always bent on grooming their outer appearances to look faithful.

Among them are sinners on the way to Jericho, the ones who are beaten up by thieves and left almost dead. We have to know how fragile we are before God.

We should admit before Him, "Lord, I will go to hell if You do not save me. Please save me. I will go wherever You want, whether it hails or storms, if I can only hear the true gospel. If You leave me alone, I will go to hell. I beg You to save me."

Those who know that they are heading for hell and give up trying to pursue their own righteousness, while hanging on to the Lord, are the ones who can be saved. We can never be saved by our own efforts.

We must understand that we are like the man who fell among thieves. ✉

SERMON 4

The Eternal Redemption

The Eternal Redemption

< John 8:1-12 >

"But Jesus went to the Mount of Olives. But early in the morning He came again into the temple, and all the people came to Him; and He sat down and taught them. Then the scribes and Pharisees brought to Him a woman caught in adultery. And when they had set her in the midst, they said to Him, 'Teacher, this woman was caught in adultery, in the very act. Now Moses, in the law, commanded us that such should be stoned. But what do You say?' This they said, testing Him, that they might have something of which to accuse Him. But Jesus stooped down and wrote on the ground with His finger, as though He did not hear. So when they continued asking Him, He raised Himself up and said to them, 'He who is without sin among you, let him throw a stone at her first.' And again He stooped down and wrote on the ground. Then those who heard it, being convicted by their conscience, went out one by one, beginning with the oldest even to the last. And Jesus was left alone, and the woman standing in the midst. When Jesus had raised Himself up and saw no one but the woman, He said to her, 'Woman, where are those accusers of yours? Has no one condemned you?' She said, 'No one, Lord.' And Jesus said to her, 'Neither do I condemn you; go and sin no more.' Then Jesus spoke to them again, saying, 'I am the light of the world. He who follows Me shall not walk in darkness, but have the light of life.'"

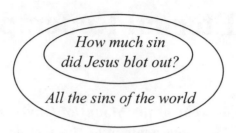

How much sin did Jesus blot out?

All the sins of the world

Jesus gave us eternal redemption. There is no one in this world who cannot be redeemed if anyone believes in Jesus as his/her Savior. He redeemed us all. If there is a sinner who agonizes over his/her sins, it is because of the person's misconception of how Jesus has delivered him/her from all sins with His baptism and crucifixion.

We should all know and believe in the secret of salvation. Jesus took over all our sins with His baptism and has born the judgment for our sins by dying on the Cross.

You should believe in the salvation of the water and the Spirit; the eternal redemption from all sins. You should believe in His great love that has already made you righteous. Believe in what He has done for your salvation at the Jordan river and on the Cross.

Jesus knew about all our concealed sins, too. Some people have a misconception about sin. They think that some sins cannot be redeemed. Jesus has redeemed all sins, every single one of them.

There is not a sin in this world that He has left out. Because He has blotted out all the sins in this world, the truth is that there are no more sinners. Do you realize that the gospel has redeemed all your sins, even your future sins? Believe in it and be saved, and give all of the glory to God.

The Woman Who Was Caught in the Act of Adultery

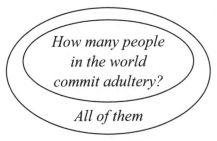

How many people in the world commit adultery?

All of them

In John 8, there is a story of a woman who was caught in the act of adultery and we see how Jesus saved her. We'd like to share the grace that she received. It isn't too much to say that all human beings commit adultery at some point in their lives. Every single person commits adultery.

If you don't think so, it is only because we do it so often that it appears as though we don't. Why? We live with so much adultery in our lives.

Taking a look at the woman in John 8, I contemplate on whether or not there is a person among us who hasn't committed adultery. There is no one who has not committed adultery, just as the woman who was caught in the act of adultery. All of us have done it, but we pretend that we haven't.

Do you think I am wrong? No, I am not. Look carefully within. Everyone on the face of the earth has done it. They commit adultery while gazing at women on the street, in their thoughts and in their acts, anytime, anywhere.

They just don't realize they are doing it. There are a lot of people who don't realize until the day they die that they have innumerably committed adultery throughout their lives. Not just those who have been caught, but all of us who have never been caught. All people do it in their minds, and in their acts. Is this not a part of our lives?

Are you upset? It is the truth. We are just discreet about it because we are embarrassed. The truth is that people these days commit adultery all the time, but do not realize that they are doing it.

People commit adultery in their souls, too. We, who were created by God, live on this earth without ever realizing that we also commit spiritual adultery. Worshiping other gods is the same as committing spiritual adultery because the Lord is the only Husband of all mankind.

The woman who was caught in the act was a human being, just like the rest of us, and she received the grace of God, just as we who were redeemed did. But the hypocritical Pharisees made her stand in their presence and pointed fingers at her as if they were judges, about to throw stones at her. They were about to rebuke and judge her as if they themselves were pure, and had never committed adultery.

Fellow Christians, those who know themselves to be a mass of sin do not judge others before God. Rather, knowing that they, too, commit adultery all their lives, they receive the grace of God which has redeemed us all. Only those who realize that they are sinners who have committed adultery all along are eligible to be redeemed before God.

Who Receives God's Grace?

Who receives God's grace?

The unworthy

Does one who lives purely without committing adultery

receive His grace, or does the unworthy one who admits oneself to be so sinful receive His grace? The one who receives grace is the one who receives the abundant grace of His redemption. Those who cannot help themselves, the weak and helpless, receive redemption. They are the ones who are in His grace.

Those who think that they are without sin cannot be redeemed. How can they receive the grace of His redemption when there is nothing to redeem?

The scribes and Pharisees dragged the woman who had been caught in the act of adultery before Jesus and set her in their midst and asked Him, *"Teacher, this woman was caught in adultery, in the very act. Now, what do You say?"* Why did they bring the woman before Him and test Him?

They themselves had also committed adultery many times, but they were trying to judge and kill her through Jesus while trying to put the blame on Him.

Jesus knew what was on their minds and knew all about the woman. So He said, *"He who is without sin among you, let him throw a stone at her first."* Then the scribes and Pharisees, starting from the oldest to the youngest, left one by one and only Jesus and the woman were left.

The ones who left were the scribes and Pharisees, the religious leaders. They were about to judge the woman who had been caught in the very act of adultery, as if they themselves were not sinners.

Jesus proclaimed His love in this world. He was the Host of love. Jesus gave people food, brought back the dead, gave life back to the son of a widow, revived Lazarus of Bethany, healed lepers, and performed miracles for the poor. He took all the sins of sinners away and gave them salvation.

Jesus loves us. He is the almighty One who can do

anything, but the Pharisees and scribes thought Him to be their enemy. That is why they brought the woman before Him and tested Him.

They asked, *"Teacher, Moses, in the law, commanded us that such should be stoned. But what do You say?"* They thought that He would tell them to stone her. Why? If we were to judge according to what is written in the law of God, everyone who has committed adultery would be stoned to death without exception.

All have to be stoned to death and all are destined to go to hell. The wages of sin is death. However, Jesus didn't tell them to stone her. Instead, He said, *"He who is without sin among you, let him throw a stone at her first."*

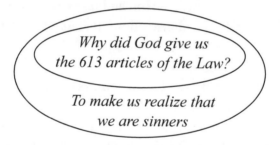

Why did God give us the 613 articles of the Law?

To make us realize that we are sinners

The Law brings about wrath. God is holy and so is His Law. This Holy Law came to us in 613 articles. The reason God has given us 613 articles of the Law is to make us realize that we are sinners; that we are incomplete beings. It teaches us that we have to long for God's grace to be redeemed. If we didn't know this and thought about only what was written in the Law, we would've had to be stoned to death, just as the woman who was caught in the act.

The scribes and Pharisees who didn't know the truth of His Law might have thought that they could throw stones at the woman and, probably at us, too. But, who could dare to throw stones at a helpless woman as the same sinful being? Even if she was caught in the act, no one in this world could throw stones at her.

If the woman and each one of us were judged only according to the Law, we, as well as the woman, would have received a terrible judgment. But Jesus saved us, we who are sinners, from our sins and from the just judgment. With all our sins, if the law of God is applied strictly to the letter, who among us could stay alive? Every single one of us would end up in hell.

But the scribes and Pharisees knew of the Law only as it was written. If His Law was applied correctly, it would kill them just as surely as the one judged by them. In fact, the law of God was given to men so that they could realize their sins, but they have suffered because they have misunderstood and misapplied it.

The Pharisees of today, just as the Pharisees in the Bible, only know the Law as it is written. They should understand the grace, the justice and the truth of God. They have to be taught the gospel of redemption to be saved.

The Pharisees said, *"The law commanded us that such should be stoned. But what do You say?"* They asked, confidently holding their stones. They thought for sure that Jesus wouldn't have anything to say about it. They were waiting for Jesus to take their bait.

If Jesus had judged according to the Law, they would also have stoned him. Their purpose was to stone both of the woman and Jesus. If Jesus had said not to stone the woman, they would have said that Jesus scorned the Law of God, and stoned Him for blasphemy. It was a terrible plot!

But Jesus stooped down and wrote on the ground with His finger, and they continued asking Him, "What do You say?

What are You writing on the ground? Just answer our question. What do You say?" They pointed their fingers at Jesus and kept harassing Him.

Then, Jesus stood up and told them that the one among them without sin should throw a stone at her first. Then He stooped down and continued writing on the ground. Those who heard it, being convicted by their consciences, left one by one, beginning with the oldest, to the very last person. Jesus was left alone, with the woman standing in His presence.

"He Who Is without Sin among You, Let Him Throw a Stone at Her First"

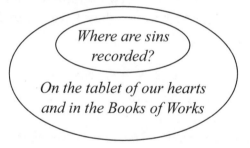

Jesus told them, *"He who is without sin among you, let him throw a stone at her first,"* and He kept on writing on the ground. A couple of older ones started to walk away. The older Pharisees, who had committed more sins, might go away first. The young ones left as well. Let's suppose Jesus was standing among us, and we were standing around the woman. If Jesus had said to us that one who was among us should throw a stone first, what would you have done?

What had Jesus been writing on the ground? God, who created us, writes our sins in two different places.

First, He writes our sins on the tablet of our hearts. *"The sins of Judah is written with a pen of iron; with the point of a diamond it is engraved on the tablet of their heart, and on the horns of your altars" (Jeremiah 17:1).*

God talks to us through Judah, who is our representative. The sins of human beings are engraved with a pen of iron, with the point of a diamond. They are recorded on the tablet of our hearts. Jesus stooped down and wrote on the ground that all men are sinners.

God knows that we sin and He engraves sins on the tablet of our hearts. First, He records our works, the sins that are committed, because we are fragile before the Law. As the sins are recorded in our hearts, we realize that we are sinners when we look at the Law. Since He recorded them in our hearts and consciences, we know that we are sinners before Him.

Jesus stooped down the second time to write on the ground. The Scripture also says that all our sins are recorded in the Books of Works before God (Revelation 20:12). Every sinner's name and his/her sins are recorded in the Book. They are also recorded on the tablet of the person's heart. Our sins are recorded both in the Book of Works and on the tablet of our hearts.

The sins are recorded on the tablet of everyone's heart, young or old. That is why they had nothing to say about their sin before Jesus. They, who tried to stone the woman, were helpless before His words.

When are our sins which are recorded in two places erased?

When we accept the redemption of the water and the blood of Jesus in our hearts.

Free book request www.bjnewlife.org

However, when you receive His salvation, all your sins in the Book of Works are erased and your name will be listed in the Book of Life. Those whose names appear in the Book of Life go to Heaven. Their good deeds, the things they have done in this world for the kingdom of God and His righteousness are also recorded in the Book of Life. They are accepted into Heaven. Those who are delivered from their sins will enter the place of eternity.

Remember that all the sins of every person are recorded in two places, so no one can deceive God. There isn't anyone who has not sinned or committed adultery in his or her heart. All people are sinners and are imperfect.

Those who have not accepted the redemption of Jesus in their hearts cannot but agonize over their sins. They are not confident. They are afraid of God and others because of their sins. But the moment they accept the gospel of the redemption of the water and the Spirit in their hearts, all the sins recorded on the tablets of their hearts and in the Book of Works are wiped clean. They are delivered from all their sins.

There is the Book of Life in Heaven. The names of those who believe in the redemption of the water and the Spirit are recorded in the book, so they will enter Heaven. They enter Heaven not because they haven't sinned in this world, but because they have been delivered from all their sins by believing in the redemption of the water and the Spirit. It is 'the law of faith' (Romans 3:27).

Fellow Christians, the scribes and Pharisees were sinners, just as the woman who was caught in the very act of adultery was.

In fact, they might have committed more sins because they deceived themselves and other people into believing that they were not sinners. The religious leaders were thieves with formal permits. They were thieves of souls, in other words, the thieves of life. They dared to teach others authoritatively, even though they themselves had not yet been redeemed.

There is no one who is without sin according to the Law. But a person can become righteous, not because he/she has not committed sin, but because he/she has been redeemed from all sins. Such a person is recorded in the Book of Life. The important thing is whether one's name has been recorded in the Book of Life or not. Since people cannot live without committing sins all their lives, they must eternally be redeemed in order to be recorded in the book.

Whether you will be accepted into Heaven depends upon whether you believe in the true gospel or not. Whether or not you receive the grace of God depends upon your acceptance of Jesus' salvation. What happened to the woman who was caught? She might have thrown herself down on her knees and closed her eyes because she knew she was going to die. She was probably crying in fear and repentance. People become honest with themselves when they face death.

"Oh, God, it is proper that I have to die. Please accept my soul into Thy hands, and take pity on me. Please take pity on me, Jesus." She pleaded to Jesus for the love of redemption. "God, if You judge me, I will be judged, and if You say I am without sin, then my sins will be erased. It is up to You." She was probably saying all of these things. She may have confessed that everything was left up to Jesus.

The woman who was brought before Jesus didn't say, "I did wrong, please forgive me for my adultery." She said, "Please save me from my sins. If You redeem my sins, I will be saved. If not, I will go to hell. I need your redemption. I need the love of God, and I need Him to take pity on me." She closed her eyes and confessed her sinfulness.

And Jesus asked her, *"Where are those accusers of yours? Has no one condemned you?"* She answered, *"No one, Lord."*

And Jesus said to her, *"Neither do I condemn you."* Jesus didn't condemn her because He had already taken away all her sins through His baptism at the Jordan river, and she was already redeemed. Now, Jesus, not the woman, had to be judged for her sins.

He Said, *"Neither Do I Condemn You."*

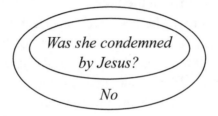

Was she condemned by Jesus?

No

This woman was blessed with the salvation in Jesus. She was redeemed of all her sins. Our Lord Jesus tells us that He redeemed all our sins and that we are all righteous.

He tells us so in the Bible. He died on the Cross to pay for our sins, which He took away with His baptism at the Jordan River. He clearly tells us that He redeemed all who believe in the redemption of His baptism and judgment on the Cross. All of us need the written Word of Jesus and need to hold on to the Word. Then, we will all be blessed with redemption.

"God, I have no merit before You. I have nothing good inside me. I have nothing to show You but my sins. But I believe that Jesus is my Lord of redemption. He took away all my sins at the Jordan River and atoned for them on the Cross. He took away all my sins with His baptism and His blood. I do believe in You, Lord."

This is how you are saved. Jesus does not 'condemn us.'

He gave us the right to be God's children: To those who believe in the redemption of the water and the Spirit, He has taken away all their sins and made them righteous.

Dear friends! The woman was redeemed. The woman who was caught in adultery was blessed with the redemption of our Lord Jesus. We can also be blessed like that. Anyone who knows of his/her sins and asks God to take pity on him/her, and anyone who believes in the redemption of the water and the Spirit in Jesus receives the blessing of redemption from God. Those who admit their sinfulness before God can be redeemed, but those who do not realize their own sins cannot be blessed with redemption.

Jesus took away the sins of the world (John 1:29). Any sinner in the world can be redeemed if he/she believes in Jesus. Jesus said to the woman, *"Neither do I condemn you."* He said that He did not condemn her because all her sins had already been born onto Him through His baptism. He took all our sins onto Himself, and He was judged for them instead of us.

We Have to Be Redeemed before Jesus

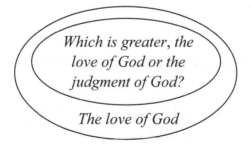

Which is greater, the love of God or the judgment of God?

The love of God

The Pharisees, with stones in their hands, as well as the religious leaders of today, interpret the Law to the letter. They believe that since the Law tells us not to commit adultery, one who commits such sins will be stoned to death. They steal a glance at women with lewd eyes while pretending not to commit adultery. They cannot be redeemed nor saved. The Pharisees and scribes were the moralists of this world. They were not the ones Jesus called. These people never heard from Him, "I will not condemn you."

Only the woman who was caught in adultery heard those joyous words. If you are honest before Him, you can also be blessed like her. "God, I cannot but commit adultery all my life. That I am not aware of it is just because I do it so often. I commit such a sin several times each day."

When we accept the Law and the fact that we are sinners who must die and honestly face God, saying, "God, this is what I am. Please save me," God will bless us with His redemption.

The love of Jesus, the gospel of the water and the Spirit has won over the just judgment of God. *"Neither do I condemn you."* He does not condemn us. He says, "You are redeemed." Our Lord Jesus Christ is the God of compassion. He has delivered us from all the sins of the world.

Our God is the God of Justice and the God of Love. The love of the water and the Spirit is even greater than His judgment.

His Love Is Greater Than His Justice

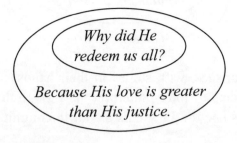

Why did He redeem us all?

Because His love is greater than His justice.

If God had enforced His judgment to complete His justice, He would have judged all sinners and sent them to hell. But because the love of Jesus, which saves us from the judgment, is greater, God sent His only Son, Jesus. Jesus took all our sins onto Himself and received just judgment for all of us. Now, anyone who believes in Jesus as their Savior becomes His child and righteous. Since His love is greater than His justice, He redeemed us all.

We must thank God that He doesn't judge us only with His justice. Once Jesus told the scribes, the Pharisees, and their disciples, "But go and learn what this means: 'I desire mercy and not sacrifice.' For I did not come to call the righteous, but sinners, to repentance" (Matthew 9:13). Some people may still kill a cow or a goat everyday and offer it before God, praying, "God, forgive my sins everyday." God does not want our offerings, but rather, our belief in the redemption of the water and the Spirit. He wants us to be redeemed and delivered. He wants to give us His love and accept our faiths. Can you all see this? Jesus has given us His perfect salvation.

Jesus hates sin, but He has a burning love for human beings, who were created in the image of God. He had decided even before Creation to make us His children, and blotted out all our sins with His baptism and blood. God created us to eventually redeem us, to clothe us in Jesus, and to make us His children. This is the love He has for us, His creations.

If God only judged us according to His just Law, we, the sinners, would all have to die. But He delivered us through the baptism and the judgment of His Son at the Cross. Do you believe? Let's confirm it in the Old Testament.

Aaron Laid His Hands on the Scapegoat

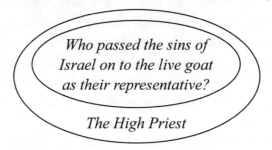

Who passed the sins of Israel on to the live goat as their representative?

The High Priest

All the sins of this world were expiated through the faith in the ordination of the Old Testament and the baptism of the New Testament. In the Old Testament, all the yearly sins of Israel were atoned through the High Priest, who laid his hands on the head of a live goat without any blemishes.

"And Aaron shall lay both his hands on the head of the live goat, confess over it all the iniquities of the children of Israel, and all their transgressions, concerning all their sins, putting them on the head of the goat, and shall send it away into the wilderness by the hand of a suitable man" (Leviticus 16:21).

This is how they were atoned in the days of the Old Testament. To be redeemed from the daily sins, one brought a lamb or a goat without blemishes to the tabernacle and offered it at the altar. He put his hands on the head of the offering, and then his sins were passed on to the sacrifice. Then, the sacrifice was killed and the priest put its blood on the horns of the altar.

There were horns on the four corners of the altar. These horns symbolize the Books of Works written in Revelations 20:12. The sacrifice's remaining blood was sprinkled on the ground too. The ground represented the heart of man because man was created from dust. The people atoned for their daily sins this way.

However, they could not make sin offerings daily, so, God allowed them to be atoned once a year for all their yearly sins. This was performed on the tenth day of the seventh month, the Day of Atonement. On that day, the High Priest, the representative of all Israelites, brought two goats and laid his hands on them to pass all the sins of the people on to them and offered them before God to make atonement for the people of Israel.

"Aaron laid both his hands on the head of the live goat, confessed over it all the iniquities of the children of Israel, and all their transgressions, concerning all their sins, putting them on the head of the goat."

God had appointed Aaron, the High Priest of Israel, to be the representative. Instead of everyone having to lay his hands on the offerings individually, the high priest, as the representative of all people, laid his hands on the head of the live goat for the remission of the year's sins.

He would narrate all the sins of Israel before God, "O God, Your children of Israel have sinned. We have worshiped idols, broken all articles of Thy Law, called Thy name in vain, created other idols and loved them more than Thee. We didn't keep the Sabbath holy, didn't respect our parents, killed, committed adultery and thievery.... We indulged in jealousy and quarrels."

He listed all the sins. "God, neither the people of Israel nor I have been able to keep any of Thy Law. To be redeemed of all these sins, I lay my hands on the head of this goat and pass onto it all those sins." The high priest laid his hands on the offering for all the people and passed all the sins onto the head of the offering. Ordination, or the laying on of hands means 'to pass' (Leviticus 1:1-4, 16:20-21).

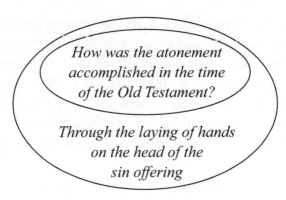

*How was the atonement
accomplished in the time
of the Old Testament?*

*Through the laying of hands
on the head of the
sin offering*

God had given the sacrificial system to the people of
Israel so that they could pass on all their sins and be redeemed.
He specified that one should prepare a sin offering without
blemishes and that the sin offering should die instead of the
person. The redemption of individual sinners was like that.

However, on the Day of Atonement, the sin offering was
killed and its blood was taken inside the Holy Place and
sprinkled on the mercy seat seven times. Thus, the people of
Israel atoned for a year's sin on the tenth day of the seventh
month.

The high priest entered the Holy Place alone to offer the
sacrifice, but people gathered outside and listened to the sound
of the golden bells on the hem of the robe of the ephod of the
High Priest. The golden bells rang seven times as the blood
was sprinkled on the mercy seat. Then, the people would
rejoice that all their sins were atoned. The sound of the golden
bells implies the sound of the joyous gospel.

It is not true that Jesus loves some selected people and
redeems only them. Jesus took away all the sins of the world
all at once with His baptism. He wanted to deliver us once and
for all. Our sins could not be redeemed every day, so they were
blotted out all at once.

In the Old Testament, atonement was given through

ordination and the blood of the sin offering. Aaron laid his hands on the head of a live goat in front of all the people and listed all the sins that people had committed during the year. He passed the sins onto the goat in front of all Israelites. Where did the sins of the people go after the laying hands of the High Priest on the scapegoat? They were all passed onto the goat.

Then, the goat was led away by a 'suitable man.' The goat, with all the sins of Israel upon it, was led to the desert where there was no water and no grass. The goat, then, would wander the desert under the burning sun and finally die. The goat died for the sins of the Israelites.

This is the love of God, the love of redemption. This is how they atoned for a year's worth of sins in those days. But we are living in the time of the New Testament. It has been about 2000 years since Jesus came down to our world. He came and fulfilled the promise that He had made in the Old Testament. He came and redeemed all our sins.

To Redeem Us All

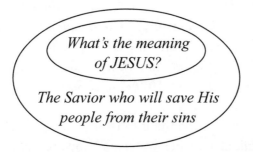

What's the meaning of JESUS?

The Savior who will save His people from their sins

Let's read Matthew 1:20-21. *"But while he thought about these things, behold, an angel of the Lord appeared to him in a dream, saying, 'Joseph, son of David, do not be afraid to take to you Mary your wife, for that which is conceived in her is of the Holy Spirit. And she will bring forth a Son, and you shall call His name Jesus, for He will save His people from their sins'" (Matthew 1:20-21).*

Our Father in Heaven borrowed the Virgin Mary's body to send His Son to this world to wash away all the sins of the world. He sent an angel to Mary and told her, *"And behold, you will conceive in your womb and bring forth a Son, and shall call His name JESUS."* It meant that the Son coming through Mary would become the Savior. Jesus Christ means the one who will save His people, in other words, the Savior.

Then, how did Jesus save all of us from sin? The way Jesus took away all the sins of the world was through His baptism at the Jordan River. When John the Baptist baptized Him, all the sins of the world were passed onto Him. Let's read Matthew 3:13-17.

"Then Jesus came from Galilee to John at the Jordan to be baptized by him. And John tried to prevent Him, saying 'I have need to be baptized by You, and are You coming to me?' But Jesus answered and said to him, 'Permit it to be so now, for thus it is fitting for us to fulfill all righteousness.' Then he allowed Him. Then Jesus, when He had been baptized, came up immediately from the water; and behold, the heavens were opened to Him, and He saw the Spirit of God descending like a dove and alighting upon Him. And suddenly a voice came from heaven, saying, 'This is My beloved Son, in whom I am well pleased.'"

Jesus went to John the Baptist to redeem all of us from our sins. He walked into the water and lowered His head before John. "John, baptize Me now. It is fitting for us to fulfill all righteousness. As I am to take away all the sins of the world and deliver all sinners from their sins, I need to take away their sins with baptism. Baptize Me now! Allow it!"

Thus, it was fitting to fulfill all righteousness. Jesus was baptized by John the Baptist in the Jordan River and right at that moment, all the righteousness of God that redeemed our sins was fulfilled.

This is how He took away all our sins. All your sins were passed onto Jesus, too. Do you understand this?

Believe in the redemption of Jesus' baptism and the Spirit and be saved.

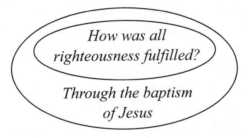

How was all righteousness fulfilled?

Through the baptism of Jesus

God had first promised Israel that all the sins of the world would be washed away with the laying on of hands and the sacrifice of the sin offering. However, as it was impossible for everyone to lay hands on the head of the goat individually, God consecrated Aaron to be the high priest so that he could offer the sacrifice for all the people. Thus, he passed all their yearly sins onto the head of the sin offering all at once. This was His Wisdom and the Power of redemption. God is wise and amazing.

He sent His Son Jesus to save the whole world. So the sin offering was ready. Now, there had to be a representative of all human beings, one who would lay his hands on the head of Jesus and pass on all the sins of the world onto Him. That representative was John the Baptist. It is written in the Bible that God sent the representative of all humankind before Jesus.

It was John the Baptist, the last high priest of man. As it is written in Matthew 11:11, *"Among those born of women there has not risen one greater than John the Baptist."* He is the only representative of humans. He sent John as the representative of all human beings so that he could baptize Jesus and pass on all the sins of the world to Him.

If six billion people on earth went to Jesus now and each had to lay their hands on Jesus to pass on their sins, what would happen to His head? If more than six billion people in this world had to lay their hands on Jesus, it would not be a pretty sight. Some enthusiastic people might press down so hard that all His hair would fall out. Thus, God, in His wisdom, appointed John to be our representative and passed all the sins of the world onto Jesus, once and for all.

It is recorded in Matthew 3:13, *"Then Jesus came from Galilee to John at the Jordan to be baptized by him."* This was when Jesus was 30 years old. Jesus was circumcised 8 days after His birth, and there are few records of Him from then until He turned 30.

The reason Jesus had to wait until He was 30 years old was to become the lawful heavenly High Priest, according to the Old Testament. In Deuteronomy, God told Moses that the high priest should be at least 30 before he could minister the high priesthood. Jesus was the heavenly High Priest. Do you believe this?

In the New Testament, in Matthew 3:13-14, it says, *"Then Jesus came from Galilee to John at the Jordan to be baptized by him. And John tried to prevent Him, saying 'I have need to be baptized by You.'"* Who is the representative of humankind? John the Baptist. Then, who is the representative of Heaven? Jesus Christ is. The representatives met. Then who is the higher? Of course, the representative of Heaven is higher.

So John the Baptist, who was so bold as to cry out to the religious leaders in those days, *"Brood of vipers! Repent!"*

suddenly became humble before Jesus. *"I have need to be baptized by You, and are You coming to me?"*

At this point, Jesus said, *"Permit it to be so now, for thus it is fitting for us to fulfill all righteousness."* Jesus came to this world to fulfill the righteousness of God, and it was fulfilled when John the Baptist baptized Him.

"Then he allowed Him. Then Jesus, when He had been baptized, came up immediately from the water and the heavens were opened up to Him, and He saw the Spirit of God descending like a dove and alighting upon Him. And suddenly a voice came from heaven, saying, 'This is My beloved Son, in whom I am well pleased.'"

This is what happened when He was baptized. The gates of Heaven were opened up when He was baptized by John the Baptist and took away all the sins of the world.

"And from the days of John the Baptist until now the kingdom of heaven suffers violence, and the violent take it by force" (Matthew 11:12).

All the prophets and the law of God had prophesied up to John the Baptist. *"And from the days of John the Baptist until now the kingdom of heaven suffers violence, and the violent take it by force."* Everyone who believes in His baptism can enter the Kingdom of Heaven without exception.

"Neither Do I Condemn You"

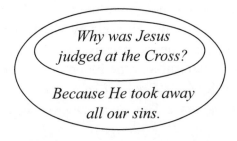

Why was Jesus judged at the Cross?

Because He took away all our sins.

Jesus was baptized by John the Baptist and took away all the sins of the world. Later, He told the woman who was caught in the act of adultery, *"Neither do I condemn you."* He didn't condemn the woman because He took away all the sins of the world at the Jordan and He Himself, not the woman, had to be judged for those sins.

Jesus blotted out all the sins of the world. We can see how afraid He was of the pain He would have to endure on the Cross because *'the wages of sin is death.'* He prayed to God three times on the Mount of Olives to take this judgment away from Him. Jesus was flesh and blood, just like other human beings, so it is understandable that He was afraid of the pain. Jesus had to bleed to fulfill the judgment.

Just as the sin offerings in the Old Testament had to bleed to pay for the sins, He had to be sacrificed on the Cross. He had already taken away all the sins of the world and now He had to give His life for our redemption. He knew that He had to be judged before God.

Jesus didn't have any sin in His heart, but as all sins were passed onto Him through His baptism, God had to judge His own Son now. Thus, in the first place, the justice of God was fulfilled and secondly, He bestowed His love on us for our salvation. Therefore, Jesus had to be judged on the Cross.

"Neither do I condemn you, nor do I judge you." All our sins, intentional or unintentional, recognized or unrecognized, had to be judged by God.

However, God did not judge us. God judged Jesus, who had taken all our sins onto Himself by His baptism. God did not want to judge sinners because of His love and His compassion. The baptism and the blood on the Cross was His redemptive love for us. *"For God so loved the world that He gave His only begotten Son, that whoever believes in Him should not perish but have everlasting life" (John 3:16).*

This is how we know of His love. Jesus didn't condemn the woman who was caught in the act of adultery.

She knew that she was a sinner for she was caught in the very adulterous act. She not only had sin in her heart, but also carried it in the flesh. There was no way she could deny her sin. However, because she believed that Jesus took away all her sins, she was saved. If we believe in Jesus' redemption, we will be saved. Believe it! It is for our own good.

Who are the most blessed?

Those who have no sin

All people sin. All people commit adultery. But all people are not judged for their sins. We have all sinned, but those who believe in the redemption of Jesus Christ are sinless in their hearts. One who believes in the salvation of Jesus is the happiest person. Those who are delivered from all their sins are the most blessed. In other words, they are now righteous in Jesus.

God tells us about happiness in Romans 4:7, *"Blessed are those whose lawless deeds are forgiven, and whose sins are covered."* We all sin until the time we die. We are lawless and incomplete before God. We continue to sin even after we are aware of His Law. We are so weak.

But God delivered us with the baptism and the blood of His only begotten Son and tells us, you and I, that we are no longer sinners, and that we are now righteous before Him. He tells us that we are His children.

The gospel of the water and the Spirit is the gospel of

eternal redemption. Do you believe it? To those who believe, He calls them the righteous, the redeemed and His children. Who is the happiest person in this world? The one who believes and has been delivered by believing in the true gospel. Have you been delivered?

Did Jesus omit taking your sins? No, He took all your sins with His baptism. Believe it. Believe and be redeemed of all your sins. Let's read John 1:29.

Just as If Swept Away with a Broom

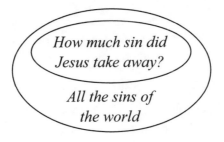

How much sin did Jesus take away?

All the sins of the world

"*The next day John saw Jesus coming toward him, and said, 'Behold! The Lamb of God who takes away the sin of the world!'*" *(John 1:29)*

"*Behold! The Lamb of God who takes away the sin of the world!*"

John the Baptist passed all the sins of the world onto Jesus at the Jordan. The next day, he witnessed that Jesus was the Lamb of God who took away all the sins of the world. He took on to His shoulders all the sins of the world.

All the sins of the world refer to all the sins that human beings commit in this world, from Creation until its end. About 2000 years ago, Jesus took away all the sins of the world and redeemed us. As the Lamb of God, He took away all our sins and was judged for us.

Any sin that we human beings commit was passed on to Jesus. He became the Lamb of God who took away all the sins of the world.

Jesus came to this world as a humble man, as the One who would save all the sinners of the world. We commit sin because we are weak, wicked, ignorant, and because we are silly and incomplete. In other words, we sin because we inherited sin from our common ancestor, Adam.   All these sins were swept up and put on the head of Jesus through His baptism at the Jordan. He ended it all with the death of His flesh on the Cross. He was buried, but God raised Him from the dead on the third day.

As the Savior of all sinners, as the Victorious, as the Judge, He now sits at the right hand of God. He does not have to redeem us again and again. All we have to do is believe in Him to be saved. Eternal life awaits those who believe, and destruction awaits those who do not believe. There is no other choice.

Jesus delivered you all. You are the happiest people on earth. You surely will commit sins in the future because of your weaknesses, but He took all those sins too.

Is there any sin left in your heart? —No—
Did Jesus take it all? —Yes! He did.—

All people are the same. No one is holier than his/her neighbor. But as so many people are hypocrites, they believe they are not sinners, when indeed, they are sinners too. This world is the greenhouse that nurtures sin.

When women step out of their houses, they put on red lipstick, powder their faces, curl their hair, dress in nice clothes, and wear high-heels.... Men also go to a barber to get their hair cut, groom themselves, put on clean shirts and fashionable ties, and shine their shoes.

But while they may look like princes and princesses on the outside, they are absolutely filthy on the inside.

Does money make men happy? Does health make men happy? No. Only the eternal redemption, the forgiveness of all sins, makes people truly happy. No matter how happy a person looks on the outside, the person is miserable if he/she has sin in his/her heart. Such a person lives in fear of judgment.

A redeemed person is bold like a lion, even in rags. There is no sin in his/her heart. "Thank you Lord, You saved a sinner like me. You blotted out all my sins. I know I am unworthy of receiving Your love, but I praise You for saving me. I am eternally redeemed of all my sins. Glory be to God!"

A person who is delivered is a truly happy one. A person who has been blessed with His grace of redemption is a truly happy one.

Because Jesus, *'the Lamb of God who takes away the sin of the world,'* has taken away all our sins, we are without sin. He *'finished'* salvation for us at the Cross. All our sins, including yours and mine, are included in *'the sin of the world,'* and therefore, we are all saved.

By God's Will

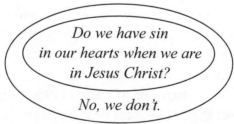

Do we have sin in our hearts when we are in Jesus Christ?

No, we don't.

Dear friends, the woman who was caught in adultery believed in the words of Jesus and she was saved. Her story is

Free book request www.nlmission.com

recorded in the Bible because she was blessed with His eternal redemption. However, the hypocritical scribes and Pharisees ran away from Jesus.

If you believe in Jesus, it is Heaven that awaits you, but if you leave Jesus, you will go to hell. If you believe in His righteous acts, it is like Heaven, but if you do not believe in His works, it is like hell. Redemption is not up to the endeavors of any individual, but to the salvation of Jesus.

Let's read Hebrews 10. *"For the law, having a shadow of the good things to come, and not the very image of the things, can never with these same sacrifices, which they offer continually year by year, make those who approach perfect. For then would they not have ceased to be offered? For the worshipers, once purged, would have had no more consciousness of sins. But in those sacrifices there is a reminder of sins every year, For it is not possible that the blood of bulls and goats could take away sins. Therefore, when He came into the world, He said: 'Sacrifice and offering You did not desire, but a body You have prepared for Me. In burnt offerings and sacrifices for sin You had no pleasure. Then I said, 'Behold, I have come—in the volume of the book it is written of Me—to do Your will, O God." He takes away the first that He may establish the second. By that will we have been sanctified through the offering of the body of Jesus Christ once for all"* (Hebrews 10:1-10).

"By God's will" Jesus offered His life to take our sins all at once, and was judged all at once and resurrected.

Therefore, we have been sanctified. *'Have been sanctified, (Hebrews 10:10)'* is written in the present complete tense. It means that our redemption was completed absolutely, and does not need to be mentioned again. You have been sanctified.

"And every priest stands ministering daily and offering

repeatedly the same sacrifices, which can never take away sins. But this Man, after He had offered one sacrifice for sins forever, sat down at the right hand of God, from that time waiting till His enemies are made His footstool. For by one offering He has perfected forever those who are being sanctified" (Hebrews 10: 11-14).

You are all sanctified forever. If you commit sins tomorrow, will you become a sinner again? Didn't Jesus take away those sins also? He did. He took away the sins of the future, too.

"But the Holy Spirit also witnesses to us; for after He had said before, 'This is the covenant that I will make with them after those days, says the Lord: I will put My laws into their hearts, and in their minds I will write them.' then He adds, 'Their sins and their lawless deeds I will remember no more.' Now where there is remission of these, there is no longer an offering for sin" (Hebrews 10:15-18).

The phrase *'there is remission of these'* means that He expiated all the sins of the world. Jesus is our Savior, both my Savior and your Savior. Believing in Jesus has saved us. This is the redemption in Jesus and the greatest grace and present from God. You and I, who have been redeemed of all sins, are the most blessed of all! ✉

SERMON 5

The Baptism of Jesus and

The Atonement of Sins

The Baptism of Jesus and The Atonement of Sins

< Matthew 3:13-17 >

"Then Jesus came from Galilee to John at the Jordan to be baptized by him. And John tried to prevent Him, saying, 'I have need to be baptized by you, and are You coming to me?' But Jesus answered and said to him, 'Permit it to be so now, for thus it is fitting for us to fulfill all righteousness.' Then he allowed Him. Then Jesus, when He had been baptized, came up immediately from the water; and behold, the heavens were opened to Him, and He saw the Spirit of God descending like a dove and alighting upon Him. And suddenly a voice came from heaven, saying, 'This is My beloved Son, in whom I am well pleased.'"

Is There Anyone Who Still Suffers from Sin?

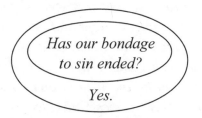

Has our bondage to sin ended?

Yes.

Our Lord God has cut off the shackles of sin for all people. All those who have a hard time under sin are slaves of sin, but With His redemption, our Lord cut them off absolutely. He removed all our sins. Is there anyone who still suffers from sin?

We have to understand that our warfare against sin has ended. We shall never suffer in sin again. Our bondage to sin ended when Jesus redeemed us with His baptism and blood. All our sins ended then and there. The Son of God has expiated all our sins. God paid for all our sins through Jesus, who set us free, forever.

Do you know how much people suffer from their sins? It started from the time of Adam and Eve. Mankind suffers from the sins inherited from Adam.

But our God made a covenant which is written in Genesis 3:15, and the covenant was that He would deliver all sinners. He said that humans would be redeemed of their sins through the sacrifice of Jesus Christ by the water and the Spirit. When the time came, God sent our Savior, Jesus, to live among us.

He also promised to send John the Baptist ahead of Jesus and He kept His promise.

Mark 1:1-8 states, *"The beginning of the gospel of Jesus Christ, the Son of God. As it is written in the Prophets: 'Behold, I send My messenger before Your face, who will prepare Your way before You.' The voice of one crying in the wilderness: 'Prepare the way of the Lord, make His paths straight.' John came baptizing in the wilderness and preaching a baptism of repentance for the remission of sins. And all the land of Judea, and those from Jerusalem, went out to him and were all baptized by him in the Jordan River, confessing their sins. Now John was clothed with camel's hair, and with a leather belt around his waist, and he ate locusts and wild honey. And he preached, saying, 'There comes One after me who is mightier than I, whose sandal strap I am not worthy to stoop down and loose. I indeed baptized you with water, but He will baptize you with the Holy Spirit.'"*

John the Baptist, the Witness and Forerunner of the Gospel, John the Baptist

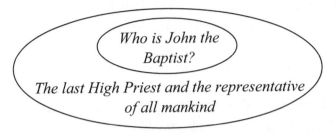

Who is John the Baptist?

The last High Priest and the representative of all mankind

Baptism in Greek, *'baptizo,'* essentially means to 'submerge', but it also implies 'to be washed, to be buried, to be immersed, or to pass on to.' When Jesus was baptized, the righteousness of God was fulfilled. 'Righteousness' is *'dikaiosune'* in Greek, which means 'to be just,' and it also means 'most proper,' 'most fitting,' or 'the fairest state'

Jesus was baptized so that He could become the Savior in the most fitting and proper manner. Therefore, those who believe in Jesus' baptism and the Cross receive the gift of redemption from God.

In the New Testament, John the Baptist is the last High Priest of the Old Testament. Let's look at Matthew 11:10-11. The Scripture says that John the Baptist is the representative of mankind and as the High Priest in the era of the New Testament, he passed all the sins of the world onto Jesus; thus ministering the high priesthood of the Old Testament.

Jesus Himself bore witness to John Himself. He said, in Matthew 11:13-14, *"For all the prophets and the law prophesied until John. And if you are willing to receive it, he is Elijah who is to come."* Therefore, John the Baptist, who baptized Jesus, was a descendant of the High Priest Aaron and the last high priest. The Bible also testified to John's being a descendant of Aaron in the Old Testament (Luke 1:5,

1 Chronicles 24:10).

Then why did John live in the wilderness alone, dressed in a cloth made from camel's hair? It was to assume the high priesthood. As the representative of all mankind, John the Baptist could not live among people. So, he cried out to the people, *"Repent, you brood of vipers!"* and baptized them for the fruit of repentance in order to return people to Jesus, who would take away all their sins. Most of all, John the Baptist passed the sins of the world onto Jesus for our salvation when he laid his hands on Jesus' head.

Two Kinds of Baptism

Why did John the Baptist baptize people?

To lead people to repent of all their sins and to believe in the baptism of Jesus for salvation

John the Baptist baptized people and then baptized Jesus. The first was 'the baptism of repentance,' which called upon sinners to return to God. Many people who heard the words of God through John abandoned their idols and returned to Him.

The second baptism was the baptism of Jesus, the baptism that passed all the sins of the world onto Jesus. John the Baptist baptized Jesus to fulfill the righteousness of God. In other words, Jesus was baptized by John the Baptist to save all people from their sins (Matthew 3:15).

Why did John have to baptize Jesus? In order to blot out

the sins of the world, God had to let John pass all sins onto Jesus so that people who believed in Him could be saved.

John the Baptist was a servant of God whose mission was to pass all the sins of the world onto Jesus through the baptism, and to bear witness to Jesus in order for all of mankind to repent and be washed of their sins by believing in the gospel of redemption. Therefore, John had to live alone in the wilderness. In the time of John the Baptist, the people of Israel were all corrupt and rotten to the core.

So God had said in the Old Testament, Malachi 4:5-6, *"Behold, I will send you Elijah the prophet before the coming of the great and dreadful day of the Lord. And he will turn the hearts of the fathers to the children, and the hearts of the children to their fathers, lest I come and strike the earth with a curse."*

In the eyes of God, all the people of Israel who had worshiped Jehovah before were corrupt. No one was righteous before Him. The religious leaders of the temple, for example, priests, lawyers and the scribes were especially rotten to the core. Israelites and their priests did not offer the lawful sacrifices according to the law of God.

The priests had abandoned the laying on of hands and the ritual of the offering of blood, which God had given them for the atonement of their sins. It is recorded that the priests in the days of Malachi had abandoned the lawful sacrificial system, the laying on of hands and the offering of the blood of the sacrificial animal.

Therefore, John the Baptist could not stay with them. He went out to the wilderness and cried out. What did he say?

It is written in Mark 1:2-3, quoting the words of the prophet Isaiah, *"Behold, I send My messenger before Your face, who will prepare Your way before You. The voice of one crying in the wilderness: 'Prepare the way of the Lord, make His paths straight.'"*

The voice in the wilderness cried out to people for the baptism of repentance. What is the 'baptism of repentance' the Bible talks about? It is the baptism which John the Baptist cried out for; the baptism that called people back to Jesus so that they would believe in Him, who would take away all their sins and be saved. The baptism of repentance was to lead them to salvation.

"Repent and be baptized. Our Savior Jesus will be baptized in the same way to take away all your sins." The cry of John the Baptist was that Jesus would take away the sins of the world and be judged on the Cross to save all people, so that they might come back to God.

"I indeed baptized you with water, but He will baptize you with the Holy Spirit." 'Baptize you with the Holy Spirit' means to wash away all your sins. To baptize means 'to wash.' The baptism of Jesus at the Jordan River tells us that the Son of God was thus baptized and took away all our sins to save us.

Therefore, we are to turn back from our sinful lives and believe in Him. He is the Lamb who took away the world's sins. This is the gospel of redemption to which John the Baptist testified.

The Task of the High Priest for the Atonement of Sins

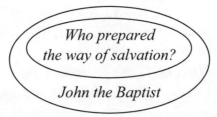

Who prepared the way of salvation?

John the Baptist

The Prophet Isaiah had prophesied, *"Speak comfort to Jerusalem, and cry out to her, that her warfare is ended, that her iniquity is pardoned; for she has received from the Lord's hand double for all her sins"* (Isaiah 40:2).

Jesus Christ took away all our sins without exception; original sin, present sins, and even future sins were washed away through His baptism. He redeemed us all. We should all know about God's redemption.

To be saved from all our sins, we must believe in the gospel that states that John the Baptist passed all sins onto Jesus through the means of baptism.

We should not misunderstand, thinking, "Since God is love, we can enter the Kingdom of Heaven only by believing in Jesus, even if we have sin in our hearts."

In order to be redeemed of all our sins, we have to believe in His baptism, through which John the Baptist passed all the sins of the world onto Jesus and the Cross. It is by 'the water' that John the Baptist passed all the sins of mankind onto Jesus.

The first thing God did to save us was to send John to this world. As the messenger of God, John the Baptist was sent as the ambassador to the King, who passed all the sins of the world onto Jesus through baptism. He ministered the high priesthood of all mankind.

God told us that He sent His messenger, John the Baptist, to us. *"I send My messenger before Your face."* Before Your face means before Jesus. Why did God send John before Jesus? It was to pass on all the sins of the world onto Jesus, the Son of God, through baptism. *"He will prepare Your way before You."* This is what the passage really means.

Who is the one who prepared the way so that we could be redeemed and go to Heaven? John the Baptist. *'Your'* means Jesus and *'My'* means God Himself. Therefore, when He said,

"I send My messenger before Your face, who will prepare Your way before You," what does it mean?

Who is to prepare our way so that we may go to Heaven? John the Baptist passed all our sins onto Jesus so that we would believe He washed them all away; his task was to pass on the sins by baptizing Jesus Christ. It was Jesus and John who made it possible for us to believe in the truth and be redeemed.

On what does our salvation depend? It depends on whether we believe in the righteous acts of Jesus, the Son of God, and the fact that the messenger of God, John the Baptist, had passed all the sins of the world onto Him. We should all know the gospel of the remission of sins. God the Father sent His messenger ahead, the one who would baptize His Son, and made him the representative of mankind. Thus, He completed the work of redemption for us.

God sent His servant John the Baptist to baptize His Son so that he could prepare the way for salvation for those who believed in Jesus. That is the reason why John baptized Jesus. The baptism of Jesus by John the Baptist was the fulfillment of God's redemption through which all the sins of mankind were passed onto Him so that all people might believe in Jesus and go to Heaven.

Even the future sins of mankind were passed onto Jesus through His baptism. Jesus and John the Baptist together prepared the way to Heaven for all of us. In this way, God revealed the secret of redemption through John the Baptist.

As the representative of humankind, John baptized Jesus so that we might believe in our redemption and go to Heaven. He passed all sin onto Jesus through baptism. This is the joyous news of redemption, the gospel.

Why Was John the Baptist Born?

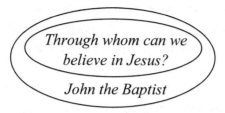

Through whom can we believe in Jesus?

John the Baptist

In Malachi 3:1, it is written, *"Behold, I send My messenger, and he will prepare the way before Me."* You have to read the Bible carefully. Why did God send His messenger before Jesus? Why was John the Baptist born prior 6 months to Jesus?

We have to understand what the Bible is all about. The Old Testament states the task of the High Priest Aaron. Aaron was the older brother of Moses. God anointed him and his sons as priests. The other Levites worked under them, bringing them assorted utensils, mixing the batter for the bread and such, while the sons of Aaron offered the sacrifice inside the holy tabernacle.

Aaron's sons were anointed to share an equal amount of work among them, but on the Day of Atonement, the tenth day of the seventh month, the High Priest alone offered the sacrifice of atonement for his people's yearly sins.

In Luke 1:5, there is a story about the lineage of John the Baptist. We have to correctly understand this messenger of God to understand Jesus properly. We tend to think a lot about Jesus, but ignore much about John the Baptist, who came before Him. I would like to help you understand.

"The beginning of the gospel of Jesus Christ, the Son of God. As it is written in the Prophets, Behold I send My messenger before Your face, who will prepare Your way before you" (Mark 1:1-2). The gospel of Heaven always starts with

John the Baptist.

When we fully learn about John the Baptist, we can clearly understand and believe in the gospel of the redemption of Jesus. It is similar to listening to the ambassadors we have dispatched all over the world in order to understand the situations of all nations. When we know about John the Baptist, we can understand the redemption of God very well.

What a pity it is, however, that so many Christians these days do not see the importance of John. God didn't send John the Baptist because He was bored and had nothing else to do. All the four Gospels of the New Testament talk about John the Baptist before talking about the redemption of Jesus.

But the evangelists of today ignore him completely and tell people that just believing in Jesus is enough to be saved. They are in fact leading people to live as sinners all their lives and end up in hell. If all the Christians just believe in Jesus without understanding the role of John the Baptist, Christianity would be depraved into a worldly religion. How can you be redeemed of your sins if you do not know the truth? It is impossible.

The gospel of redemption is neither that simple nor that easy. So many people think that redemption lies in our faiths in the Cross because Jesus died on the Cross for us. However, if you believe only in His crucifixion without knowing the whole truth of the passing on of sins, such faith will not lead to complete redemption, no matter how strong your faith may be.

God sent John the Baptist to let the world know how redemption was to be accomplished and how Jesus would take away the sins of the world. Only when we know the whole truth will we understand that Jesus is the Son of God, who took all our sins onto Himself.

John the Baptist tells us about the truth of redemption. He

tells us how he came to testify that Jesus was God and the true Light. He clearly asserted that he was not that Light, but the witness of the Light. He also testified in John 1 that it was he who prepared the gospel of redemption by baptizing Jesus Christ.

If we didn't have the testimony on redemption by John the Baptist, how could we believe in Jesus? We have never seen Jesus, and when we come from different cultures and religions, how is it possible to believe in Jehovah as our God?

Having such diverse religions throughout the world, how could we know Jesus Christ? How could we know that Jesus was in fact the Son of God, who redeemed us by taking all the sins of the world upon Himself?

We have to look into the Old Testament to find the words of redemption from the beginning and to know that Jesus is our Savior. We have to obtain the correct knowledge to have the correct faith. There's nothing we can do without true knowledge. In order to believe in Jesus and be saved, we have to know the gospel of the redemption that John the Baptist testified to and his role in it. To have complete faith in Christ, we have to know the truth about redemption.

Therefore, as Jesus said, *"And you shall know the truth, and the truth shall make you free,"* we have to know the truth of redemption in Jesus.

The Proofs in the Bible

From what point do the four Gospels start?

From the advent of John the Baptist

Free book request www.bjnewlife.org

Let us go ahead to explore all the proofs of redemption in the Bible. Let us uncover what the four Gospels say about John the Baptist, about who he was, why he was called 'the representative of mankind' or 'the last High Priest,' how all the sins of the world were passed onto Jesus through him, and whether Jesus took away all our sins onto Himself or not.

We should pay attention to the fact that all four Gospels start with John the Baptist. John 1:6 states one of the most important facts in the gospel. It tells us who performed the task of passing all the sins of the world onto Jesus. *"There was a man sent from God, whose name was John. This man came for a witness, to bear witness of the Light, that all through him might believe" (John 1:6-7).*

It says, *'all through him might believe,'* and that he was *'to bear witness of the Light.'* The Light is Jesus Christ. It means that John was to bear witness to Jesus so that all might believe through him. Now, let's take a closer look at Matthew chapter 3.

In Matthew 3:13-17, *"Then Jesus came from Galilee to John at the Jordan to be baptized by him. And John tried to prevent Him, saying, 'I have need to be baptized by You, and are You coming to me?' But Jesus answered and said to him, 'Permit it to be so now, for thus it is fitting for us to fulfill all righteousness.' Then he allowed Him. Then Jesus, when He had been baptized, came up immediately from the water, and behold, the heavens were opened to Him, and He saw the Spirit of God descending like a dove and alighting upon Him. And suddenly a voice came from heaven, saying, 'This is My beloved Son, in whom I am well pleased.'"*

Why do we have to understand the lineage of John?

Because the Bible tells us that John is the High Priest of all mankind.

John the Baptist baptized Jesus to accomplish the remission of all the sins in the world. The baptism that Jesus received from John was the most important event for our salvation. But to understand and believe the whole truth in full detail, we should closely study John the Baptist first.

In Luke 1:1-14, *"In as much as many have taken in hand to set in order a narrative of those things which are most surely believed among us, just as those who from the beginning were eyewitnesses and ministers of the word delivered them to us, it seemed good to me also, having had perfect understanding of all things from the very first, to write to you an orderly account, most excellent Theophilus, that you may know the certainty of those things in which you were instructed. There was in the days of Herod, the king of Judea, a certain priest named Zacharias, of the division of Abijah. His wife was of the daughters of Aaron, and her name was Elizabeth. And they were both righteous before God, walking in all the commandments and ordinances of the Lord blameless. But they had no child, because Elizabeth was barren, and they were both well advanced in years. So it was, that while he was serving as priest before God in the order of his division, according to the custom of the priesthood, his lot fell to burn incense when he went into the temple of the Lord. And the whole multitude of the people was praying outside at the hour of incense. Then an angel of the Lord appeared to him, standing on the right side of the altar of incense. And when Zacharias saw him, he was troubled, and fear fell upon him. But the angel said to him, 'Do not be afraid, Zacharias, for your prayer is heard; and your wife Elizabeth will bear you a son, and you shall call his name John. And you will have joy and gladness, and many will rejoice at his birth.'"*

Here, Luke, a disciple of Jesus, tells us in detail the lineage of John. Luke, a disciple of Jesus, explains the lineage of John from the beginning. Luke had taught the gospel to a man named Theophilus, who was from a different culture and didn't know about the Lord.

So, in order to teach him about Jesus, the Savior of sinners, Luke thought that he needed to explain the lineage of John the Baptist in detail. As we are also Gentiles from different races, we cannot understand the salvation of Jesus if it isn't specifically explained, step by step. Let's find out what the details are.

In Luke 1:5-9, he narrates, *"There was in the days of Herod, the king of Judea, a certain priest named Zacharias, of the division of Abijah. His wife was of the daughters of Aaron, and her name was Elizabeth. And they were both righteous before God, walking in all the commandments and ordinances of the Lord blameless. But they had no child, because Elizabeth was barren, and they were both well advanced in years. So it was, that while he was serving as priest before God in the order of his division, according to the custom of the priesthood."*

Here, an incident occurred while Zacharias was serving God, according to the custom of the priesthood. Luke testified clearly that Zacharias was a descendant of Aaron. Then, what division did Zacharias belong to? This is a very important point.

He explained, *"While Zacharias was serving as priest before God in the order of his division."* We can see that Luke knew about Zacharias so well that he explained the gospel of redemption by mentioning both Zacharias and Elizabeth.

John the Baptist was born to Zacharias and his wife Elizabeth, who was one of the daughters of Aaron. Now, let's look at the lineage of Zacharias, the father of John.

The Lineage of John the Baptist

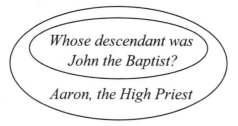

Whose descendant was John the Baptist?

Aaron, the High Priest

To understand the lineage of John the Baptist, we have to read the Old Testament, 1 Chronicles 24:1-19.

"Now these are the divisions of the sons of Aaron. The sons of Aaron were Nadab, Abihu, Eleazar, and Ithamar. And Nadab and Abihu died before their father, and had no children; therefore Eleazar and Ithamar ministered as priests. Then David with Zadok of the sons of Eleazar, and Ahimelech of the sons of Ithamar, divided them according to the schedule of their service. Now there were more leaders found of the sons of Eleazar than of the sons of Ithamar, and thus they were divided. Among the sons of Eleazar there were sixteen heads of their fathers' houses, and eight heads of their fathers' houses among the sons of Ithamar. Thus they were divided by lot, one group as another, for there were officials of the sanctuary and officials of the house of God, from the sons of Eleazar and from

the sons of Ithamar. And the scribe, Shemaiah the son of Nethaneel, one of the Levites, wrote them down before the king, the leaders, Zadok the priest, Ahimelech the son of Abiathar, and the heads of the fathers' houses of the priests and Levites, one father's house taken for Eleazar and one for Ithamar. Now the first lot fell to Jehoiarib, the second to Jedaiah, the third to Harim, the fourth to Seorim, the fifth to Malchijah, the sixth to Mijamin, the seventh to Hakkoz, the eighth to Abijah, the ninth to Jeshua, the tenth to Shecaniah, the eleventh to Eliashib, the twelfth to Jakim, the thirteenth to Huppah, the fourteenth to Jeshebeab, the fifteenth to Bilgah, the sixteenth to Immer, the seventeenth to Hezir, the eighteenth to Happizzez, the nineteenth to Pethahiah, the twentieth to Jehezekel, the twenty-first to Jachin, the twenty-second to Gamul, the twenty-third to Delaiah, the twenty-fourth to Maaziah. This was the schedule of their service for coming into the house of the Lord according to their ordinance by the hand of Aaron their father, as the Lord God of Israel had commanded him."

Let's read verse 10 again. *"The seventh to Hakkoz, the eighth to Abijah."* In the days of King David, there were numerous priests, so there was also a need to establish a regulation for their systematic services. Thus, David assigned lots to each of the sons of Aaron so that the sacrifice was offered in order. (As you all know, Aaron was the older brother of Moses. God ordained Moses as His agent, and Aaron as the High Priest of the Holy Tabernacle before the people of Israel.)

All the other Levites were put under the priests and Aaron and the priests, his sons, took charge of all the sacrifices before God. Before David assigned lots, the priests, who were the descendants of Aaron, had to draw lots each time and it had caused much confusion.

Therefore, David arranged a system by putting each

division in order. There were 24 divisions in an order, originating from the grandsons of Aaron, and the eighth was Abijah. It is said, *"A certain priest named Zacharias, of the division of Abijah."* So Zacharias was a priest of the division of Abijah, and they were both descendants of Aaron the High Priest.

It was Zacharias, a priest of the division of Abijah, who was John the Baptist's father. We know from the Bible that they used to marry within their families.

So, Jacob married his uncle's daughter from his mother's side. It is this explanation of the lineage that has profound importance. It says, *"A certain priest named Zacharias, of the division of Abijah."*

Therefore, he was definitely a descendant of Aaron. Who? Zacharias, John the Baptist's father. This is an important fact in explaining the redemption of Jesus, and the ministry of John the Baptist, and the passing of the world's sins onto Jesus.

Only the Sons of Aaron Shall Minister as Priests

Who could minister the high priesthood in the time of the Old Testament?

Aaron and his appointed descendants

Then, where in the Bible does it specify that the sons of Aaron should minister as priests? Let's look it up.

In Numbers 20:22-29, *"Then the children of Israel, the whole congregation, journeyed from Kadesh and came to*

Mount Hor. And the Lord spoke to Moses and Aaron in Mount Hor by the border of the land of Edom, saying: 'Aaron shall be gathered to his people, for he shall not enter the land which I have given to the children of Israel, because you rebelled against My word at the water of Meribah. Take Aaron and Eleazar his son, and bring them up to Mount Hor; and strip Aaron of his garments and put them on Eleazar his son; for Aaron shall be gathered to his people and die there.' So Moses did just as the Lord commanded, and they went up to Mount Hor in the sight of all the congregation. Moses stripped Aaron of his garments and put them on Eleazar his son; and Aaron died there on the top of the mountain. Then Moses and Eleazar came down from the mountain. Now when all the congregation saw that Aaron was dead, all the house of Israel mourned for Aaron thirty days."

In Exodus, the law of God is recorded, saying that the sons of Aaron, the High Priest, should assume the priesthood, and an appointed son had to assume the high priesthood, as his father did, when they came to the age of 30.

In Exodus 28:1-5, *"Now take Aaron your brother, and his sons with him, from among the children of Israel, that he may minister to Me as priest, Aaron and Aaron's sons; Nadab, Abihu, Eleazar, and Ithamar. And you shall make holy garments for Aaron your brother, for glory and for beauty. So you shall speak to all who are gifted artisans, whom I have filled with the spirit of wisdom, that they may make Aaron's garments, to sanctify him, that he may minister to Me as priest. And these are the garments which they shall make: a breastplate, an ephod, a robe, a skillfully woven tunic, a turban, and a sash. So they shall make holy garments for Aaron your brother and his sons, that he may minister to Me as priest. They shall take the gold and blue and purple and scarlet thread, and fine linen."*

God clearly assigned Aaron, the brother of Moses, to the high priesthood. The priesthood was not open to any other man. God ordered Moses to consecrate Aaron as the High Priest, and to make proper attire for him as defined by Him. We should never forget the words of God.

Also in Exodus 29:1-9, *"And this is what you shall do to them to hallow them for ministering to Me as priests: Take one young bull and two rams without blemish, and unleavened bread, unleavened cakes mixed with oil, and unleavened wafers anointed with oil (you shall make them of wheat flour). You shall put them in one basket and bring them in the basket, with the bull and the two rams. And Aaron and his sons you shall bring to the door of the tabernacle of meeting, and you shall wash them with water. Then you shall take the garments, put the tunic on Aaron, and the robe of the ephod, the ephod, and the breastplate, and gird him with the intricately woven band of the ephod. You shall put the turban on his head, and put the holy crown on the turban. And you shall take the anointing oil, pour it on his head, and anoint him. Then you shall bring his sons and put tunics on them. And you shall gird them with sashes, Aaron and his sons, and put the hats on them. The priesthood shall be theirs for a perpetual statute. So you shall consecrate Aaron and his sons."*

Gird them with sashes, Aaron and his sons, and put the hats on them.... The priesthood shall be theirs for a perpetual statute. So you shall consecrate Aaron and his sons.... God specified that only Aaron and his sons were to be consecrated to perpetually minister the priesthood. When He specifically said, *"for a perpetual statute,"* it implied that the priesthood was effective even after Jesus came into this world.

Luke explains in depth that Zacharias was a descendant of

Aaron the High Priest. When Zacharias was serving as the priest in charge in front of God in the temple of the Lord, an angel appeared and told him that his prayer was heard; that his wife Elizabeth would bear him a son.

Zacharias could not believe this and said, *"My wife is well advanced in years, how could she bear a son?"* Because of his doubt, God made him mute for a while to show that His words were true.

In due time, his wife became pregnant and after a while, the Virgin Mary, a virgin, also became pregnant. Both incidents were the prepared works of God for our salvation. In order to save the wretched mankind, He had to send His servant John and His only begotten Son Jesus into this world.

Therefore, God had His Son baptized by John in order to pass on all the sins of the world, so that those who believed in Him would be saved.

The Special Providence of God!

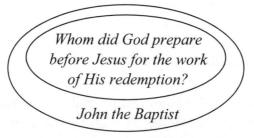

Whom did God prepare before Jesus for the work of His redemption?

John the Baptist

Jesus Christ was the Savior of mankind, who was born of the body of the Virgin Mary. Mary was betrothed to Joseph, who was a descendant of Judas. Jesus had to be born through the descendants of Judas to fulfill the Covenant of God, just as John the Baptist had to be born in the house of Aaron, the High Priest.

God prepared these two to be born into this world, in that order, John before Jesus. John was born so that he could baptize Jesus and pass all the sins of the world onto Him. A descendant of the High Priest had to offer the sacrifice of atonement in order to fulfill the Covenant of God, made in the Old and New Testament; the gospel of the redemption of Jesus had to be carried out correctly so that all the people would be delivered.

In Exodus, God gave Israel His Law and Covenants; the laws of God and the sacrificial system of the tabernacle, down to the attire of the priests, details of the sacrifices, and the succession of the priesthood to the sons of priests. God appointed Aaron and his descendants to the high priesthood in perpetuity.

Therefore, all descendants of Aaron could offer sacrifices and the high priests could come only from the house of Aaron. Do you see why this was so?

Among many descendants of Aaron, God chose a certain priest named Zacharias and his wife Elizabeth. He had said, *"Behold, I send My messenger before Your face."* When God told Zacharias that He would enable Elizabeth to have a son, and that He was to name him John, he was so astonished that he became a mute at His command until the son was born and named.

Indeed, a son was born to his house. When it was time to name the baby according to the custom of Israel, the son was named after his father, or one of his relatives.

"Now Elizabeth's full time came for her to be delivered, and she brought forth a son. When her neighbors and relatives heard how the Lord had shown great mercy to her, they rejoiced with her. Now so it was, on the eighth day, that they came to circumcise the child; and they would have called him

by the name of his father, Zacharias. And his mother answered and said, 'No; he shall be called John.' But they said to her, 'There is no one among your relatives who is called by this name.' So they made signs to his father—what he would have him called. And he asked for a writing tablet, and wrote, saying, 'His name is John.' And they all marveled. Immediately his mouth was opened and his tongue loosed, and he spoke, praising God. Then fear came on all who swelt around them; and all these sayings were discussed throughout all the hill country of Judea. And all those who heard them kept them in their hearts, saying, 'What kind of child will this be?' And the hand of the Lord was with him" (Luke 1:57-66).

Zacharias was still mute when his son was born. When it was time to name the baby, the relatives suggested that the baby should be called Zacharias. But his mother insisted that his name should be John. At this, the relatives said that there was no one by that name in the family and that the baby should be named after his father.

When Elizabeth kept on insisting on the name, the relatives went to Zacharias and asked what the name of the baby should be. Zacharias, since he could not yet speak, asked for a writing tablet and wrote *'John'*. All the relatives wondered at this unusual choice of name.

But after the naming, Zacharias' mouth opened immediately. He praised God and he was filled with the Holy Spirit and prophesied.

Thus, Luke tells of the birth of John the Baptist in the house of Zacharias. *"There was a certain priest named Zacharias, of the division of Abijah."* In the special providence of God, John the Baptist, the representative of mankind was born to Zacharias, a descendant of Aaron.

Through John the Baptist and Jesus Christ, God had

accomplished the salvation of mankind. We are saved from all our sins by believing in the work of redemption, carried out through John and Jesus Christ.

The Baptism of Jesus

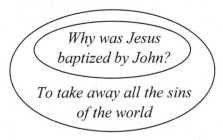

Why was Jesus baptized by John?

To take away all the sins of the world

John the Baptist testified that Jesus was the Son of God and He took away all our sins. He was John the Baptist, the servant of God who was sent to bear witness to God's salvation. It does not mean that God doesn't tell us Himself that He is our Savior. God works through His servants in the church, and through the mouths of all His people who have been saved.

God says, *"Speak comfort to Jerusalem, and Cry out to her, that her warfare is ended, that her iniquity is pardoned; for she has received from the Lord's hand double for all her sins...The grass withers, the flower fades, but the word of our God stands forever" (Isaiah 40:2, 8).*

God had already promised about seven hundred years before the birth of Christ, "You are not sinners anymore. I have atoned for all your sins and the warfare has ended." Thus, the voice of the gospel of redemption keeps crying out to us. This is what is called the prepared gospel.

When we understand the works of John the Baptist and really understand that all the sins of the world were passed onto Jesus through John the Baptist, we can all be freed from our sins.

All four Gospels tell us about John the Baptist, and Malachi, the last prophet of the Old Testament also testifies that John the Baptist is the prepared servant of God. The New Testament begins with the birth of John the Baptist and the passing on of sins through him.

Then why do we call him John the Baptist? It is because he baptized Jesus. What does baptism mean? It means 'to pass on to, to be buried, to be washed'—the same as 'the laying on of hands' in the Old Testament.

In the Old Testament, when a man sinned, he passed his sins on to the sacrificial animal without blemish by laying his hands on the head of it, and the sacrifice died with those sins. 'The laying on of hands' means 'to pass on to.' Therefore, 'the laying on of hands' and 'baptism' has the same implications, even though they are apparently different.

Then, what was the meaning of the baptism of Jesus? His baptism was the only way for us to receive the remission of sins. God had established the law that sin might be transferred to a sacrifice through 'the laying on of hands.' Thus, in the days of the Old Testament, sinners had to lay their hands on the head of a sacrifice in order to pass their sins onto its head. After that, they had to cut its throat and the priests placed the blood on the horns of the altar of the burnt offering. This was the way to atone for daily sins.

Then, how did they atone for yearly sins?

In this case, Aaron the High Priest offered the sacrifice for all the people of Israel. Because John the Baptist was born to the house of Aaron, it was proper for him to be the high priest, and God predestined him to be the last High Priest, according to His promise of redemption.

John the Baptist was the representative of all mankind and

the last high priest because the Old Testament ended when Jesus Christ was born. Who else but John the Baptist could have passed all the sins of the world onto Jesus in the New Testament, just as Aaron had atoned for the sins of his people in the Old Testament? As the last high priest in the Old Testament and the representative of all mankind, John the Baptist passed all the sins of the world onto Jesus when he baptized Him.

Because John passed all the sins of the world onto Jesus, believing in the gospel of the water and Spirit can redeem us. Jesus became the Lamb in order to save all sinners, thus carrying out the work of redemption as God had planned. Jesus told us that John the Baptist was the last prophet, the last high priest who passed all the sins of the world onto Him.

Why couldn't Jesus do it by Himself? Why did He need John the Baptist? There was a reason for John the Baptist to be born six months prior to Jesus; it was to fulfill the law of the Old Testament, to accomplish its promises.

Jesus was born to the Virgin Mary, and John the Baptist was born to an old and barren woman named Elizabeth.

These were the works of God and He planned them to save all sinners. To save us from a perpetual war against sin, along with all the sufferings of our sinful existences, He sent His servant John, and then His Own Son, Jesus. John the Baptist was sent as the representative of all mankind, the last High Priest.

The Greatest Man Born of Women

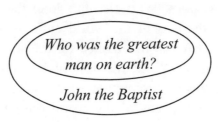

Who was the greatest man on earth?

John the Baptist

Let's look at Matthew 11:7-14. *"As they departed, Jesus began to say to the multitudes concerning John: What did you go out into the wilderness to see? A reed shaken by the wind? But what did you go out to see? A man clothed in soft garments? Indeed, those who wear soft clothing are in kings' houses. But what did you go out to see? A prophet? Yes, I say to you, and more than a prophet. For this is he of whom it is written: 'Behold, I send My messenger before your face, who will prepare Your way before You.' Assuredly, I say to you, among those born of women there has not risen one greater than John the Baptist; but he who is least in the kingdom of heaven is greater than he. And from the days of John the Baptist until now the kingdom of heaven suffers violence, and the violent take it by force. For all the prophets and the law prophesied until John. And if you are willing to receive it, he is Elijah who is to come."*

People went out to the wilderness to see John the Baptist, who cried out, *"Repent, you brood of vipers!"* And Jesus said, *"But what did you go out to see? A man clothed in soft garments? Indeed, those who wear soft clothing are in kings' houses."*

Jesus Himself testified to John's greatness. "What did you go out to see? A barbarian who dresses in camel hair and shouts at the top of his lungs? He must have worn the hair of a camel. What did you go out to see? A man clothed in soft garments? Those who wear soft clothing live in kings' houses. But he is greater than the king," testified Jesus. *"Indeed, those who wear soft clothing are in kings' houses. But what did you go out to see? A prophet? Yes, I say to you, and more than a prophet."*

In the old days, prophets were considered to be greater than kings. John the Baptist was more than a king, and more than a prophet. He was more than all the prophets of the Old Testament. In fact, John, the last high priest and the representative of mankind, was more important than Aaron, the first High Priest. Jesus Himself testified that John was as such.

Who is the representative of mankind? Except Christ Himself, who is the greatest man on earth? John the Baptist. *"I say to you, and more than a prophet. 'Behold, I send My messenger before Your face, who will prepare Your way before You.'"*

John the Baptist testified that the war against sin had ended. *"Behold, the Lamb of God who takes away the sin of the world!"* It was John the Baptist who testified that Jesus took away the sins of the world.

In Matthew 11:11, *"Assuredly, I say to you, among those born of women there has not risen one greater than John the Baptist."* Has there been anyone greater than John the Baptist among those born of women?

What does it mean to be *'born of women?'* It refers to all humankind. Except for Adam and Eve, all human beings were born from women. Yes, among those born of women, there has not risen a greater person than John the Baptist. Therefore, he is the last High Priest and the representative of mankind. John the Baptist was the High Priest, prophet and the representative of all humankind.

In the Old Testament, Aaron and his sons were ordained

by God to serve in perpetuity. All sins had to be washed away through Aaron and his sons. It was as God had ordered.

If some other Levites had come forward and dared to step into their priesthood, they would have certainly died. All they were able to do was to collect wood for the fire on the altar, skin the animals, pick out the fat, clean the intestines and bring its offal outside the camp. If they had been presumptuous enough to try to physically do the work of priests, they would have died. It is the law of God. They could not cross the line.

On earth, there has not risen a man greater than John the Baptist. He was the greatest among all mortals. *"And from the days of John the Baptist until now the kingdom of heaven suffers violence, and the violent take it by force."*

The redemption of mankind was accomplished when John the Baptist baptized Jesus, and those who believe in Jesus can enter the Kingdom of Heaven because they become righteous by faith.

Now, let's see how John's father testified to his son.

The Testimony of Zacharias, the Father of John

What did Zacharias prophesy about his son?

John will prepare the Lord's way by giving knowledge of salvation to His people.

Let's read Luke 1:67-80. *"Now his father Zacharias was filled with the Holy Spirit, and prophesied, saying: 'Blessed is the Lord God of Israel, for He has visited and redeemed His people, and has raised up a horn of salvation for us in the house of His servant David, as He spoke by the mouth of His holy prophets, who have been since the world began, that we should be saved from our enemies and from the hand of all who hate us, to perform the mercy promised to our fathers and to remember His holy covenant, the oath which He swore to our father Abraham: to grant us that we, being delivered from the hand of our enemies, might serve Him without fear, in holiness and righteousness before Him all the days of our life. And you, child, will be called the prophet of the Highest; for you will go before the face of the Lord to prepare His ways, to give knowledge of salvation to His people by the remission of their sins, through the tender mercy of our God, with which the Dayspring from on high has visited us; to give light to those who sit in darkness and the shadow of death, to guide our feet into the way of peace.' So the child grew and became strong in spirit, and was in the deserts till the day of his manifestation of Israel."*

Zacharias prophesied two things. He prophesied that the King of all people would come. From verses 68 to 73, he prophesied with joy that God did not forget His promises and that Jesus, as God promised to Abraham, was born to the Virgin Mary in order to save his descendants from their enemies' hands.

From verse 74, *"To grant us that we, being delivered from the hand of our enemies, might serve Him without fear."* This is a reminder of the Promise of God to Abraham and the people of Israel, and he prophesied, *"to grant us that we might serve Him without fear."*

From verse 76, he prophesied to his son. *"And you, child, will be called the prophet of the Highest; for you will go before the face of the Lord to prepare His ways, to give knowledge of salvation to His people by the remission of their sins, through the tender mercy of our God, with which the Dayspring from on high has visited us; to give light to those who sit in darkness and the shadow of death, to guide our feet into the way of peace."*

Here he said, *"To give knowledge of salvation to His people by the remission of their sins."* By whom did he say the knowledge of salvation was to be given? John the Baptist. Can you all see this? John the Baptist, through the words of God, was to give us the knowledge that Jesus is God's Son, who took away the sins of the world.

Now, let's look at Mark 1. *"The beginning of the gospel of Jesus Christ, the Son of God. As it is written in the Prophets: 'Behold, I send My messenger before Your face, who will prepare Your way before You. The voice of one crying in the wilderness: 'Prepare the way of the Lord, make His paths straight.' John came baptizing in the wilderness and preaching a baptism of repentance for the remission of sins. And all the land of Judea, and those from Jerusalem, went out to him and were all baptized by him in the Jordan River, confessing their sins"* (Mark 1:1-5).

When the Israelites heard from John the Baptist, they turned from worshipping the idols of Gentiles and were baptized by John the Baptist. But John testified, "I baptize you with water so that you may return to God. But the Son of God will come and be baptized by me so that all your sins will be passed onto Him in this same manner. And if you believe in His baptism as you are being baptized by me, all your sins will be passed onto Him, just as the sins were passed on through the laying on of hands in the Old Testament." That was what John testified to.

The fact that Jesus was baptized in the Jordan means that He was baptized in the river of death. We sing at a funeral, *"♪In the sweet by and by, we shall meet on that beautiful shore. We shall meet on that beautiful shore.♪"* When we die, we will cross the Jordan River. The Jordan River is the river of death. Jesus was baptized in this river of death, for He took all the sins of the world there and *"the wages of sin is death."*

The Baptism That Passes on Our Sins

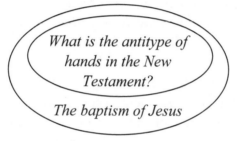

What is the antitype of hands in the New Testament?

The baptism of Jesus

In Matthew 3:13-17, we read, *"Then Jesus came from Galilee to John at the Jordan to be baptized by him. And John tried to prevent Him, saying, 'I have need to be baptized by You, and are You coming to me?' But Jesus answered and said to him, 'Permit it to be so now, for thus it is fitting for us to fulfill all righteousness.' Then he allowed Him. Then Jesus, when He had been baptized, came up immediately from the water; and behold, the heavens were opened to Him, and He saw the Spirit of God descending like a dove and alighting upon Him. And suddenly a voice came from heaven, saying, 'This is My beloved Son, in whom I am well pleased.'"*

Jesus went to the Jordan and was baptized by John the Baptist. He ordered John, "Baptize Me." John replied, "But I need to be baptized by You, and are You coming to me?" The high priests of heaven and earth met together.

As stated by Hebrews, Jesus Christ is the High Priest forever, according to the order of Melchizedek. This means that Jesus is without human genealogy. He is not a descendant of Aaron, or of any person on earth. He is the Son of God, our Creator. He is who He is; therefore, He has no genealogy. Jesus threw away the glory of heaven and came down to earth to save His people.

The reason He descended into this world was to save all sinners who suffered from the deception of Satan. In addition, He took away all the sins of the world by being baptized by John the Baptist. *"But Jesus answered and said to him, 'Permit it to be so now, for thus it is fitting for us to fulfill all righteousness.' Then he allowed Him."*

"Permit it to be so now." Permit it! Jesus ordered the representative of all mankind and bowed His head to be baptized. In the Old Testament, when a sacrifice was offered to God, either the sinner or the high priest laid his hands on its head and passed on the sins. 'To lay one's hands on' means 'to pass.'

John the Baptist baptized Jesus. It was the same as the laying on of hands in the Old Testament. 'To pass on to,' 'to be buried,' 'to be washed,' and 'to sacrifice' are also the same. The New Testament is the reality while the Old Testament is its shadow.

When a sinner laid his hands on a lamb in the Old Testament, his sin was passed onto the lamb and the lamb had to be killed. When the lamb was dead, it was buried. The sins of the one who laid his hands on the lamb were passed onto the sacrificial animal, so the lamb was to be killed due to the sins! If the sins were passed onto the lamb, could the one who offered the lamb according to the sacrificial system be without sin? Yes.

Let's say that this handkerchief is sin and this microphone, the lamb. When I lay my hands on this microphone, this sin is passed onto it, the lamb. God Himself decided that it would be so. "Lay your hands on." In order to be redeemed of sins in the days of the Old Testament, one had to lay his hands on the head of a sacrifice. After that, he could be without sin. Likewise, the baptism of Jesus was to wash, bury and pass the sins of the world onto Him. This is exactly what it means.

What does it mean to fulfill all righteousness?

It's to wash away all sins by passing the sins onto Jesus.

So, when Jesus was baptized to take away all the sins of the world, were they all indeed passed onto Him? All the sins of the world were passed onto Jesus and all people were redeemed. It is the same as the passing of sins to the sacrifices in the Old Testament. Jesus came from Galilee to the Jordan and said to John, *"Permit it to be so now, for thus it is fitting for us to fulfill all righteousness" (Matthew 3:15).*

Then, John baptized Jesus. He told John that it was fitting for them to fulfill all righteousness by His baptism. *'All righteousness'* means 'the most proper and fitting.' *'For thus,'* in other words, by the means of baptism, all righteousness was fulfilled. This meant that it was right for John to baptize Jesus, and Jesus to be baptized by John, so as to pass all the sins of the world onto Him.

God grants redemption on the basis of Jesus' baptism, His sacrifice on the Cross and our faiths. "All people suffer from sin and are tormented by the devil because of their sins. Therefore, in order for them to be saved and sent to Heaven, you, as the representative of mankind and a descendant of Aaron, should baptize Me for all people. I shall be baptized by you, John. Then, the work of redemption will be fulfilled."

"I understand," replied John.

So John baptized Jesus. He laid his hands on Jesus' head and passed all the sins of the world onto Him. Thus, Jesus became the Savior who washed away all our sins. Now, believing in His redemption can save us. Do you believe?

After His baptism at the Jordan, through the hands of the representative of all mankind, Jesus traveled and preached the gospel for three-and-a-half years with all the sins of the world on His body as His first public works in ministry.

He told the woman who was caught in the act of adultery, *"Neither do I condemn you."* He could not condemn her because He had taken all her sins onto Himself and was about to die on the Cross for them. While He was praying at a place called Gethsemane, He prayed three times, begging for the Father to let the cup of God's judgment pass from Him, but soon gave up and said, *"Not as I will, but as You will."*

"Behold! The Lamb of God Who Takes Away the Sin of the World!"

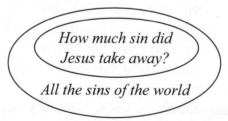

How much sin did Jesus take away?

All the sins of the world

John 1:29 states, *"The next day John saw Jesus coming*

toward him, and said, 'Behold! The Lamb of God who takes away the sin of the world!'" John the Baptist baptized Jesus and the next day, Jesus came toward him, so he told people, *"Behold! the Lamb of God who takes away the sin of the world!'"* It was his testimony.

The Son of God came to this world and took away all its sins. John the Baptist testified again. In John 1:35-36, *"Again, the next day, John stood with two of his disciples. And looking at Jesus as He walked, he said, 'Behold the Lamb of God!'"*

The Lamb of God refers to the fact that Jesus is the true and real entity of the sacrifice mentioned in the Old Testament, which died for the sins of Israel. For you and I, the Son of God and our Creator, came down to this world to take away all our sins; all sins from the creation of the world until the day that it ends, from original sin to all our iniquities, from our shortcomings to our faults. He redeemed all of us with His baptism and blood on the Cross.

Jesus took away all our sins and gave us, the believers, perfect redemption. Do you understand this? *"The Lamb of God who takes away the sin of the world."*

About 2000 years has passed since He was born into this world and in 30 A.D., Jesus took away all our sins. The year 1 A.D. was the year that Jesus was born. We call the time before Christ: B.C. Almost 2000 years has passed since Jesus came to this world.

In 30 A.D., John the Baptist baptized Jesus and the next day, John cried out to the people, *"Behold! The Lamb of God who takes away the sin of the world!"* *"Behold!"* He told people to believe in Jesus, who took away all their sins. He testified that Jesus was the Lamb of God, the One who saved us from all our sins.

Jesus took away all our sins and ended our perpetual war

against sin. We are now without sin since the Son of God took them away. John the Baptist testified that Jesus had taken away all our sins, the sins of both you and I. *"This man (John) came for a witness, to bear witness of the Light, that all through him might believe" (John 1:7).*

Without the testimony of John, how could we have known that Jesus took away all our sins? The Bible tells us often that He died for us, but only John the Baptist clearly testified that He took away all our sins.

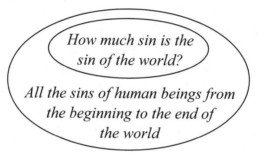

How much sin is the sin of the world?

All the sins of human beings from the beginning to the end of the world

Many testified the fact after Jesus' death, but only John testified it while He was alive. Of course, the disciples of Jesus also testified to the redemption of Jesus. They testified that Jesus took away our sins, that He is our Savior.

Jesus took away the world's sins. Now reader, you are not yet 100 years old are you? Jesus took away the sins of the world when He was 30 years old. Consider this diagram.

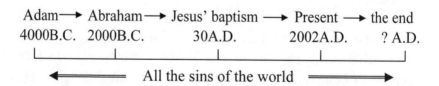

Adam⟶ Abraham⟶ Jesus' baptism ⟶ Present ⟶ the end
4000B.C. 2000B.C.   30A.D.   2002A.D.   ? A.D.

⟵ ══ All the sins of the world ══ ⟶

Let's say that it was 4,000 years before Jesus came that the first man was created. And it has been just a little over 2000 years since Jesus came. We do not know how long the world will last, but the end is sure to come. He says, *"I am the Alpha and the Omega, the Beginning and the End, the First and the Last" (Revelation 22:13).*

So, there will surely be an end. We are now at the point indicated by the year 2002. Christ took away our sins in 30 A.D., and it was 3 years before He died at the Cross.

"Behold! The Lamb of God who takes away the sin of the world." He took away the sins of the world, the sins of you and I. We are over 2000 years away from the birth of Jesus and are living our lives about 2000 years after Jesus took away our sins. We still live and commit sins day in and day out, however, Jesus is the Lamb of God who already took away the world's sins.

We begin to live and sin in this world from the moment we are born. Do we all sin from the moment we are born, or do we not? —We do.— Let's go through the whole process. From the day we are born until we are 10, do we sin, or do we not? —We do.— Then, were those sins passed onto Jesus or not? —They were.— Since all sins were passed onto Jesus, He is our Savior. If not, how could He be our Savior? All the sins were passed onto Jesus.

From the age of 11 to 20, do we sin, or do we not? We sin in our hearts and in our acts.... We are very good at it. We have been taught not to sin, but are prone to commit sins by nature.

God tells us that all those sins were passed onto Jesus. He knew what we were sinful, so He took away all those sins beforehand.

And how long do we usually live in this world? Let's say it is about 70 years. If we added together all the sins we committed during those 70 years, how heavy would our load be? If we packed them into 8-ton trucks, we would probably end up with more than 100 truckloads.

Try to imagine how much sin we will commit during our whole lifetimes. Are those the sins of the world, or are they not? They are a part of the sins of the world. We sin from birth, up to 10, 10 to 20, 20 to 30... until the day we die, but all those sins are included in the sins of the world that already passed onto Jesus through His baptism.

The Savior of Man, Jesus Christ

How much sin did Jesus take away?

All the sins of our ancestors, of us and our descendants until the end of the world

Jesus tells us that He came in flesh to wash away all those sins. But, Jesus couldn't baptize Himself, so God sent His servant John ahead, the elected representative of all human beings. As it is written, *'His name will be called Wonderful, Counselor, Mighty God.'* By Himself, by His wisdom and by His council, He sent the representative of mankind ahead, and Jesus Himself, the Son of God, came in the flesh to take away all the sins of the world. Isn't this a wonderful salvation of God's profound providence?

It is wonderful, isn't it? So, just by being baptized by John the Baptist, He washed away all of mankind's sins throughout the whole world and delivered everyone from sin by being crucified, once and for all. He delivered us all. Think about it. Let's take a look at all your sins from 20 to 30, 30 to 40, 40 to

60, to 70, to 100, and also those of your children. Did He blot out all those sins, or did He not? Yes, He did. He is Jesus Christ, the Savior of mankind.

Since John the Baptist passed all our sins onto Jesus, and because God had planned it so, we can be delivered by believing in Him. Are you and I sinners? Were all our sins passed onto Jesus or not? —We are not sinners anymore because our sins were already passed onto Jesus.—

Who dares to say that there's sin in this world? Jesus took away all the sins of the world. He knew that we would sin, and thus, also took the sins of the future. Some of us are not yet 50 and some haven't even lived half of our lives yet, but some of us we talk about ourselves, including myself, as if we would live forever.

There are so many of us who lead turbulent lives. Let me explain it this way. What is half the life span of a mayfly? It is about 12 hours.

"My goodness! I met such and such a man and he swung a flyswatter at me! I was almost crushed to death, and you know, I've never met such a cruel man during my half life." It had only lived 12 hours and couldn't stop talking. But already, half of its life had passed.

By 7 or 8 in the evening, it faces the twilight of its life, and in a short while, death. Some mayflies survive for 20 hours, some 21, and some live to the ripe old age of 24 hours. They may talk of their lifelong experiences, but what does it look like to us? As we live to 70, or 80 years old, we may say, "Don't make me laugh." Their experience is nothing at all in our eyes.

Let's apply this parable to the relationship between God and us. God is eternal. He lives for eternity. He decides the beginning and the end of the world. As He lives forever, He lives in eternity beyond the time frame of eternity. He looks at us from the position of His eternity.

Once upon a time, He took away all the sins of the world, died on the Cross, and said, *"It is finished."* He was resurrected on the third day and went up to Heaven. He now resides in eternity. Now, He is looking down at each of us.

One man might say, "Oh, dear, I have sinned so much. Even though I have lived only 20 years, I have sinned so much." "I have lived for 30 years and have sinned too much. It is just too much. How can I ever be without sins?"

But our Lord in His eternity would say, "Don't make Me laugh. I have not only redeemed your sins up to now, but also the sins of your ancestors before you were born, and the sins of all the generations of your descendants who will live after your death." He says this to you from the eternal time frame. Do you believe this? Believe it and receive the gift of salvation given freely to you. Enter the Kingdom of Heaven.

Do not bound yourself with your thoughts, but believe in the words of God. *'It is fitting for us to fulfill all righteousness.'* The Lamb of God, who took away the sins of the world, already fulfilled all righteousness. Jesus took away all the sins of the world. Did He, or did He not? He did.

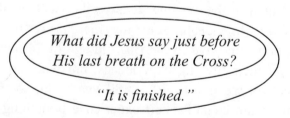

What did Jesus say just before His last breath on the Cross?

"It is finished."

Jesus Christ took away all the sins of the world through His baptism, was sentenced to death in the court of Pontius Pilate and was crucified on the Cross.

"And He bearing His Cross, went out to a place called the

place of the Skull, which is called in Hebrew, Golgotha, where they crucified Him, and two others with Him, one on either side, and Jesus in the center. Now Pilate wrote a title and put it on the Cross. And the writing was: JESUS OF NAZARETH, THE KING OF THE JEWS. Then many of the Jews read this title, for the place where Jesus was crucified was near the city; and it was written in Hebrew, Greek, and Latin" (John 19:17-20).

Let's take a look at what happened after He was crucified on the Cross. *"After this, Jesus, knowing that all things were now accomplished, that the Scripture might be fulfilled."* He had taken over all our sins according to the Scripture. *"He said, 'I thirst!' Now a vessel full of sour wine was sitting there; and they filled a sponge with sour wine, put it on hyssop, and put it to His mouth. So when Jesus had received the sour wine, He said, 'It is finished!' and bowing His head, He gave up His spirit" (John 19:28-30).*

After He had received the sour wine, He cried out, *"It is finished!"* and bowed His head and passed away. He was actually dead. Jesus Christ resurrected on the third day and ascended to Heaven.

Let us turn to Hebrews 10:1-9. *"For the law, having a shadow of the good things to come, and not the very image of the things, can never with these same sacrifices, which they offer continually year by year, make those who approach perfect. For then would they not have ceased to be offered? For the worshipers, once purged, would have had no more consciousness of sins. But in those sacrifices there is a reminder of sins every year. For it is not possible that the blood of bulls and goats could take away sins. Therefore, when He came into the world, He said: Sacrifice and offering You did not desire, but a body You have prepared for Me. In burnt offerings and sacrifices for sin You had no pleasure. Then I said, 'Behold, I have come—in the volume of the book it is written of Me—to do Your will, O God.' Previously saying, 'Sacrifice and offering, burnt offerings, and offerings for sin You did not desire, nor had pleasure in them' (which are offered according to the law), then He said, 'Behold, I have come to do Your will, O God.' He takes away the first that He may establish the second."*

The Eternal Redemption

How can we solve the problem of daily sin after coming to believe in Jesus?

By confirming that Jesus has already blotted out all sin through His baptism

The law, in other words, the sacrificial system, was a shadow of the good things to come. The sacrifices of the Old Testament, of sheep and goats, revealed to us that Jesus Christ would come and take away our sins in the same manner in order to blot out all our sins.

All the people of the Old Testament, David, Abraham, and all the others, knew and believed what the sacrificial system meant to them. It revealed that the Messiah, Christ (Christ means 'the Anointed King') would come some day to wash away all their sins. They believed in their redemption and were saved by their faiths.

The law was a shadow of the good things to come. Offering sacrifices for their sins day after day, year after year could never completely redeem them. Therefore, the complete and eternal Being, the One without blemish, the Son of God, had to come to earth.

Jesus said that He had come to do His Father's will, as written in the Book, which was written of Him. *"And then I said, 'Behold, I have come to do Your will, O God.' He takes away the first that He may establish the second."* We are redeemed of our sins because Jesus Christ took away our sins, as written in the Old Testament, and because we believe in Him.

Let's read Hebrews 10:10. *"By that will we have been sanctified through the offering of the body of Jesus Christ once for all."* By that will we have been sanctified through the offering of the body of Jesus Christ once for all. Have we been sanctified or not? —We have.—

What does this mean? God the Father sent His Son and passed all our sins onto Him through the baptism. He received and judged Him once and for all on the Cross. Thus, He delivered all of us who were suffering from sin. It was the Will of God.

In order to deliver us, Jesus offered Himself as the eternal sacrifice, once and for all, so that we could be sanctified. We have been sanctified because Jesus sacrificed Himself for all our sins and died for us so that we need not be judged.

The sacrifice of the Old Testament was offered every day because all the daily sins needed another offering to be washed away.

The Spiritual Meaning of Jesus' Washing Peter's Feet

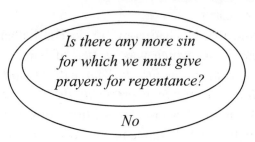

Is there any more sin for which we must give prayers for repentance?

No

In John 13, there's a story of Jesus washing Peter's feet. He washed Peter's feet in order to show him that Peter would commit sins in the future and to teach him that He had already redeemed all those sins too. Jesus knew that Peter would sin again in the future, so He poured water into a basin and washed his feet.

Peter tried to refuse, but Jesus said, *"What I am doing you do not understand now, but you will know after this."* What this passage means is, 'You will sin again after this. You will deny Me and sin again after I wash all your sins. You will sin even after My Ascension. Therefore, I wash your feet to warn Satan not to test you because I have already taken away even your future sins.'

Do you think He washed Peter's feet in order to tell us that we have to repent everyday? No. If we had to repent everyday to be redeemed, that means that Jesus would not have taken away all our sins once and for all.

But Jesus said that He sanctified us once for all. If we were to repent every day, we might as well go back to the time of the Old Testament. Then who could become righteous? Who could be redeemed completely? Even if we believed in God, who could live without sin?

Who can become sanctified by repentance? We sin

ceaselessly each day, so how can we ask for forgiveness for each and every sin? How can we become so thick-skinned and pester Him every day for our redemptions? We tend to forget our sins committed in the mornings by the end of the day, and the sins of the evening by the next morning. It is impossible for us to completely repent for all our sins.

Therefore, Jesus was baptized once and offered Himself on the Cross once so that we might become sanctified all at one time. Can you understand this? We were redeemed from all our sins once and for all. We are not redeemed every time we repent.

We have been saved from our sins by believing that Jesus took away all our sins, yours and my sins.

"And every priest stands ministering daily and offering repeatedly the same sacrifices, which can never take away sins. But this man, after He had offered one sacrifice for sins forever, sat down at the right hand of God, from that time waiting till His enemies are made His footstool. For by one offering He has perfected forever those who are being sanctified. And the Holy Spirit also witnesses to us; for after he had said before, 'This is the covenant that I will make with them after those days, says the Lord: I will put My laws into their hearts, and in their minds I will write them,' then He adds, 'Their sins and their lawless deeds I will remember no more.' Now where there is remission of these, there is no longer an offering for sin" (Hebrews 10:11-18).

What does it mean, *"Now where there is remission of these"* in verse18 above? It means that the sin itself, any sin at all, was expiated forever, without exception. God has blotted them out and forgiven us all. Do you believe this? *"Now where there is remission of these, there is no longer an offering for sin."*

Let us summarize everything so far. If John the Baptist had not laid his hands on Jesus, in other words, if he had not baptized Jesus, could we have been redeemed? No, absolutely not! Let's think backwards. If Jesus had not elected John the Baptist as the representative of all human beings and taken away all sin through him, could He have washed away all our sins? He couldn't have.

The Law of God is just. It is fair. He could not just say that He was our Savior and that He took away all our sins. He had to take away our sins practically. Why did Jesus, God, come to us in the flesh? He came in order to take away all the sins of mankind through His baptism. Jesus knew that all the sins from our hearts and flesh could not be blotted out, unless He came in the flesh to be offered as the eternal sacrifice.

If Jesus Christ had not been baptized, our sins would still remain. If He had been crucified without first taking away our sins, His death would have been meaningless. It wouldn't have had anything to do with us. It would have been completely meaningless.

So, when He started His public ministry at the age of 30, He went to John the Baptist at the Jordan to be baptized. His public ministry started at the age of 30 and ended at 33. When He was 30, He went to John the Baptist to be baptized. "Permit it to be so now, for it is fitting for us to do thus so that all people can be saved and become righteous. It is the proper thing for us to do. Now, baptize Me." Yes, Jesus Christ was baptized for the redemption of all people.

Since Jesus was baptized and took away all our sins, and because all our sins were passed onto Him through the hands of John the Baptist, God Himself turned His eyes away when Jesus was dying on the Cross. Even though Jesus was His only begotten Son, He had to sacrifice His Son.

God is love, but He had to let His Son die. So, for three hours, there was darkness over all the land. Jesus cried out just before He died, *"Eli, Eli, lama sabachthani?"* that is, *"My God, My God, why have You forsaken Me?"* Jesus shouldered all our sins and received the vicarious judgment on the Cross for us. Thus, He saved us all. Without the baptism of Jesus, His death would have been meaningless.

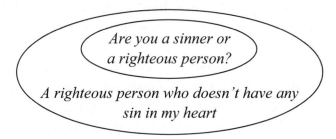

Are you a sinner or a righteous person?

A righteous person who doesn't have any sin in my heart

If Jesus had died on the Cross without taking away all our sins through His baptism, His death would not have accomplished the redemption. In order to perfectly redeem us, Jesus was baptized by John, the representative of all human beings, and received the judgment on the Cross so that all those who believe in Him might be saved.

Therefore, from the days of John the Baptist until now, the Kingdom of Heaven has suffered violence. Because John the Baptist passed all the sins of the world onto Jesus, our sins have been atoned. You and I can now call God our Father and boldly enter the Kingdom of Heaven.

In Hebrews 10:18, *"Now where there is remission of these, there is no longer an offering for sin."* Are you still a sinner? Now that Jesus has already paid off all your debts, do you still have to pay debts?

There was a man whose heavy drinking put him in debt to many creditors. Then, one day, his son made a fortune and paid off his father's entire debts. His father would no longer have a debt no matter how much he had owed every public house there.

This is what Jesus did for us. He paid more than enough in advance for all our sins. Not just the sins of our lifetimes, but all the sins of the world. They were all passed onto Jesus when He was baptized. So are you still sinners now? No, you are not.

If we had known this gospel of redemption from the beginning, how easy it would have been for us to believe in Jesus. But as it is, it sounds so new that many people wonder about it.

But this is not something new. It has existed since the beginning of human history. We just didn't know of it before. The gospel of the water and the Spirit has always been recorded in the Scriptures and has always been in effect. It has been there all the time. It was here in the Bible before you and I were born. It has been here since the creation of the earth.

The Gospel of Eternal Redemption

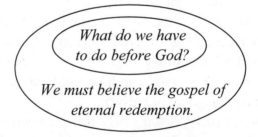

What do we have to do before God?

We must believe the gospel of eternal redemption.

Jesus Christ, who washed away all our sins, did it even before you and I were born. He took them all away. Are you still with sin? —No— Then what about the sins you will commit tomorrow? They are also included in the sins of the world.

Let's take off the sins of tomorrow now. The sins we have committed until now were also included in the sins of the world, weren't they? Were they passed onto Jesus or not? Yes, they were.

Then, were the sins of tomorrow also passed onto Him? Yes, He took them all, without exception. He has not left even one sin behind. The gospel tells us to believe wholeheartedly that Jesus took away all our sins, all at once, and paid for them all.

'The beginning of the gospel of Jesus Christ, the Son of God.' (Mark 1:1) The gospel of Heaven is the joyous news. He asks us, "I took away all your sins. I am your Savior. Do you believe in Me?" Among a countless number of people, only a few have answered, "Yes, I believe. I believe as You have told us. It was so simple that I could understand it immediately." Those who confess their faiths like this become righteous just like Abraham.

But others say, "I cannot believe it. It sounds so new and strange to me."

Then, He asks, "Just tell Me, did I take away all your sins or not?"

"I was taught that You took away only the original sin, but not my daily sins."

"I see that you are too smart to believe as you are told. You must go to hell because I have nothing to say to you."

Believing in His complete redemption has saved us. All of those who insist that they have sin must go to hell. They made their own choice.

The gospel of redemption starts from the testimony of John the Baptist. Since Jesus washed all our sins away through His baptism by John the Baptist, we become sanctified when we believe.

The Apostle Paul talked a lot about the baptism of Jesus in his Epistles. In Galatians 3:27, *"For as many of you as were baptized into Christ have put on Christ."* 'Being baptized into Christ' means that we are in union with Christ by believing in His baptism. When Jesus was baptized, all our sins were passed onto Him through John the Baptist, and they were completely washed away.

In 1 Peter 3:21, *"There is also an antitype which now saves us, namely baptism (not the removal of the filth of the flesh, but the answer of a good conscience toward God), through the resurrection of Jesus Christ."*

Only those who believe in the testimony of John the Baptist, the baptism of Jesus and the blood on the Cross have the grace of redemption from above.

Receive the baptism of Jesus as the antitype of salvation in your heart and be saved. ✉

SERMON 6

Jesus Christ Came by Water, Blood, and the Spirit

Jesus Christ Came by Water, Blood, and the Spirit

< 1 John 5:1-12 >

"Whoever believes that Jesus is the Christ is born of God, and everyone who loves Him who begot also loves him who is begotten of Him. By this we know that we love the children of God, when we love God and keep His commandments. For this is the love of God, that we keep His commandments. And His commandments are not burdensome. For whatever is born of God overcomes the world. And this is the victory that has overcome the world—our faith. Who is he who overcomes the world, but he who believes that Jesus is the Son of God? This is He who came by water and blood—Jesus Christ; not only by water, but by water and blood. And it is the Spirit who bears witness, because the Spirit is truth. For there are three who bear witness in heaven: the Father, the Word, and the Holy Spirit; and these three are one. And there are three that bear witness on earth: the Spirit, the water, and the blood; and these three agree as one. If we receive the witness of men, the witness of God is greater; for this is the witness of God which He has testified of His Son. He who believes in the Son of God has the witness in himself; he who does not believe God has made Him a liar, because he has not believed the testimony that God has given of His Son. And this is the testimony: that God has given us eternal life, and this life is in His Son. He who has the Son has life; he who does not have the Son of God does not have life."

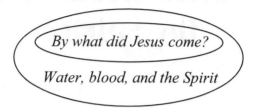

Did Jesus come by water? Yes, He did. He came by His baptism. The water symbolizes the baptism of Jesus by John the Baptist at the Jordan River. It was the baptism of redemption with which He took away all the sins of the world.

Did Jesus come by blood? Yes, He did. He came in the flesh of a man and was baptized to take away all the sins of the world, then paid off the wages of sin by bleeding on the Cross. Jesus came by blood.

Did Jesus come by the Spirit? Yes, He did. Jesus was God, but He came as the Spirit in the flesh to be the Savior of sinners.

Many people do not believe that Jesus came by water, blood and Spirit. Only a few believe that Jesus is truly the King of kings and the God of gods. The majority of people still wonder, 'Is Jesus truly the Son of God, or the son of man?' And many, including theologians and ministers, believe in Jesus as a man rather than as God, the Savior and the absolute Being.

But God said that anyone who believes that Jesus is the King of all kings, the true God and the true Savior would be born of Him. Those who love God love Jesus and those who truly believe in God believe in Jesus in the same way.

People cannot overcome the world unless they are born again. Thus, the Apostle John told us that only true Christians could overcome the world. The reason why the faithful can overcome the world is that they have faith in the water, the blood, and the Spirit. The power to overcome the world cannot spring from a person's will, endeavor or passion.

"Though I speak with the tongues of men and of angels, but have not love, I have become as sounding brass or a clanging cymbal. And though I have the gift of prophecy, and understand all mysteries and all knowledge, and though I have all faith, so that I could remove mountains, but have not love, I am nothing. And though I bestow all my goods to feed the poor, and though I give my body to be burned, but have not love, it profits me nothing" (1 Corinthians 13:1-3).

'The love' referred to here means that Jesus came by the water, blood and Spirit. In the Bible, the word 'love' always refers 'the love of the truth' (2 Thessalonians 2:10). Actually, God's love was manifested through His only begotten Son (1 John 4:9).

Only He Who Believes in the Water and the Blood Can Overcome the World

Who can overcome the world?

Those who believe in the redemption of Jesus' baptism, of His blood and of the Spirit

1 John 5:5-6 state, *"Who is he who overcomes the world, but he who believes that Jesus is the Son of God? This is He*

who came by water and blood—Jesus Christ."

Fellow Christians, the One who overcame Satan and the world was Jesus Christ. Those who believe in the word of the water, the blood and the Spirit of Jesus can also overcome the world. How did Jesus overcome the world? Through the redemption of the water, the blood and the Spirit

In the Bible, 'water' refers to 'the baptism of Jesus' (1 Peter 3:21). Jesus came to this world in the flesh. He came to save the sinners of the world; He was baptized to take away the sins of all the sinners and died on the Cross to atone for those sins.

The blood on the Cross refers to the fact that He came to this world in the flesh of a man. He came in the likeness of sinful flesh to save sinners and was baptized with water. Therefore, Jesus came to us by both water and blood. In other words, He took away all the sins of the world with both the water of His baptism and the blood of His death.

How did Satan rule over the world? Satan caused humankind to doubt the Word of God and planted the seeds of disobedience in their hearts. Satan tries to turn people into his servants by deceiving them into disobeying the Word of God.

However, Jesus came into this world and blotted out all their sins with the water of His baptism and His blood on the Cross: He overcame Satan and blotted out all the sins of the world.

This occurred because Jesus Christ was the Savior of sinners. He became our Savior because He came by water and blood.

Jesus Took Away All the Sins of the World with His Baptism of Redemption

What does it mean by Jesus' overcoming the world?

It means that He took away all the sins of the world.

Since Jesus was baptized to take away all the world's sins and died to expiate them, He was able to deliver us from all sins. Because Jesus was baptized in the Jordan River by John the Baptist, the representative of all human beings, all the sins of the world were passed onto Him. Jesus gave His life on the Cross for the wages of sin. He overcame the power of Satan with His death and resurrection. Jesus paid the wages of all our sins with His death.

Jesus Came to Sinners by the Water of His Baptism and the Blood on The Cross

How did He overcome the power of Satan?

Through His baptism, the blood and the Spirit

The Apostle John said that redemption is not just of water, but both of water and blood. Therefore, as Jesus had taken away all sins and removed our sins forever, all sinners would be saved from sin by believing in Him, and being faithful to His Words.

When Jesus came down to the world, He not only took away our sins, but He also paid them off by bleeding to death on the Cross. He took away all our sins with His baptism in the Jordan and paid the wages of those sins on the Cross; He paid for our sins with His death. The just law of God which said that the *'wages of sin is death' (Romans 6:23)* was fulfilled.

What did Jesus mean by overcoming the world? The faith that overcomes the world is the faith in the gospel of redemption, which Jesus bestowed to us by water and blood. He came in the form of flesh and testified to salvation with His baptism of water and His death on the Cross.

Jesus overcame the world, namely Satan. The disciples of the early church stood fast even in the face of martyrdom without submitting to the Roman Empire or to any of the temptations of this world.

This was all a result of their belief that Jesus came by water (He was baptized to take away all our sins), and by His blood on the Cross (He paid the wages of all our sins with His death).

Jesus came in the Spirit (He came in the flesh of man), and took away the sins of sinners with His baptism and His blood on the Cross so that all of us who are to be redeemed could overcome the world.

There Is Also an Antitype Which Now Saves Us, Namely Baptism, through the Resurrection of Jesus Christ <1 Peter 3:21>

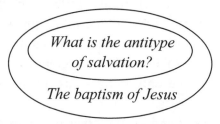

What is the antitype of salvation?

The baptism of Jesus

It is said in 1 Peter 3:21, *"There is also an antitype which now saves us, namely baptism (not the removal of the filth of the flesh, but the answer of a good conscience toward God), through the resurrection of Jesus Christ."* The Apostle Peter testified that Jesus was the Savior and that He came by the water of baptism and blood.

As a result, we should believe in Jesus, who came by water and blood. We should also know that the water of the baptism of Jesus is the antitype of our salvation. The Apostle Peter told us that the 'water' of baptism, the 'blood,' and 'the Spirit' are 'the absolute factors' in redemption.

Jesus' disciples believed in the blood on the Cross through the baptism of Jesus. To believe only in the blood is to possess only half of the true faith. Faith based on a half or incomplete truth fades with time. However, the faiths of those who believe in the gospel of the water, the blood and the Spirit will grow stronger with time.

The voice of the gospel of only the blood is continually growing in the world these days. Why is this so? People do not know the Word of truth, the redemption of the water and the Spirit, so they cannot be born again.

At one time, the churches of the West had fallen victim to superstition. They seemed to be prospering for a while, but the servants of Satan helped to turn their faiths into superstition.

Superstition is to believe that the devil will flee if one draws a cross on a piece of paper or make it with wood, and that Satan will be driven off if one confesses his/her faith in the blood of Jesus. Through these and other superstitious beliefs, Satan deceived people into believing that they only had to believe in the blood of Jesus. Satan pretends to be afraid of the blood, saying that the only thing Jesus did for sinners was to shed blood on the Cross.

However, Peter and all the other disciples testified to the true gospel of the baptism of Jesus and the blood on the Cross. But, what do Christians these days testify to? They testify only to the blood of Jesus.

We should believe in the words written in the Bible and have faith in the salvation of the Spirit, of the baptism of Jesus, and of His blood. If we ignore the baptism of Jesus and only testify to the fact that Jesus died for us on the Cross, our salvation cannot be complete.

The 'Word of Testimony' for God's Salvation of the Water

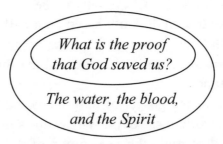

What is the proof that God saved us?

The water, the blood, and the Spirit

In 1 John 5:8, the Lord says, *"There are three that bear witness on earth."* The first is the Spirit, the second is the water of Jesus' baptism, and the third is His blood on the Cross. All three of these things are as one. Jesus came to this world to save all of us from these sins. He alone did this with all three, the baptism, the blood, and the Spirit.

'There are three that bear witness.' There are three things that prove that God saved us. These three elements of proof are the water of Jesus' baptism, His blood, and the Spirit. These three things are what Jesus did for us in this world.

If one of these three things were to be omitted, salvation would not be complete. There are three that bear witness on earth: the Spirit, the water, and the blood.

Jesus Christ, who came to us in the flesh, is God, the Spirit, and the Son. He came down to this world as the Spirit in the flesh of man and was baptized in the water to take away all the sins of the world. He took all sins onto His flesh and saved us sinners by bleeding to death on the Cross. He fully paid off all our sins. It is the gospel of complete redemption by the water, the blood, and the Spirit.

Even if just one of these were omitted, it would be the same as refusing God's salvation, which has saved us from all sin. If we were to agree with the majority of believers today, we would have to say 'there are two that bear witness on earth: the blood and the Spirit.'

But the Apostle John said that there were three things that bore witness: the water of Jesus' baptism, the blood on the Cross and the Spirit. The Apostle John was very explicit in his testimony.

The faith that redeems a sinner is the faith in the Spirit, the water, and the blood. What kind of faith enables one to overcome the world? And where can we find such faith? It is right here in the Bible. It is to believe in Jesus, who came by water, blood and the Spirit. Have faith in them to receive salvation and eternal life.

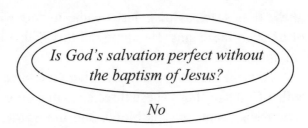

Is God's salvation perfect without the baptism of Jesus?

No

A long time ago, before I was born again, I, too, was a Christian who believed only in the blood on the Cross and the Spirit. I believed that He came down as the Spirit and died for me on the Cross to save me from all sins. I only believed in these two things and was presumptuous enough to preach them to all people.

I had planned to study theology to become a missionary in order to work and die for all the lost souls, as Jesus had done. I had planned all sorts of grand things.

But, since I believed in only two things, there was always sin remaining in my heart. As a result, I could not overcome the world. I could not be free of sin. When I only believed in the blood and the Spirit, I still had sin in my heart.

The reason why I still had sin in my heart, even though I believed in Jesus, was that I didn't know about the water, the baptism of Jesus. My deliverance was not complete until I was redeemed by my complete faith in the water of baptism, the blood, and the Spirit.

I was not able to overcome the sins of the flesh because I didn't know the meaning of Jesus' baptism. Even now, many people believe in Jesus, but still commit sins of the flesh. They still have sin in their hearts and try in vain to revive the first love they had for Jesus.

They cannot revive the passion of their first enthusiasms because they have never been washed completely of their sins with the water. They do not realize that all their sins were passed onto Jesus when He was baptized, and they cannot recover their faiths again after a fall.

I would like to make this clear to all of you. We can live in faith and overcome the world when we believe in Jesus. However insufficient we are, no matter how often we commit sin in this world, as long as we believe in Jesus as our Savior, who made us completely free of sin with His baptism and bloodshed, we can stand victorious.

Nonetheless, if we believe in Jesus without the water of His baptism, we cannot be delivered completely. The Apostle John told us that the faith that overcomes the world is the faith in Jesus Christ, who came by the water of baptism, the blood and the Spirit.

God sent His only begotten Son to redeem those who believe in the baptism and His blood. Jesus took away all our sins with His baptism. Jesus, the only Son of God, came to us in the Spirit (in the flesh of a man). Then, He bled on the Cross to pay off the wages of sin. Thus, Jesus delivered all human beings from sin.

The faith that leads us to overcome the world comes from believing in the truth that Jesus came to us by water, blood, and the Spirit, which completely freed us from all sins.

If there had not been the water of baptism and the blood on the Cross, there would be no true salvation. Without one or the other of the three components, we could not have true salvation. True salvation can't be achieved without the water, the blood and the Spirit. Therefore, we have to believe in the water, the blood and the Spirit. Know this and you will have true faith.

I Tell You That It Is Not True Salvation without the Witness of the Water, the Blood, and the Spirit

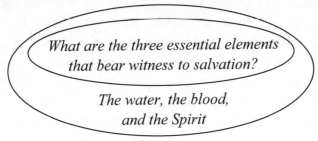

What are the three essential elements that bear witness to salvation?

The water, the blood, and the Spirit

One may think of the above question like this. "Jesus is my Savior. I believe in the blood on the Cross and I want to die as a martyr. I believe in Jesus even though I have sin in my heart. I have repented diligently and worked hard to act in a good, just and charitable manner everyday. I have given my life and all my worldly possessions for You. I even chose not to marry. How can God not know me? Jesus died for me on the Cross. Our Holy God came down as a man and died for us on the Cross. I believed in You, sacrificed for You, and did my work faithfully for You. Although I may be unworthy and still have some sin in my heart, will Jesus send me to hell for that? No, He won't."

There are so many people who think this way. They do not believe that Jesus was baptized to take away all the sins of the world. When these nominal Christians, who believe in Jesus but still have sin, die, where do they go? They go to hell. They are mere sinners!

They, who think as they please and presume that God must think the same, will go to hell. Moreover, some say that because Jesus took away all sins when He died on the Cross, there's no sin in the world. However, this is only talking about the blood and the Spirit. This is not the faith that leads people to complete redemption.

We should believe that Jesus took away our sins with His baptism, was judged, and died on the Cross for us, and that He rose again the third day after His death.

Without such faith, complete redemption would not be possible. Jesus Christ was baptized, died on the Cross, and was resurrected. Jesus Christ came to us by water, blood, and the Spirit. He took away all the sins of the world.

There are three vital elements that bear witness to His salvation on earth: the Spirit, the water and the blood.

Firstly, the Holy Spirit testifies that Jesus is God and that He descended in the flesh of a man.

The second element is the witness of the 'water.' The water is the baptism of Jesus in the Jordan by John the Baptist, through which our sins were passed onto Jesus. All our sins were passed onto Him when He was baptized (Matthew 3:15).

The third witness is the 'blood' that stands for Jesus' acceptance of responsibility for the judgment of our sins. Jesus died, accepted His Father's judgment for us and was resurrected on the third day to give us new lives.

God the Father sends the Spirit into the hearts of those who believe in the baptism and blood of His Son to testify to our redemption.

The ones who have been born again have the Word, with which they overcome the world. The redeemed will overcome Satan, the lies of false prophets, and the obstacles, or pressures of the world that ceaselessly attack them. The reason we have this power is because we have three witnesses in our heart: the water of Jesus, His blood, and the Spirit.

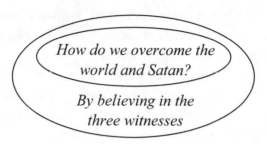

How do we overcome the world and Satan?

By believing in the three witnesses

We can overcome Satan and the world because we believe in the Spirit, the water, and the blood. Those who believe in the baptism and blood of Jesus are able to overcome all the deceptions of false prophets. Our faith, with this power to overcome, lies in the water, the blood, and the Spirit. Do you believe in this?

You can neither be born again nor overcome the world if you do not have faith in redemption through the baptism of Jesus, His blood, and the belief that Jesus is the Son of God and our Savior. Is such faith in your heart?

Do you have the Spirit and the water in your heart? Do you believe that all your sins were passed onto Jesus? Do you have the blood of the Cross in your heart?

You will overcome the world if you have faith in the water and the blood of Jesus in your heart. If you believe that Jesus died on the Cross for you and took the judgment for you, you will overcome.

The Apostle John overcame the world because he had all of these three essential elements in his heart. He also talked about redemption to all his brothers in faith who endured obstacles and threats in their work. He testified, "This is how you too can overcome the world. Jesus came by the Spirit, the water, and the blood. As He overcame the world, so too will the faithful be able to overcome the world. This is the only way for the faithful to overcome the world."

In 1 John 5:8, it is said, *"And there are three that bear witness on earth: the Spirit, the water, and the blood; and these three agree as one."* Many still only talk about the blood and the Spirit while omitting the water of Jesus' baptism. If they take out the 'water,' they are still deceived by Satan. They should come out from behind their own self-deceptions and repent; they should believe in the 'water' of Jesus' baptism, of being born again.

No one can overcome the world without believing in the water and the blood of Jesus. I say to you again, no one! We have to fight using the water and the blood of Jesus as our powerful weapons. His Word is the sword of the Spirit, the Light.

There are still too many who do not believe in the baptism of Jesus, which washed away all our sins. There are still too many who believe in only two things. So, when Jesus tells them to *'arise and shine,'* they cannot shine at all. They still have sin in their hearts. Although they believe in Jesus, they still end up in hell.

The Gospel of the Baptism and the Blood of Jesus Should Definitely Be Testified to So That People Can Hear, Believe, and Be Saved

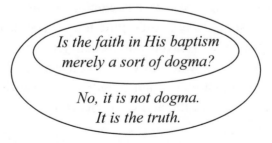

Is the faith in His baptism merely a sort of dogma?

No, it is not dogma. It is the truth.

When we testify to the gospel, it has to be definite. Jesus

came by the Spirit, the baptism (which took away all our sins), and by the blood (which paid for all our sins). We must believe in all three of these.

If we don't, we aren't preaching the gospel, but rather simple religion. Most Christians regard today's Christianity as just a religion, but Christianity cannot be classified as a religion. It is the faith of redemption built on the truth, the faith of looking up to God. It cannot be a religion.

Religion is something created by humans, while faith is looking up to the salvation that God granted us. This is the difference. If you ignore this truth, you treat Christianity as just another religion and preach by means of morals and ethics.

Jesus Christ didn't come to establish a religion in this world. He never established a religion called Christianity. Why do you believe that it is a religion? If it is all the same, why not believe in Buddhism instead? Do you think that I am wrong in saying this?

Some people believe in Jesus as a religious way of life, and end up saying, "What is the difference? Heaven, Nirvana, paradise.... They are all the same thing, they just have different names. We will all end up in the same place anyway."

Fellow Christians, we should stand firm on the truth. We should *'arise and shine.'* We should be able to tell the truth without hesitation.

When someone says, "That cannot be the only way to Heaven," you should say in a definite tone, "Yes! It is the only way. You can go to Heaven only when you believe in Jesus Christ, who came by water, blood, and the Spirit." You should shine so brightly that other souls may want to hear the Word of redemption, be born again, and go to Heaven.

Have Correct Faith:
Unrequited Lovers of Jesus Who Don't Know the Redemption of Jesus' Baptism and His Blood Will Perish

Who will perish even though he/she believes in Jesus?

Those who don't believe in the baptism of Jesus

Just claiming to arbitrarily believe in Jesus is to have an unrequited love for Jesus and is a shorter way to be a Christian-religionist.

A ship crossing the Pacific went down and a few survivors were left adrift on a rubber raft. They sent out an SOS signal, but rough seas prevented other ships from coming to their aid. Then, a helicopter came and threw down a rope. If one of the men held onto the rope with his hands instead of tying it around his body, it would be like falling into an unrequited love with Jesus; believing in God as he pleases. He is not safe yet, but he says, "I believe. Save me. I believe, so I guess I will be saved."

One who does not understand the truth of the baptism of Jesus and His blood believes that he/she will be saved just by holding onto the rope.

But as he is pulled up, his hands will lose their grip on the rope. He will be holding on with only his own strength. It is too far to the coast for him to hold onto the rope to the end. When his strength runs out, he will lose his grip and fall back into the ocean.

To have an unrequited love with Jesus is like that. Many

may say that they believe in God and Jesus; that they believe in Jesus, who came by the Spirit, but this is only part of the whole equation. They can neither really believe in nor dwell in the perfect gospel, so they force themselves to say over and over that they 'believe' in Him.

To believe and to try to believe is not the same thing. They say that they will follow Jesus to the end, but they will be cast away on the last day because of the sins that remain in their hearts. They love Jesus without knowing that He came by His baptism, blood, and the Spirit. If they love Jesus only for His blood, they will go to hell.

Tie your soul with the rope of the true gospel, the gospel of the water and the blood. When Jesus throws down the rope of salvation, those who tie themselves with the water, the blood, and the Spirit will be saved.

The rescuer from the helicopter shouted through a megaphone, "Please listen carefully to me. When I throw down the rope, tie it around your breast, under your arms. Then, just stay as you are. Don't hang onto the rope with your hands. Just tie it around your chest and relax. Then, you will be saved."

The first person followed the instructions and tied himself with the rope, and was saved. But the other man said, "Don't worry. I'm very strong. I've been working out at a health club. Look! Can you see my muscles? I can hang on for miles." He then held onto the rope with his hands as the rope was pulled up.

Both men were pulled up in the beginning. But the difference was that the one who listened to the instructions and tied the rope around his chest was pulled up without a hitch. He even lost consciousness on the way up, but he was pulled up nevertheless.

The one who had pride in his own strength eventually lost

his grip because his strength ran out. He died because he refused to listen and ignored the instructions.

To obtain complete redemption, one must believe in the redemption of the water of His baptism and the blood that saved all souls from sin. Salvation is available to those who wholeheartedly believe in the Word: "I saved you completely with My baptism by John the Baptist and with My bleeding to death on the Cross."

Those who believe only in the blood say, "Don't worry, I believe. I will be thankful to the end of my life for the blood of Jesus. I will follow Jesus to the end and my belief only in the blood will be more than enough to overcome the world and all sins for the rest of my life."

However, this is not enough. Those whom God admits to be His people are the ones who believe in all three witnesses: that Jesus came by the Spirit, that He was baptized (Jesus took away all sins with His baptism in the Jordan), that He died on the Cross to pay the wages for all sins, and that He was resurrected on the third day from the dead.

The Spirit comes only to those who believe in all three and witnesses for them. "Yes, I am your Savior. I saved you with the water and the blood. I am your God."

To those who do not believe in all three, God does not give salvation. Even if only one is omitted, God says, "No, you are not saved." All His disciples believed in all three. Jesus says that His baptism is the antitype for salvation, and that His blood is the judgment.

The Apostle Paul and Peter Also Bore Witness to Both the Baptism and the Blood of Jesus

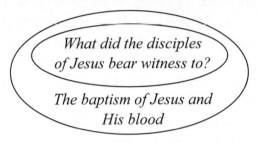

What did the disciples of Jesus bear witness to?

The baptism of Jesus and His blood

Did the Apostle Paul talk about the baptism of Jesus? Let's see how many times he talked about the baptism of Jesus. He said in Romans 6:3, *"Or do you not know that as many of us as were baptized into Christ Jesus were baptized into His death?"* And in 6:5, *"For if we have been united together in the likeness of His death, certainly we also shall be in the likeness of His resurrection."*

He also said in Galatians 3:27, *"For as many of you as were baptized into Christ have put on Christ."* Jesus' Apostles all testified to the 'water,' the baptism of Jesus. *"There is also an antitype which now saves us, namely baptism"* (1 Peter 3:21).

The Salvation of Redemption of the Lord Came by the Water and the Blood of Jesus

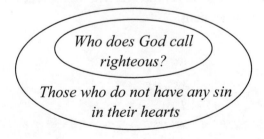

Who does God call righteous?

Those who do not have any sin in their hearts

The redemption that Jesus bestowed upon man is of the water of Jesus' baptism and His blood on the Cross. By that redemption, we can arise and shine. How? By testifying to these three things.

"Arise, shine; For your light has come! And the glory of the LORD is risen upon you" (Isaiah 60:1). God has shone the light on us and tells us to shine too. We should obey that command.

We have been preaching the gospel with all our strength. However, so many people still do not listen. Believe in Jesus and you will be redeemed. You will be righteous. If sin still remains in your heart, you are not yet righteous. You have not yet overcome the sins of the world.

You can never get rid of the sin in your heart if you do not believe in the water of Jesus (the baptism of Jesus). You can never avoid judgment if you do not believe in the blood of Jesus. You can never be saved if you do not believe in Jesus Christ, who came by the Spirit. You can never be completely righteous unless you believe in those three witnesses.

Insufficient righteousness only leads to a 'so-called righteousness.' If anyone says that he/she still has sin, but considers himself/herself a righteous person, that person is not yet in Jesus. Some people these days try to hang onto redemption through 'so-called righteousness.' They have written tons of useless articles on the subject.

Does God call a person sinless when there is sin still in his/her heart? He does not do that. He calls it as He sees it. He is almighty, but He can never lie. People do not understand the true meaning of righteousness. We call something 'clean' only when it is clean. We do not say 'righteous' when there is sin.

You may think that you are called righteous by Jesus even though you have sin in your heart, but that is incorrect.

Jesus only calls us righteous when we believe in Him as the One who came by the Spirit, the water (that He took away all our sins when He was baptized), and the blood (He came in the flesh and died for us).

Fellow Christians, 'so-called righteousness' has nothing to do with the gospel of the water and the blood. 'So-called righteousness,' or 'to be called righteous' is a dogma that was invented by men. Does God call you righteous when you have sin in your heart? God does not call someone righteous when he/she has sin in his/her heart, no matter how fervently that person may believe in Jesus. Jesus can never lie.

Yet, do you still think He calls someone righteous when there is sin in his/her heart? That's what people think, not God. God hates lies. Would He call you righteous when you only believe in the 'Spirit' and the 'blood?' Never.

There is only one kind of persons that God calls righteous. They are those who do not have any sin in their hearts. He only recognizes those who believe in all three things: that Jesus, who is God, came down to the world in the flesh, was baptized in the Jordan, and bled on the Cross to blot out all our sins.

Only those who believe in the good news of redemption are recognized to be the righteous by God. They are the ones who have the correct belief. They completely believe in all the things He did for us. They believe that Jesus came, was baptized to take away all our sins, took judgment for us by dying on the Cross, and was resurrected from the dead.

All these things were done out of God's love. Jesus came down from heaven and said, *"Come to Me, all you who labor and are heavy laden, and I will give you rest"* *(Matthew 11:28).* He did this by taking away our sins.

God doesn't recognize those who only believe in the blood of Jesus. Those who only believe in the blood of Jesus still have sin in their hearts. Who does Jesus recognize to be the redeemed?

Belief in the baptism of Jesus, His blood, and the fact that He is God are all necessities for salvation. "I took away all your sins when I came down to this world and was baptized by John the Baptist. I testify that all the sins of the world were passed on to Me. I paid for the sins on the Cross. I saved you thus."

To those who believe in all three, Jesus says, "Yes, you are saved. You are righteous and children of God." You, too, can be saved if you believe in the baptism of Jesus, His blood, and the Spirit altogether. Those who believe only in the blood and the Spirit still have sin in their hearts.

In the Kingdom of God, there is only one truth. There is justice, honesty, love, and kindness. There's not a speck of a lie. Lies and wiles do not exist in Heaven.

Who is the one 'who practices lawlessness?'

The one who doesn't believe in the baptism of Jesus

"Many will say to Me in that day. 'Lord, Lord, have we not prophesied in Your name, cast out demons in Your name, and done many wonders in Your name?" (Matthew 7:22)

God never recognizes those works of people to be eligible to enter His Kingdom. *"And then I will declare to them, 'I never knew you: depart from Me, you who practice lawlessness!'" (Matthew 7:23)*

"I offered two houses for You. I gave up even my life for You. Didn't You see me? I have never denied you until my last breath. Didn't You see me?"

"So, do you have sin in your heart?"

"Yes, Lord. I do a little."

"Then, stay away from Me! No sinner is allowed to come in here."

"But I died as a martyr to my faith in You Lord!"

"What do you mean, died a martyr? You only died of your stubbornness. Did you acknowledge My baptism and blood? Did I testify in your heart that you are My child? You do not believe in My baptism and I never testified that you are My child, yet you hung onto your belief and died for it. When did I ever testify for you? You brought it on yourself. You loved and tried alone for your own redemption. Do you understand? Now, be on your way."

Jesus told us to arise and shine. The redeemed people may cower down before many nominal Christians and many false prophets, and fail to shine brightly! But a little flame can start a big fire. If one stands bravely and testifies the truth, the whole world will brighten up.

In Isaiah 60:1-2, it says, *"Arise, shine; for your light has come! And the glory of the Lord is risen upon you. For behold, the darkness shall cover the earth, and deep darkness the people; but the Lord will arise over you and His glory will be seen upon you."*

God orders us to arise and shine because the darkness of untruth, that is, the false gospel, has covered the whole world. Only those who believe in Jesus can love Him. Those who are not redeemed can never love Jesus. How can they? They only talk of love, but can never truly love Him unless they believe in the whole truth.

There Are Three Things That Bear Witness to the Salvation of Sinners

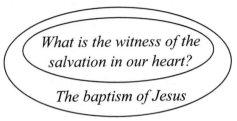

What is the witness of the salvation in our heart?

The baptism of Jesus

"And there are three that bear witness on earth: the Spirit, the water, and the blood; and these three agree as one." Jesus came to earth and He did His work with the water and the blood. He did this and saved us.

"If we receive the witness of men the witness of God is greater; for this is the witness of God which He has testified of His Son. He who believes in the Son of God has the witness in himself; he who does not believe God has made Him a liar, because he has not believed the testimony that God has given of His Son. And this is the testimony; that God has given us eternal life, and this life is in His Son. He who has the Son has life; he who does not have the Son of God does not have life" (1 John 5:9-12).

The born-again receive the witness of mankind. We are recognized as the righteous. When the born-again, who are the redeemed, speak of the truth about redemption, people cannot dispute it. They accept it. They say that we believe correctly, that we are correct in our faiths. If we tell them how we were born again, no one can stand against the true gospel we bear witness to. They say we are right. We receive the witness of men.

But this passage also says, *"The witness of God is greater; for this is the witness of God."* It says the witness of

God is of His Son. Correct? What is the witness of His Son? The witness that God saved us is that Jesus came by the Spirit, the water of redemption, and the blood on the Cross. God witnesses that this is the way He saved us, and that we are His people because we believe in it.

"He who believes in the Son of God has the witness in himself; he who does not believe God has made Him a liar, because he has not believed the testimony that God has given of His Son."

This passage tells us precisely who the delivered ones are. It says that one who believes in the Son of God has the witness in oneself. Do you have the witness in your heart? It is in you and it is in me. Jesus came to the earth for us. (He came in the flesh through the body of Mary by the Holy Spirit.) When He was 30 years old, He was baptized to take all our sins upon Himself. And with all our sins, He was judged on the Cross. He was resurrected the third day to give us eternal life. Jesus saved us thus.

What would have happened if He had not been resurrected? How could He have testified for me in the grave? That is why He is my Savior. This is what we believe.

Just as He said, He saved us with His baptism and blood. And because we believe, you and I are saved. The witness is in me and it is in you. The redeemed can never ignore the 'water' of His baptism. We never omit the things that He did to save us.

"For thus it is fitting for us to fulfill all righteousness" *(Matthew 3:15)*. We never deny that Jesus took away all our sins at the Jordan when John the Baptist baptized Him. The redeemed can never deny the 'water,' the baptism of Jesus.

Those Who Believe, but Are Not Redeemed, Deny the Baptism of Jesus to the End

Who makes God a liar?

He who does not believe in the baptism of Jesus

How precise he was when the Apostle John said, *"He who does not believe God has made Him a liar."* If the Apostle John were living here and now, what would he tell us, today's Christians? He would ask whether or not 'Jesus took away all our sins when He was baptized.'

Wouldn't John the Baptist also testify to the gospel that Jesus redeemed us with His baptism? "Were not your sins passed onto Jesus' head and did He not bear your sins on His back when He was baptized by me?" Thus, he explicitly testified that Jesus had been baptized to save all of us (John 1:29. 1 John 5:4-8).

Those who do not believe in God, in other words, who do not believe in everything He did to save us, make Him a liar. When we say that Jesus took away all our sins when He was baptized, they say, "Oh, dear me! He couldn't have taken away all our sins! He only took away original sin, so all our daily sins still remain"

So, they insist that they have to offer prayers of repentance for their daily sins in order to be redeemed. This is what they believe. Do you all believe so too? The ones who do not believe that our sins were washed away with Jesus' baptism make God a liar.

Jesus Redeemed Us Once and for All When He Was Baptized and Bled on the Cross

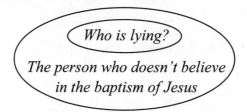

Who is lying?

The person who doesn't believe in the baptism of Jesus

Jesus was baptized and took away all sins once and for all. God saves those who believe in the baptism and the blood of Jesus, but abandons those who do not believe. They go to hell. Therefore, whether we are saved or not depends on what we believe. Jesus delivered the world from all sins. Those who believe are saved, and the ones who do not believe are not yet saved because they have made God a liar.

People do not go to hell for their weaknesses, but for their lack of belief. *"He who does not believe God has made Him a liar" (1 John 5:10).* Those who do not believe that all their sins were passed onto Jesus still have sin in their hearts. They cannot say that they don't have sin.

Once, I met a deacon and asked him, "Deacon, were all your sins gone when you believed in Jesus?"

"Of course they were."

"Then, since Jesus took all the sins of the world and said that *'it was finished,'* you have been saved. Isn't that right?"

"Yes, I have been saved."

"Then you must be without sin."

"Yes, I am."

"What happens if you sin again?"

"We are only human. How could we not sin again? So we have to repent and wash away our sins every day."

This deacon still has sin in his heart because he does not

know the complete truth of redemption.

The likes of him are the ones who mock God and make Him a liar. Did Jesus, who is God, fail to get rid of all the sins of the world? It is very upsetting. If Jesus had not gotten rid of all sins, how could He be the God of Salvation? How could He tell us to believe in Him? Are you going to make Him a liar? I advise you not to do that!

The Bible tells us not to mock Him. This means to not make Him a liar and try to deceive Him. He is not like us.

The Apostle John tells us precisely about the gospel of redemption. Many people do not want to believe in the things that God did for us—the fact that Jesus Christ came by water, blood, and the Spirit.

There are two groups of Christians: those who do not believe as the Bible says and confess, "I am a sinner," and those who believe in all the things that God has done for them and confess with faith, "I am righteous." Which group do you think is telling the truth?

Those who do not believe in the things that God did, in other words, who do not admit the witness of the water, the blood, and the Spirit, are lying. They have false faiths. The ones who do not believe make God a liar.

Do not make Him a liar. Jesus came to the Jordan River and thus, (by being baptized) fulfilled all righteousness (took away the sins of the world).

The Unbelievers Deny the Baptism of Jesus and His Holiness

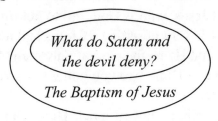

What do Satan and the devil deny?

The Baptism of Jesus

A believer in His Son has the witness in him. A born-again believes that his/her sins were passed on to Jesus when He was baptized, and that he/she was delivered with the water and the blood of Jesus. Born-again Christians believe that Jesus was born into this world through the body of the Virgin Mary, that He was baptized in the Jordan before He died on the Cross, and that He was resurrected.

The righteous have the witness in their hearts. The proof of our salvation is in our faith in Jesus, who came by water, blood, and the Spirit. The witness is in you. I advise you to have the witness in yourself. I say to you. It is not salvation if there is no witness, the proof of salvation, within you.

The Apostle John said, *"He who believes in the Son of God has the witness in himself" (1 John 5:10).* Is it to have the witness to believe only in the blood on the Cross? Or, to believe in the water, but not the blood? You should believe in all three to be recognized by God.

Only then will Jesus testify for you that 'you are saved.' Are you saying that you will have the witness if you believe in only two of three? It would be to believe in God in your own way. It would be to 'testify for yourself.'

There are so many like this. There are so many in the world who believe only in two out of the three. They testify that they have been saved and write books about it. How fluent they are! It is so frustrating. They call themselves 'the Evangelicals.' They feel that they are not just 'the Evangelicals,' but also 'the religious.' They do not believe in the 'water,' but still boast of their salvation! They may sound logical, but they do not have the witness of God in their minds. It is only a hypothesis.

How can you call it salvation? Only those who believe in Jesus, who came by the Spirit, water, and blood, have the witness of God and men.

The Apostle Paul said, *"For our gospel did not come to you in word only, but also in power, and in the Holy Spirit and in much assurance" (1 Thessalonians 1:5).* Satan is delighted when people believe only in the blood of Jesus. "Oh, you fools, you are deceived by me, ha-ha!" There are many who believe that when people praise the blood of Jesus, Satan goes away. They think Satan may be afraid of the Cross. But you should keep in mind that Satan is only putting on a show. We should not be fooled by it.

When a demon possesses a man, he may become crazed and foam at the mouth. It is not a difficult feat for the devil because it has the power to make a man do almost anything. The devil only has to use his brain a little. God gave the devil all sorts of powers, except the power to kill. The devil can make someone tremble like an aspen leaf, scream, and foam at the mouth.

When this happens, believers shout, "Be gone in the name of Jesus! Be gone!" And when the man regains his senses and comes back to his normal self, they say to him that it was the blood of Jesus that had the power to save him. But this is not the power of His blood. It is only the devil putting on a 'show'.

Satan is most afraid of those who believe in Jesus, who has washed us clean with His baptism, who took the judgment for us with His blood and on the third day, was resurrected. Satan cannot stay around a witness of the baptism of Jesus and the salvation of the blood.

As you know, Catholic priests sometimes minister exorcisms. We have seen it in the movies. In the movie, 'The Omen,' a priest holds up a wooden cross and shakes it, but the priest dies anyway. Someone who is born again would not be defeated like this.

A born-again believer confidently talks about the blood and the water of Jesus. When the devil tries to torment him/her, he/she would ask the devil, "Do you know that Jesus took away all my sins?" The devil would then run away. The devil hates to be around 'the born-again.' If 'a born-again' just sat there, the devil would try to escape. It is said that those who do not believe in God make Him a liar. They do not believe in the witness of His Son, the witness of the water and the blood.

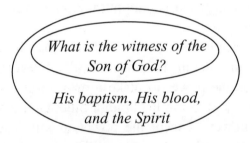

What is the witness of the Son of God?

His baptism, His blood, and the Spirit

What is the witness of the Son of God? It is that He came by the Spirit and took away our sins with water. He took all the sins of the world onto Himself and bled on the Cross for all of us. Isn't that the redemption of the water, the blood, and the Spirit?

People tell lies before God because they do not believe in the true gospel of the water and the blood, the gospel of redemption. All the other gospels are false. Their beliefs are false, and they propagate these false gospels in vain.

Let's return to 1 John 5. The 11th verse says, *"And this is the testimony: that God has given us eternal life, and this life is in His Son."* It tells us that God has given us eternal life, and the life is in the one who receives it. Also, this life is in His Son.

Those who receive eternal life are the ones who are redeemed by believing in the baptism of Jesus and His blood. The redeemed receive eternal life and live forever. Have you received eternal life?

In the 12th verse, *"He who has the Son has life; he who does not have the Son of God does not have life."* In other words, he who believes in the things the Son did on earth—His baptism, death on the Cross, and His resurrection—has eternal life. But he who omits even one of these will not have life, nor will he be redeemed.

The Apostle John distinguished the people of God on the basis of their belief in the things that Jesus did: the water, the blood, and the Spirit. These things tell us whether they have the Word in them or not. He identifies the redeemed by their belief in the water of Jesus' baptism, His blood, and the Spirit.

Those Who Are Not Born Again Cannot Discern a Sheep from a Goat

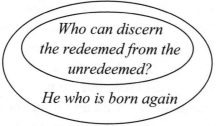

Who can discern the redeemed from the unredeemed?

He who is born again

The Apostle John clearly identified the righteous ones

who were redeemed. The Apostle Paul did too. How can the servants of God keenly distinguish between a sheep and a goat? How do they distinguish the true servants of God from the pretenders? Those who are redeemed by believing in the water and the blood of Jesus receive the power to see.

Whether a man is a pastor, an evangelist, or an elder, if he cannot identify the redeemed, or if he cannot distinguish between a sheep and a goat, he has not been born again yet, and he does not have the life in him. But those who have truly been born again can explicitly see the difference. Those who are lifeless can neither see the difference nor acknowledge it.

Though we cannot distinguish colors in the dark, green is green and white is white. But, if you close your eyes, you can neither see nor acknowledge the colors.

But those with their eyes open can recognize even the tiniest variation in color. They can tell which is green and which is white. Similarly, there is an obvious difference between the redeemed and those who are not redeemed.

We have to preach the gospel of redemption, the gospel of the water, the blood, and the Spirit. We have to arise and shine. When we gather people around us to propagate the true faith, we do not speak with the words of man. In the Bible, 1 John 5 explains its meaning. We should explain it step by step so that there is no confusion.

The Word that we are preaching, that is, the Word of the water, the blood, and the Spirit of Jesus is the light of redemption. To make the 'water' of Jesus known to people, we must shine brightly. To make the 'blood' of Jesus known is to shine brightly. We have to make it very clear so that there is no one on earth who does not know this truth.

If the born again do not arise and shine, many people will die without redemption and God will not be pleased. He would call us lazy servants. We must spread the gospel of the water and the blood of Jesus.

The reason why I am repeating myself so many times is because the baptism of Jesus is very important to our salvation. When we speak to children, we have to explain things over and over, going through every point so that we are sure they understand.

If we were trying to teach an illiterate man, we would probably start with the alphabet. Then, we could gradually teach him how to write words with this alphabet. When he is able to put words together such as 'punishment,' we would begin to explain the meaning of these words. This is exactly how we should talk to people about Jesus to make sure that they truly understand.

We should clearly explain the baptism of Jesus. He came into this world by water, blood, and the Spirit. I pray that you will believe in Jesus as your Savior and be redeemed.

The redemption of the water and the Spirit springs from the faith in the baptism of Jesus, His blood on the Cross, and from the belief that Jesus is God, our Savior. ⊠

SERMON 7

The Baptism of Jesus Is
The Antitype of Salvation
For Sinners

The Baptism of Jesus Is The Antitype of Salvation For Sinners

< 1 Peter 3:20-22 >

"A few, that is, eight souls, were saved through water. There is also an antitype which now saves us, namely baptism (not the removal of the filth of the flesh, but the answer of a good conscience toward God), through the resurrection of Jesus Christ, who has gone into heaven and is at the right hand of God, angels and authorities and powers having been made subject to Him."

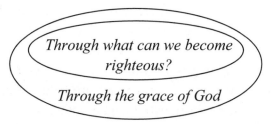

Through what can we become righteous?

Through the grace of God

God already knew us even before we were born on this earth. He knew that we would be born sinners and saved all of us believers through His baptism, which took away all the sins of the world. He saved all believers and made them His people.

All this is the result of God's grace. As it is said in Psalms 8:4, *"What is man that He is mindful of us?"* The redeemed who are saved from all sins are the recipients of His special love. They are His children.

What were we, who believed only in His blood and the

Spirit, before we became God's children, before we became the righteous and were saved and granted the right to call Him Father? We were sinners, mere sinners who were born to live in this world for about 70 years, or 80 years if healthy.

Before we were washed of our sins, and before we had the faith in the gospel of the baptism of Jesus and His blood, we were unrighteous people who were sure to perish.

The Apostle Paul said that it was owing to His grace that he was what he was. Likewise, it is absolutely due to His grace that we are what we are now. We thank Him for His grace. The Creator came down to this world and saved us, making us His children, His people. We thank Him for the grace of the salvation of the water and the Spirit.

What is the reason that He allows us to be His children, the righteous ones? Is it because we are beautiful to look at? Is it because we are so worthy? Or is it because we are so good? Let us think about it and give thanks where it is due.

The reason is that God created us to make us His people and to let us live in the Kingdom of Heaven with Him. God made us His people to allow us to eternally live with Him. That is the only reason why God blessed us with eternal life. He didn't make us His people because we are better looking, more worthy, or live more virtuously than any other of His creations. The only reason is that He loves us.

"There is also an antitype which now saves us, namely baptism" (1 Peter 3:21). "A few, that is, eight souls, were saved through water" (1 Peter 3:20).

Only a few, one in a city and two in a family have been saved. Then, are we any better than others? Not at all. We are not all that special, but we have been saved anyway through our faith in the water and the Spirit.

It is a miracle amongst miracles that we have been saved,

and it is an unconditional gift and blessing from God that we can call Him our Father, our Lord. We can never deny this. How could we call Him our Father or our Lord if we were still sinners?

When we think about the fact that we have been saved, we know that God has loved us unconditionally. Can we not thank Him? We would have been born and died after living desperate lives, ending up in hell, if it had not been for His love and blessings. We thank God again and again for His blessings and the love that made us worthy to be His children in His eyes.

The Precious Salvation Given to Us through the Baptism of Jesus

Why did the people at the time of Noah perish?

Because they didn't believe in the water (the baptism of Jesus).

"There is also an antitype which now saves us, namely baptism." It is written in 1 Peter that only eight souls were saved through water. How many people would there have been in Noah's time? We have no way of knowing how many there were, but let's suppose that there were about a million. Only 8 people in Noah's family out of a million were saved.

The ratio would be about the same today. They say that there are more than 6 billion people on the earth right now. How many people have been washed of their sins among those who believe in Jesus today? If we were to take a look at only one city, there would be very few of them.

In my city, which consists of about 250,000 people, how many are redeemed from their sins? Perhaps 200? Then, what would the ratio be? It would mean that less than one out of a thousand has received the blessing of redemption.

It is estimated that there are about 12 million Christians in Korea, including Catholics. Out of these, how many among them have been born again of water and the Spirit? We should keep in mind that there were only 8 saved out of the earth's entire population in Noah's time. We should know and believe that Jesus washed away the sins of all those who believe in His baptism, through which He took away all sins.

There aren't many who believe that Jesus redeemed all of us with His baptism and His blood on the Cross. Look at the famous picture of 'The Resurrection of Jesus.' How many resurrected people are shown there? You can see them coming down from the castle of Jerusalem toward the figure of Jesus, who has His arms open wide for them. Guess how many among them are theologians or ministers.

Today, there are plenty of theologians in the world, but we find so few who know and believe in the baptism of Jesus as the pivotal truth of redemption. Some theologians say that the reason Jesus was baptized was because He was humble, and some say that He was baptized to become more like us, the human beings.

But it is written in the Bible that all the Apostles, including Peter and John, testified to Jesus' baptism as the transferal of our sins to Him, and we believe it too.

The Apostles testify in the Scriptures that our sins were passed onto Jesus with His baptism. It is such an amazing testimony to the grace of God that we can be delivered just by believing in it.

There's No 'Maybe' about the Baptism of Redemption

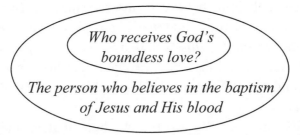

Who receives God's boundless love?

The person who believes in the baptism of Jesus and His blood

People are apt to believe that just believing in Jesus will save us. All denominations are convinced of salvation in their beliefs, and many people think that the baptism of Jesus is merely a dogma of a Christian community. But it is not true. Among the thousands of books that I've read, I have not been able to find any book about salvation that specifies the relationship between the redemption in the baptism and blood of Jesus and God's salvation.

Only 8 were saved at the time of Noah. I don't know how many are saved today, but probably not many. Those who are saved are the ones who believe in the baptism and the blood of Jesus. While visiting many churches, I recognize again and again that there are so few who preach the gospel of the baptism of Jesus, which is the gospel of truth.

If we don't believe in the redemption of the baptism and the blood of Jesus, we are still sinners and not saved, no matter how faithfully we attend church. We may faithfully attend church all our lives, but if we still have sin in our hearts, we are still sinners.

If we have attended church for 50 years, but still have sin in our hearts, our faith of 50 years is nothing but a falsehood. It is far better to have only one day of true faith. Among those who believe in Jesus, only those who correctly believe in the meaning of the baptism of Jesus and His blood shall enter the Kingdom of Heaven.

True faith is to believe in the fact that the Son of God descended to this world and was baptized to take away all the sins of the world. It is this faith that leads us to the Kingdom of Heaven. We should also believe that Jesus bled on the Cross for you and me. We should also know this in order to thank and glorify Him.

What are we? We are the children of men and women who were saved with Jesus' baptism and blood. How can we not thank Him? Jesus was baptized in the Jordan when He was 30 years old in order to save us. By this, He took away all our sins and received judgment for us on the Cross.

When we think about it, we cannot but humbly thank Him. We should know that everything Jesus did in this world was for our salvation. First, He came down to this world. He was baptized, crucified on the Cross, resurrected from the dead on the third day, and now sits at the right hand of God.

The redemption of God is for each and every one of us without exception. The salvation of Jesus is all for you and me. We praise God for His love and His blessings.

We know a gospel song that goes like this. *"♪There's a beautiful story. ♪Among so many people in the world, I am the one who has His love and salvation. ♪O how amazing His love is! ♪His love for me, His love for me. There's a beautiful story. ♪Among so many people in the world, we are the ones who are saved, who became His people. We are wearing His love. ♪O the love of God, the grace of God.♪ O how amazing His love is! His love for me.♪ "*

Jesus came down to save you and me, and the redemption of His baptism is also for us. The gospel is not just some fairy tale; it is the truth that lifts us out of our lives of drudgery into the beautiful Kingdom of God. You should keep in mind that the faith is the relationship between God and yourself.

He came down to this world in order to save us. He was baptized and received the judgment of the Cross to wash away our sins.

What a blessing it is when the faithful can call God their Father! How can we believe in Jesus as our Savior and be saved from sin with our faiths? It is possible because of His boundless love for us. We have been saved because of Him, who loved us first.

Jesus Washed Away all Our Sins Once and for All

"For Christ also suffered once for sins, the just for the unjust, that He might bring us to God" (1 Peter 3:18). Jesus Christ was baptized for our redemption and died once on the Cross in order to save you and me, the unjust.

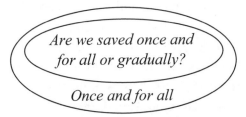

He died once on this earth in order to avert us from God's judgment. So that we may enter the Kingdom of Heaven and live forever before God, He came down to this world in the flesh and completely washed away all our sins all at once with His baptism, His death on the Cross, and His resurrection.

Do you believe that Jesus Christ saved us completely with His baptism and blood? If you do not believe in the gospel of His baptism and blood, you cannot be saved. Because we are so weak, we cannot be born again if we do not believe that Jesus completely washed away all our sins once and for all with His baptism and blood.

He was baptized to take away all our sins and was judged on the Cross for us. Jesus washed away all the sins of sinners once and for all with the redemption of His baptism and blood.

It would be impossible for us as human beings to be redeemed if we had to repent every time we sinned, to be good and benevolent all the time, and to offer many things to the church as well.

Therefore, the belief in the baptism of Jesus and the blood on the Cross is a must for our salvation. We must believe in the water and the blood. Simply doing good works has nothing to do with the remission of our sins.

It wouldn't do any good for your salvation to buy expensive suits for the poor or to serve delicious food for pastors. Jesus saves only those who believe in His baptism and blood. If we believe that God saved us through Jesus with His baptism and His blood once and for all, we will be saved.

Some may think that even though God said thus in the Bible, they have to give it further thought. This is up to them, but we should believe in His word as it is written.

In Hebrews 10:1-10, it is written that He saved us all at once. It is true that God saved those who believed in the baptism and the blood of Jesus all at once. We should also believe it thus. *"♪He died once, saved us all at once. O brothers, believe and be redeemed. Put your burdens down under the baptism of Jesus.♫"* Jesus saved us from all impiousness and sins once and for all by being baptized once and bleeding once.

"The just for the unjust" (1 Peter 3:18) Jesus is God without sin, and He has never sinned. He came down to us in

the flesh to save people from their sins. He was baptized and took away all our sins. He saved us from sin and injustice.

All the sins of people from their birth to death were passed onto Jesus when He was baptized, and all were saved from the judgment when He bled and died on the Cross. He was baptized for sinners and died vicariously in their place.

This is the redemption of His baptism. Jesus saved all of us, who were sinners, once and for all. How weak each of us is! Jesus redeemed all of our sins from our births to our deaths and offered Himself for the judgment on the Cross. We who believe in Jesus should believe that He saved us once and for all with His baptism and blood.

We are weak, but Jesus is not. We are not faithful, but Jesus is. God saved us once and for all. *"For God so loved the world that He gave His only begotten Son, that whoever believes in Him should not perish but have everlasting life"* *(John 3:16).* God gave us His only begotten Son. He had His Son baptized in order to pass all the sins of the world onto Him, so that He might receive the judgment for all human beings.

What an amazing salvation this is! What an amazing love this is! We thank God for His love and salvation. God saves those who believe in the water and the blood of Jesus: the baptism and the bloodshed of Jesus, and the fact that Jesus is the Son of God.

Those who believe in Jesus can be saved by believing in the truth of the baptism and the blood of Jesus and have everlasting lives as the righteous. We must all believe it.

Who saved us? Was it God who saved us, or was it one of His creations that saved us? It was Jesus, who is God, who saved us. We were saved because we believed in the redemption of God, and this is the salvation of redemption.

Jesus Is the Lord of Salvation

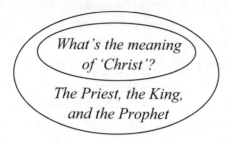

What's the meaning of 'Christ'?

The Priest, the King, and the Prophet

Jesus Christ is God. Jesus means the Savior, and Christ means 'one who is anointed.' As Samuel anointed Saul in the Old Testament, kings were anointed, priests were anointed and for a prophet to minister his mission, he had to be anointed.

Jesus came to this world and was anointed for three duties: that of the Priest, the King, and the Prophet. As the heavenly Priest, He was baptized to take away the sins of all human beings.

Obeying the will of His Father, He presented Himself as the sin offering before the Father. *"I am the way, the truth, and the life. No one comes to the Father except through Me."* Jesus saved those of us who believe in Him by taking away all our sins through His baptism and by being crucified.

"For the life of the flesh is in the blood" (Leviticus 17:11). Jesus bled on the Cross after His baptism; thus, offering His life before God as the wages for our sins so that we believers might be saved.

He was resurrected on the third day after He died on the Cross and preached the gospel to the spirits shut away in jail. Those who are not yet redeemed are like spiritual prisoners in the jail of sin, and to them, Jesus preaches the gospel of truth, the gospel of the water and the blood. God has given us the gospel of the water and the Spirit to save us. Anyone who believes in it can be born again.

The Baptism and the Blood of Jesus Saves Sinners

How can we have a good conscience before God?

By having faith in the baptism and the blood of Jesus

Jesus Christ is our Savior, and it is testified in 1 Peter 3:21, *"There is also an antitype which now saves us, namely baptism (not the removal of the filth of the flesh, but the answer of a good conscience toward God)."* The water of the baptism of Jesus is a must for the salvation of sinners.

Jesus washed away the sins of all sinners by taking these sins upon Himself through His baptism. Do you believe in the baptism of Jesus? Do you believe that our hearts are washed clean of all sins through His baptism? Our hearts are washed clean of all sins, but our flesh still sins.

To be 'born again' does not mean that a person will not sin again. We, the born-again, also commit sins, but our hearts stay clean of sin because of our faiths in His baptism. Thus, the above passage states, *"Not the removal of the filth of the flesh, but the answer of a good conscience toward God"* (1 Peter 3:21).

Since Jesus washed away my sins, and since God accepted judgment for me, how can I not believe in Him? Knowing that Jesus, who is God, saved me through His baptism and blood, how can I not believe in Him? We were saved before God and now our consciences are clean. We can no longer say before God that Jesus didn't completely wash away our sins, just as we cannot say that God doesn't love us.

Our consciences become far more sensitive to sin after being born again and they tell us whenever we do wrong. If our consciences are bothered even a little, we cannot be completely free of sin unless we remind ourselves of the power of Jesus' baptism. It is the only way we can have good consciences.

When our consciences bother us, it means that something is wrong. The water of Jesus' baptism cleans away all the dirt of sin. Jesus took away all our sins with His baptism and washed us clean, even to our consciences. When we really believe this, our consciences can truly be cleansed. How can our consciences be cleansed? By believing in the baptism and the blood of Jesus. Everyone has an evil and dirty conscience from birth, but if we believe that all our sins were passed onto Jesus, we can blot out that stain.

This is the faith of the born-again. It is not autohypnosis, something that you consciously admit. Is your conscience clean? Is it clean because you have lived a good life, or is it clean because all your sins were passed onto Jesus and you believe in Him? It is only through this faith that you can obtain a clean conscience.

There are words with life and words without life. How can the consciences of all people be cleansed? The only way that we can be righteous and have clean consciences is to believe in the complete redemption of Jesus.

When believing in His baptism sanctifies us, it does not mean that the filth of the flesh has been removed, but that our consciences are clean toward God. For that, He came, was baptized, died on the Cross and was resurrected from the dead and now sits at the right hand of God.

When the time comes, He will come to this world again. *"To those who eagerly wait for Him He will appear a second time, apart from sin, for salvation" (Hebrews 9:28).* We believe that He will come to take us, who eagerly wait for Him, and are sinless by believing in His baptism and blood.

A Clinical Experiment of Faith

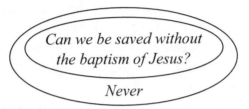

Can we be saved without the baptism of Jesus?

Never

We conducted a clinical and unplanned experiment at our Daejeon Church.

Rev. Park of Daejeon Church told a couple that there was no sin in the world without mentioning the meaning of Jesus' baptism. The husband used to sleep during the sermons when he had attended other churches because all the pastors preached the gospel while omitting the redemption through the baptism of Jesus, thus forcing him to repent everyday.

But here in our Taejon Church, he listened to the sermon with both eyes wide open because he was told that all his sins were passed onto Jesus. It made it easy for his wife to persuade him to come to church with her.

One day, he was sitting in church and heard Romans 8:1. *"There is therefore now no condemnation to those who are in Christ Jesus."* Then, he immediately thought, 'Ah, if one believes in Jesus, one is without sin. Since I believe in Jesus, I am also without sin.'

So he phoned his brother-in-law and many of his friends one by one and said, "Do you have sin in your heart? Then your faith is not correct." At this, Rev. Park was at a loss. The husband didn't know about the baptism of Jesus but he insisted that he was now without sin.

Then, the couple started having problems. The wife used to be more religious, but she still had sin in her heart while her husband said that he was without sin. The husband went to church only a few times, but he was already without sin.

The wife was sure that both of them still had sin in their hearts. They started arguing about it. The husband insisted that he was without sin because *'There is no condemnation to those who are in Christ Jesus.'* And the wife argued that she still had sin in her heart.

Then one day, his wife was so piqued about it that she decided to go and ask Rev. Park what he meant when he said that all sins were passed onto Jesus.

So one day, after the evening worship service, she sent her husband home and stayed behind to ask Rev. Park a question. She said, "I know you are trying to tell us something, but I am sure there is one important part hidden. Please tell me what it is." Then, Rev. Park told her about being born again of water and the Spirit.

She realized at once why it was written in Romans 8:1, *"There is therefore no condemnation to those who are in Christ Jesus."* She believed at once and was saved. She realized at last that all our sins were passed onto Jesus through His baptism so that those who are in Christ would not be condemned.

She started to understand the written Word. She finally found out that the key to redemption was the baptism of Jesus and that we could become righteous through the redemption of His baptism.

In fact, her husband did not go home but was waiting for her outside. He listened to her testimony that her sins were all cleansed, and asked exultantly, "Well, are you redeemed now?"

But after listening to what his pastor told his wife, he became confused. He had never heard about the gospel of Jesus' baptism before. He was sure that he no longer had sin in his heart even without the baptism of Jesus. So at home, they argued again.

This time, the position was reversed. The wife pressed the husband whether he had sin in his heart or not. She asked him how he could be without sin when he did not believe in the baptism of Jesus. She urged him to look closely into his conscience. Then, he realized while examining his conscience that he still had sin in his heart.

So, he went to Rev. Park and confessed that he had sin in his heart. He asked, "When they put their hands on the head of the scapegoat, was it before they killed it, or after they killed it?" He had never heard of the gospel of the water and the Spirit, so he was terribly confused.

That was the point of this spiritual experiment. Jesus had to be baptized to have all the sins of the world passed on to Him. Only then could he have died on the Cross because the wages of sin is death.

"Did they lay their hands on the head of the offering before, or after it was killed?" He asked this because he was confused about the laying on of hands and the baptism of Jesus. So Rev. Park explained the redemption of the baptism of Jesus in detail to him.

On that day, the husband heard for the first time the gospel of the water and the Spirit and was redeemed. He heard the gospel only once and was delivered.

That was the experiment on the omitting of Jesus' baptism. We may say that we have no sin, but we surely still have sin in our consciences without the baptism of Jesus. People usually say that Jesus cleansed all sin by dying on the Cross, but only those who believe in the baptism and the blood of Jesus can say that they actually have no sin before God.

Rev. Park proved with this couple that we cannot be completely redeemed of our sins without the redemption through faith in the baptism of Jesus.

The Antitype of Salvation: the Baptism of Jesus

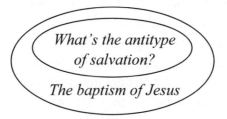

What's the antitype of salvation?

The baptism of Jesus

"There is also an antitype which now saves us, namely baptism." Jesus came down to our world to wash away all our sins and to make our consciences as white as snow. We are cleansed of all sins because Jesus took them all upon Himself through His baptism. He saved us with His baptism and blood. Therefore, all creations should kneel before Him.

Believing in Jesus saves us. We become God's children and go to Heaven by believing in Jesus. We become righteous by believing in Jesus. We are the royal priesthood. We can call God our Father. We live in this world, but we are kings.

Do you truly believe that God saved those of us who believe in the redemption of the water and the Spirit? Our redemption can never be complete without the baptism of Jesus. The faith that God and Jesus admit to be true is the belief in the gospel of His baptism, His Cross, and the Spirit, which saved us completely. This is the only true faith.

Our sins were washed away when Jesus took them away

with His baptism and all our sins were paid off when He bled on the Cross. Christ Jesus saved us with the water and the Spirit. Yes! We believe! ⊠

SERMON 8

The Gospel of the

Abundant Atonement

The Gospel of the Abundant Atonement

< John 13:1-17 >

"Now before the feast of the Passover, when Jesus knew that His hour had come that He should depart from this world to the Father, having loved His own who were in the world, He loved them to the end. And supper being ended, the devil having already put it into the heart of Judas Iscariot, Simon's son, to betray Him, Jesus, knowing that the Father had given all things into His hands, and that He had come from God and was going to God, rose from supper and laid aside His garments, took a towel and girded Himself. After that, He poured water into a basin and began to wash the disciples' feet, and to wipe them with the towel with which He was girded. Then He came to Simon Peter. And Peter said to Him, 'Lord, are You washing my feet?' Jesus answered and said to him, 'What I am doing you do not understand now, but you will know after this.' Peter said to Him, 'You shall never wash my feet!' Jesus answered him, 'If I do not wash you, you have no part with Me.' Simon Peter said to Him, 'Lord, not my feet only, but also my hands and my head!' Jesus said to him, 'He who is bathed needs only to wash his feet, but is completely clean; and you are clean, but not all of you.' For He knew who would betray Him; therefore He said, 'You are not all clean.' So when He had washed their feet, taken His garments, and sat down again, He said to them, 'Do you know what I have done to you? You call Me Teacher and

**Lord, and you say well, for so I am. If I then, your Lord
and Teacher, have washed your feet, you also ought to wash
one another's feet. For I have given you an example, that
you should do as I have done to you. Most assuredly, I say
to you, a servant is not greater than his master; nor is he
who is sent greater than he who sent him. If you know these
things, happy are you if you do them.'"**

Why did Jesus wash Peter's feet on the day before the
feast of the Passover? Just before washing his feet, Jesus said,
"You do not understand now, but you will know after this."
Peter was the best of Jesus' disciples. He believed that Jesus
was the Son of God and testified that Jesus was the Christ. As
Jesus washed his feet, there must have been a good reason for
doing so. When Peter confessed his belief that Jesus was the
Christ, it meant that he believed Jesus to be the Savior who
would save him from all his sins.

*Why did Jesus wash
the disciples' feet before
He was crucified?*

*Because He wanted them to understand
His perfect salvation.*

Why did He wash Peter's feet? Jesus knew that Peter
would soon deny Him three times and that he would continue
to sin in the future.

If, after Jesus went up to Heaven, Peter had had any sin
left in his heart, he wouldn't have been able to be united with

Jesus. But Jesus knew all of His disciples' weaknesses and He didn't want their sins to come between Him and His disciples. Therefore, He needed to teach them that all their iniquities had already been washed away. That was the reason He washed His disciples' feet. Jesus, before He died and left them, wanted to make sure that they would stand firm on the gospel of His baptism and also, the complete remission of all their lifelong sins.

John 13 talks about the perfect salvation that Jesus had fulfilled for His disciples. While washing their feet, Jesus told them about the wisdom of the gospel of His baptism through which all men could be washed of their trespasses.

"Do not be deceived by the devil in the future. I have taken away all your sins with My baptism in the Jordan River and I shall take the judgment for them on the Cross. Then, I shall be resurrected from the dead and fulfill the salvation of being born again for all of you. To teach you that I have already washed away even your future sins, to teach you the original gospel of the remission of sins, I am washing your feet before my crucifixion. This is the secret of the gospel of being born again. You should all believe thus."

We should all understand the reason why Jesus washed the disciples' feet and know why He said, *"What I am doing you do not understand now, but you will know after this."* Only then can we believe in the gospel of being born again and be born again ourselves.

He Said in John 13:12

What are the trespasses?

They are the sins which we commit every day due to our weakness.

Before He died on the Cross, Jesus had the feast of Passover with His disciples and convinced them of the gospel of the remission of sins by washing their feet with His own hands.

"Jesus, knowing that the Father had given all things into His hands, and that He had come from God and was going to God, rose from supper and laid aside His garments, took a towel and girded Himself. After that, He poured water into a basin and began to wash the disciples' feet and to wipe them with the towel with which He was girded. Then He came to Simon Peter. And Peter said to Him, 'Lord, are you washing my feet?' Jesus answered and said to Him, 'What I am doing you do not understand now, but you will know after this'" (John 13:3-7).

He taught His disciples the gospel of baptism and the atonement for sins through the water of His baptism.

At the time, being faithful to Jesus, Peter was not able to understand the reason why Jesus the Lord washed his feet. After Peter really understood what Jesus had done for him, the way in which he believed in Jesus had changed. Jesus wanted to teach him about the remission of sins, about the gospel of the water of His baptism.

He was worried that Peter might not be able to come to Him because of all his future sins, in other words, the sins of his flesh in the future. Jesus washed their feet so that the devil couldn't take away the disciples' faiths. Later, Peter came to understand why.

Jesus prepared the way so that anyone who believed in the water of His baptism and blood might be redeemed of his sins forever.

In John 13, the words He spoke while washing His disciples' feet are recorded. They are very important words that only the born-again can truly understand.

The reason Jesus washed His disciples' feet after the Passover feast was to help them realize that He had already washed away all their lifelong sins. Jesus said, "Why I am washing your feet you do not understand now, but you will know after this." These words to Peter contained the truth of eternal redemption in Him.

We should all know and believe in the baptism of Jesus, which has washed away all our sins and iniquities. The baptism of Jesus at the Jordan was the gospel of the passing of sins by the laying on of hands. We should all believe in the words of Jesus. He took away all the sins of the world through His baptism and accomplished the remission of sins by being judged and crucified. Jesus was baptized to rid all people of their sins.

The Remission of All Our Lifelong Trespasses Was Fulfilled with the Baptism and the Blood of Jesus

What is 'the snare' of the devil against the righteous?

The devil tries to deceive the righteous in order to make them sinners again.

Jesus knew well that, after He was crucified, resurrected and went up to Heaven, the devil and the propagators of the untrue faith would come and try to deceive the disciples. We can see by the testimony of Peter, *"You are the Christ, the Son of the living God,"* that he believed in Jesus. But still, Jesus wanted to remind Peter once more to keep the gospel of the remission of sins in mind. That gospel was the baptism of Jesus, through which He took away all the sins of the world. He wanted to teach it once more to Peter, the disciples and even to us who would come later. *"What I am doing you do not understand now, but you will know after this."*

Whenever the disciples of Jesus sinned, the devil would tempt and condemn them, saying, "Look! If you still commit sins, how can you say that you are without sin? You have not been saved. You are merely a sinner." To prevent that kind of infection, Jesus told them that their faiths in the baptism of Jesus had already washed away all their lifelong sins—past, present, and future.

"You all know that I was baptized! The reason I was baptized at the Jordan was to wash away all your lifelong sins, as well as the original sin of humankind. Are you able to understand now why I was baptized, and why I have to be crucified and die on the Cross?" Jesus washed His disciples' feet to show them that He had taken away all their daily sins through His baptism, and that He would take the judgment for them on the Cross.

Now, you and I have been redeemed of all our sins by our faiths in the gospel of Jesus' baptism and blood, which enables us to receive the remission of all our sins. Jesus was baptized and crucified for us. He has washed away all our sins with His baptism and blood. Anyone who knows and believes in the gospel of the atonement of sins and who believes in the truth is redeemed of all his/her sins.

Then, what should the born-again do after being saved? They have to admit their sins everyday and believe in the salvation of the baptism and blood of Jesus, the gospel of the atonement for all their sins. The gospel of the remission of sins is what we, the born-again, should deeply impress on our minds.

Just because you sin again, does that mean that you are a sinner again? No. Knowing that Jesus took away all our sins, how could we become sinners again? The baptism of Jesus and His blood on the Cross was the gospel of the atonement for all our sins. Anyone who believes in this original gospel of the remission of sins can be born again, without exception, as 'a righteous person.'

The Righteous Can Never Become Sinners Again

Why can the righteous never become sinners again?

Because Jesus has already atoned for all their lifelong sins.

If you believe in the gospel of the remission of sins, of the water and the Spirit, but still feel that you are a sinner because of your everyday trespasses, then you have to go to the Jordan, where Jesus was baptized to take away all your sins. If you became a sinner again after receiving the remission of sins, Jesus would have to be baptized all over again. You have to have faith in the remission of your sins in the gospel of the baptism of Jesus. You have to keep in mind that Jesus took away all your sins all at once through His baptism. You have to have an unwavering faith in Jesus Christ as your Savior.

Believing in Jesus as your Savior means that you believe in the baptism of Jesus, which took away all your lifelong sins. If you really believe in His baptism, the Cross, the death, and the resurrection of Jesus, you can never become a sinner again, no matter what kind of sin you have committed. You have been redeemed of all the sins in your whole life through faith.

Jesus Christ washed away the sins of the future as well, even the sins we commit out of our own weaknesses. Since Jesus had to emphasize the importance of His baptism, He washed His disciples' feet with water to symbolize the gospel of the remission of sins, that is, His baptism. Jesus Christ was baptized, crucified, resurrected, and ascended to Heaven to fulfill God's promise of abundant atonement for all the sins of the world and to save all humankind. As a result, His disciples were able to preach the gospel of the atonement for sins, the baptism of Jesus, the Cross, and the resurrection, right up until the end of their lives.

The Weakness of Peter's Flesh

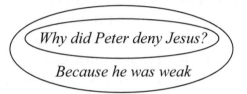

Why did Peter deny Jesus?

Because he was weak

The Bible tells us that when Peter was confronted by the servants of Caiaphas, the high priest, and was accused of being one of the followers of Jesus, he denied it twice, saying, *"No, I do not know the Man."* Then, he cursed and swore it for the third time.

Let us read the passage from Matthew 26:69. *"Now Peter sat outside in the courtyard. And a servant girl came to him, saying, 'You also were with Jesus of Galilee.' But he denied it before them all, saying, 'I do not know what you are saying.' And when he had gone out to the gateway, another girl saw him and said to those who were there, 'This fellow also was with Jesus of Nazareth.' But again he denied with an oath, 'I do not know the Man!' And after a while those who stood by came to him and said to Peter, 'Surely you also are one of them, because your speech betrays you.' Then he began to curse and swear, saying, 'I do not know the Man!' And immediately a rooster crowed. And Peter remembered the word of Jesus who had said to him, 'Before the rooster crows, you will deny Me three times.' Then he went out and wept bitterly" (Matthew*

26:69-75).

Peter really believed in Jesus and followed Him faithfully. He believed that the Lord Jesus was his Savior and 'the Prophet' to come. But when Jesus was taken to the court of Pilate and it became dangerous for him to disclose his relationship with Jesus to the authorities, he denied and cursed Him before them.

Peter didn't know that he would deny Jesus, but Jesus knew that he would. Jesus knew Peter's weakness thoroughly. Therefore, Jesus washed Peter's feet and engraved the gospel of salvation on his memory, as written in John 13, "You will sin in the future, but I have already washed away even all your future sins."

Peter did indeed deny Jesus when his life was in danger, but it was due to the weakness of his flesh that made him do this. Therefore, to save His disciples from all their future iniquities, Jesus washed their feet in advance.

"I shall expiate all your future sins, too. I am to be crucified because I was baptized and took away all your sins, and I shall pay them all off to become the true Savior for all of you. I am your God, your Savior. I shall pay in full for all your sins, and I shall become your Shepherd through My baptism and blood. I am the Shepherd of your salvation."

To plant this truth firmly in their hearts, Jesus washed their feet after the feast of the Passover. This is the truth of the gospel.

Because our flesh is weak even after being born again, we will sin again. Of course, we shouldn't sin, but when we are faced with severe crises as Peter was, we tend to sin without really intending to do so. We live in the flesh, so sometimes we are led to destruction by our sins. The flesh will sin as long as we live in this secular world, but Jesus remitted all those sins with His baptism and blood on the Cross.

We do not deny that Jesus is our Savior, but when we live in the flesh, we keep on committing sins against God's will. It is because we are born of the flesh.

Jesus knew well that we would commit sins while living in the flesh, so He became our Savior by paying off our sins with His baptism and blood. He has rid the sins of all those who believe in His salvation and resurrection.

That is why all the four Gospels start with the baptism of Jesus by John the Baptist. The purpose of His human life was to fulfill the gospel of being born again, the gospel of salvation.

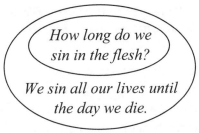

How long do we sin in the flesh?

We sin all our lives until the day we die.

When Peter denied Him not once, nor twice, but three times before the rooster crowed, how it must have broken his heart! How ashamed must he have felt? He had sworn before Jesus that he would never betray Him. He sinned because of the weakness of his flesh, but how miserable he must have felt when he succumbed to his weakness and denied Jesus not only once, but three times? How embarrassed he must have felt when Jesus looked at him with compassion once again?

But Jesus knew all of these things and more. Therefore, He said, "I know that you will sin again and again. But I have already taken away all those sins with My baptism, lest your sins make you stumble and turn you back into a sinner, lest you find it impossible to come back to Me. I have become the complete Savior for you by being baptized and judged for all your sins. I have become your God, your Shepherd. Believe in the gospel of the remission of your sins. I will keep on loving you even if you continuously commit the sins of the flesh. I have already washed away all your iniquities. The gospel of the remission of sins is effective forever. My love for you is also everlasting."

Jesus told Peter and the disciples, *"If I do not wash your feet, you have no part with Me."* The reason He spoke of this gospel in John 13 was that it was important for people to be born again of water and the Spirit. Do you believe in this?

In verse 9, *"Simon Peter said to Him, 'Lord, not my feet only, but also my hands and my head!' Jesus said to him, 'He who is bathed needs only to wash his feet, but is completely clean.'"*

Dear friends, will you commit sins 'of the flesh' in the future, or will you not? You surely will. But Jesus said that He had already washed away even the sins of the future, all the iniquities of our flesh with His baptism and blood, and He clearly told His disciples the word of truth, of the gospel of atonement, before He was crucified.

Because we live in our flesh with all our weaknesses, we cannot help but sin. Jesus washed away all the sins of the world with His baptism. He has not only washed our heads and bodies, but also our feet, that is, all our sins of the future. This is the gospel of being born again, of the baptism of Jesus.

After Jesus was baptized, John the Baptist testified, *"Behold! The Lamb of God who takes away the sin of the world!" (John 1:29)* We ought to believe that all the sins of the world were washed away by being passed onto Jesus during His baptism.

While living in this sinful world, we cannot help but sin. That is an obvious fact. Whenever our weaknesses of the flesh surface, we have to remind ourselves that Jesus washed away all our sins and all the sins of the world through the gospel of remission and paid for them with His blood. We should give thanks to Him from the bottom of our hearts. Let us confess with faith that Jesus is our Savior and God. Praise the Lord.

Everyone in this world cannot help but to commit sins with the flesh. People continuously sin with their flesh and die of their lifelong sins.

Evil Thoughts in the Hearts of People

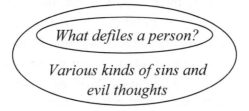

Jesus says in Matthew 15:19-20. *"For out of heart proceed evil thoughts, murders, adulteries, fornications, thefts, false witness, blasphemies. These are the things which defile a man, but to eat with unwashed hands does not defile a man."* Because various kinds of sin in the heart of a person defile him/her, he/she is unclean.

One Has to Recognize One's Own Evil Nature

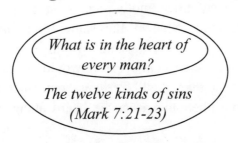

We have to be able to say, "Those twelve kinds of sins are in the hearts of people. I have all of them in my heart. I have the twelve kinds of sins inside me that are written about in the Bible." Before we are born again of water and the Spirit, we have to admit that the sins are originally in our hearts. We have to acknowledge that we are complete sinners before God, but we do not often do that. Most of us make excuses for our sins, saying, "I have never had those thoughts in my heart, I was just momentarily led astray."

But what did Jesus say about human beings? He clearly stated that what comes out of a person's heart 'defiles' him/her. He told us that people have evil thoughts inside of them. What do you think? Are you good or evil? Do you know that everyone has evil thoughts? Yes, everyone's thoughts are evil.

A few years ago, a huge department store in Seoul suddenly collapsed. The families who lost their loved ones were in deep agony, but many people went there to enjoy the tragic spectacle.

Some thought, "How many died? 200? No, that is too low of a number. 300? Maybe? Well, it would have been much more interesting and spectacular if the number of people dead had been at least a thousand...." The hearts of people can be as evil as that. We have to accept it. How disrespectful it was to the dead! How devastating it was for the families! Some were financially ruined.

Some of the spectators were not very sympathetic. "It would have been much more interesting if more had died! What a spectacle! What if the same thing happened at a ballpark full of people? Thousands would be buried under the rubble, wouldn't they? Oh, yes! It would certainly be much more interesting than this!" Perhaps some had thoughts like this. The same phenomena can be heard about car accidents.

The curious spectators are prone to be disappointed at minor crashes.

We all know how evil we can be sometimes. Of course, we would never say such evil thoughts aloud. We may click our tongues and express our sympathies when we take a look at an accident by chance, but secretly, in our hearts, we long for it to be more spectacular. We want to see terrible tragedies, where thousands of people are killed, as long as it does not go against our interests. This is the way the hearts of people work. Most of us are like this before being born again.

Murder in the Heart of Every Person

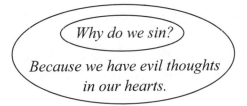

Why do we sin?

Because we have evil thoughts in our hearts.

God told us that there is murder inside the hearts of every person. But many would deny it before God saying, "How can You say that! I don't have any murderous thoughts in my heart! How can You even regard me to be such a person!" They would never admit that they have murder in their hearts. They think murderers are of a different breed from them.

"That serial killer in the news the other day, the mobs who have murdered and burned people in their basements are the ones who have murder in their hearts! They are of a different breed. I could never be like them! They are rogues! Murderers!" They become indignant with the criminals and yell, "Those born of evil seeds should be wiped off the face of this earth! They should all be sentenced to death!"

But unfortunately, the thought of murder is inside the hearts of those indignant people, as well as in the hearts of serial killers and murderers. God tells us that in the hearts of all people, there is murder. We have to accept the Word of God, who sees even the things hidden inside our minds. Thus, we have to admit, "I am a sinner with murder in my heart."

Yes, God told us that there are evil thoughts, including murder, inside the hearts of all people. Let us accept the Word of God. As the generations of people become more evil, all sorts of personal protection equipment become tools for murder. This is a result of the murder in our hearts. You can murder in a fit of anger, or fear. I am not saying that every one of us would actually kill others, but we think about it in our hearts.

We all are born with evil thoughts in our hearts. Some do indeed end up killing, not because they are especially born as murderers, but because all of us are capable of becoming murderers. God tells us that we have evil thoughts and murder in our hearts. It is the truth. None of us is the exception to this truth.

Therefore, the correct path for us to take is to accept the word of God and obey. We sin in this world because we have evil thoughts in our hearts.

Adultery in Our Hearts

God says that there is adultery in the heart of every person. Do you agree? Do you admit that you have adultery in your heart? Yes, there is adultery in the heart of every person.

That is why prostitution and other sexual offenses flourish in our society. It is one of the surest ways of making money in every period in human history. Other businesses might suffer from economic depression, but these vile businesses do not suffer as much because there is adultery dwelling in the heart of every single person.

The Fruit of Sinners Is Sin

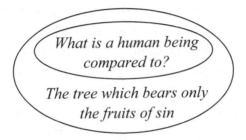

What is a human being compared to?

The tree which bears only the fruits of sin

Just as apple trees bear apples, pear trees pears, date trees dates, and persimmon trees persimmons, we, who are born with the 12 kinds of sins in our hearts, cannot but bear the fruits of sin.

Jesus says that what comes out of the heart of a person defiles him/her. Do you agree? We can only agree to the words of Jesus and say, "Yes, we are a brood of sinners, evildoers. Yes, You are right, Lord." Yes, we have to admit our evils. We have to admit the truth to ourselves in front of God.

Just as Jesus Christ obeyed the will of God, we have to accept the Word of God and obey Him. It is the only way we can be saved from all our sins through the water and the Spirit. These are the gifts from God.

My country is blessed with four beautiful seasons. As the seasons progress, various kinds of trees bear their fruits. In the same way, the twelve sins in our hearts have a hold on us and constantly lead us to sin. Today, it may be murder that has a grip on our hearts and tomorrow, it may be adultery.

Then, the next day, evil thoughts, then fornication, theft,

false witness...and so on. We go on sinning all year round, every month, every day, every hour. Not a day passes without our committing some kind of sin. We keep on swearing to ourselves that we won't commit sin, but we can't help it because we are born this way.

Have you ever seen an apple tree refuse to bear apples because it didn't want to? "I don't want to bear apples!" Even if it made up its mind to refuse to bear fruit, how could it not bear apples? The flowers would inevitably bloom in the spring, the apples would grow and ripen in the summer, and the fruit would be ready to be picked and eaten in the fall.

It is the provision of nature, and the life of sinners must also follow the same law of nature. Sinners cannot help but bear the fruits of sin.

'The Baptism and the Cross of Jesus' Was to Atone for Our Sins

What does it mean by Jesus' atonement?

It is the payment of the wages of sin by the baptism of Jesus (the laying on of hands) and His blood on the Cross.

Let us read a passage from the Bible to find out how sinners, the brood of evildoers, can atone for their sins before God and live out their lives in happiness. This is the gospel of the atonement for sins.

In Leviticus 4, it is said, *"If anyone of the common people sins unintentionally by doing something against any of the commandments of the Lord in anything which ought not to be done, and is guilty, or if his sin which he has sinned comes to his knowledge, then he shall bring as his offering a kid of the goats, a female without blemish, for his sin which he has sinned. And he shall lay his hand on the head of the sin offering, and kill the sin offering in the place of the burnt offering. Then the priest shall take some of its blood with his finger, put it on the horns of the altar of burnt offering, and pour its remaining blood at the base of the altar. He shall remove all its fat, as fat is removed from the sacrifice of peace offering; and the priest shall burn it on the altar for a sweet aroma to the Lord. So the priest shall make atonement for him, and it shall be forgiven him" (Leviticus 4:27-31).*

During the days of the Old Testament, how did the people atone for their sins? They laid their hands on the head of the sin offering first, and passed their sins onto it.

It is written in Leviticus. *"When any one of you brings an offering to the Lord, you shall bring your offering of the livestock of the herd and of the flock. If his offering is a burnt sacrifice of the herd, let him offer a male without blemish; he shall offer it of his own free will at the door of the tabernacle of meeting before the Lord. Then he shall put his hand on the head of the burnt offering, and it will be accepted on his behalf to make the atonement for him" (Leviticus 1:2-4).*

When a person of that era recognized sin in his heart, he had to prepare sin offerings that would be used to atone for the sin. He had to 'lay his hands' on the head of the sin offering to pass on the sins he had committed. Inside the court of the holy tabernacle, there was the altar of burnt offering. It was box-styled, a little bigger than the pulpit table, and it had horns on every corner. The people of Israel atoned for their sins by passing their sins onto the head of the sin offering and burning its meat on the altar of burnt offering.

God said in Leviticus for people to *"Offer it of his own free will at the gate of the court of the tabernacle before the Lord."* Their sins were passed onto the sin offering when they laid their hands on its head, and then the sinner would cut the throat of the offering and put its blood on the horns of the altar of burnt offering.

After that, the body of the offering was cleaned of its internal organs, and its meat was cut into pieces and burnt to ashes on the altar of burnt offering. Then, the sweet aroma of the meat was offered to God for their atonement. This was how they atoned for their daily sins.

God allowed another sacrifice of atonement for their yearly sins. It differed from the sacrifice of atonement for daily sins. In this case, the High Priest alone laid his hands on the sin offering on behalf of all the people of Israel and he sprinkled the blood on the east of the mercy seat seven times. Also, the laying of his hands on the head of the live goat was done in front of the people of Israel on the tenth day of the seventh month every year (Leviticus 16:5-27).

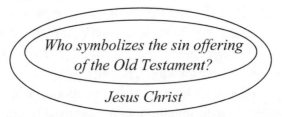

Who symbolizes the sin offering of the Old Testament?

Jesus Christ

Now, let us find out how the sacrificial system changed in the New Testament and how the eternal statute of God has remained constant over the years.

Why did Jesus have to die on the Cross? What did He do wrong on this earth that God had to let His Son die on the

Cross? Who forced Him to die on the Cross? When all the sinners of the world, meaning all of us, had fallen into sin, Jesus came to this world to save us.

He was baptized by John the Baptist at the Jordan River and took the punishment on the Cross for all sins on behalf of humankind. The way Jesus was baptized and the way He bled on the Cross was similar to the sacrifice of atonement in the Old Testament, the laying of hands on the sin offering and the shedding of its blood.

This was the way it had been done in the Old Testament. A sinner laid his hands on the sin offering and confessed his sins, saying, "Lord, I have sinned. I have committed murder and adultery." Then, his sins were passed onto the sin offering.

Just as the sinner cut the throat of the sin offering and offered it before God, Jesus was offered in the same way to atone for all our sins. Jesus was baptized and bled on the Cross to save us and atoned for all our sins through His sacrifice.

In fact, Jesus died because of us. When we think about it, what was the meaning of offering those animals without blemish as sacrifices for all the sins of the people? Had all those animals known what sin was? Animals do not know sin. They had to be without blemish.

Just as those animals were completely without blemish, so, too, was Jesus without sin. He is the Holy God, the Son of God, and He has never sinned. So, He took away all our sins through His baptism in the Jordan River when He was 30 years old.

Jesus died on the Cross because of the sins He took away from us. It was His ministry for salvation that washed away all the sins of humankind.

The Beginning of the Gospel of the Atonement for Sins

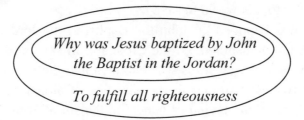

Why was Jesus baptized by John the Baptist in the Jordan?

To fulfill all righteousness

It is written in Matthew 3, *"Then Jesus came from Galilee to John at the Jordan to be baptized by him. And John tried to prevent Him, saying, "I have need to be baptized by You, and are You coming to me?' But Jesus answered and said to him, 'Permit it to be so now, for thus it is fitting for us to fulfill all righteousness'"* (Matthew 3:13-15).

We have to know and understand why Jesus was baptized when He was 30. He was baptized to atone for the sins of all people and to fulfill all the righteousness of God. To save all people from their sins, Jesus Christ, the One without blemish, was baptized by John the Baptist.

Thus, He took away the sins of the world and offered Himself up to atone for the sins of all human beings. In order to be saved from sin, we should know the whole truth and believe in it. It is up to us to believe in His salvation and be saved.

What does the baptism of Jesus mean? It is the same as the laying on of hands in the Old Testament. In the Old Testament, the sins of all the people were passed onto the head of the sin offering by the laying on of the High Priest's hands. Similarly, in the New Testament, Jesus took away the sins of the world by presenting Himself as the sin offering and being baptized by John the Baptist.

John the Baptist was the greatest man among all human beings, the representative of mankind ordained by God. As the representative of mankind, the High Priest of humanity, he laid his hands on Jesus and passed all the sins of the world onto Him. 'Baptism' implies, 'to pass on to, to be buried, and to be washed.'

Do you know why Jesus came to this world and was baptized by John the Baptist? Do you believe in Jesus, knowing the meaning of His baptism? The baptism of Jesus was to take away all our sins, the sins that we, the brood of evildoers, commit with our flesh throughout our lives. John the Baptist baptized Jesus for the fulfillment of the original gospel of atonement for all our sins.

In Matthew 3:13-17, it begins with *'Then,'* and it refers to the time Jesus was baptized, the time all the sins of the world were passed onto Him.

'Then,' Jesus took away all the sins of humankind, died on the Cross after three years, and was resurrected on the third day. To wash away all the sins of the world, He was baptized once and for all, died on the Cross once and for all, and was resurrected from the dead once and for all. For those who want to be redeemed of their sins before God, He took all the sin of the world and saved them once and for all.

Why did Jesus have to be baptized? Why did He have to put on the crown of thorns and be judged at the court of Pilate like a common criminal? Why did He have to be crucified on the Cross and bleed to death? The reason for all the above is because He took away all the sins of the world, the sins of you and I, onto Himself through His baptism. For our sins, He had to die on the Cross.

We have to believe in the word of salvation that God has saved us and be grateful to Him. Without the baptism of Jesus, His Cross, and His resurrection, there would be no salvation for us.

When Jesus was baptized by John to take away all the sins of the world, He took away our sins and thus, saved us who believe in His gospel of salvation. There are people who think, "Jesus took away only the original sin, didn't He?" But they are wrong.

It is recorded clearly in the Bible that Jesus took away all the sins of the world once and for all when He was baptized. All our sins, including the original sin, have been washed away. Jesus says in Matthew 3:15, *"For thus it is fitting for us to fulfill all righteousness."* To fulfill all righteousness means that all sins, without exception, have been taken away from us.

Has Jesus washed away all our lifelong sins, too? Yes, He has. Let us find the proof of it in Leviticus first. It tells us about the High Priest and the sacrifice of the Day of Atonement.

The Sacrifice of Atonement for the Yearly Sins of All Israelites

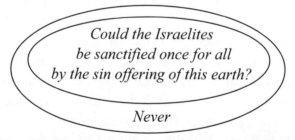

Could the Israelites be sanctified once for all by the sin offering of this earth?

Never

"Aaron shall offer the bull as a sin offering, which is for himself, and make atonement for himself and for his house. He shall take the two goats and present them before the Lord at the door of the tabernacle of meeting. Then Aaron shall cast lots for the two goats: one lot for the Lord and the other lot for the scapegoat. And Aaron shall bring the goat on which the Lord's lot fell, and offer it as a sin offering. But the goat on

which the lot fell to be the scapegoat shall be presented alive before the Lord, to make atonement upon it, and to let it go as the scapegoat into the wilderness" (Leviticus 16:6-10). Here, Aaron took two goats at the door of the tabernacle of meeting to atone for the yearly sins of Israelites.

"Then Aaron shall cast lots for the two goats: one lot for the Lord and the other lot for the scapegoat."

A sacrificial animal was needed for the lawful atonement for daily sins in order to pass the sinner's sin onto it by laying his hands on the head of the offering. But for the yearly sins of the Israelites, the High Priest, on behalf of all the people, passed the yearly sins onto the sin offering on the tenth day of the seventh month every year.

In Leviticus 16:29-31, it is written, *"In the seventh month, on the tenth day of the month, you shall afflict your souls, and do no work at all, whether a native of your own country or a stranger who sojourns among you. For on that day the priest shall make atonement for you, to cleanse you, that you may be clean from all your sins before the Lord. It is a sabbath of solemn rest for you, and you shall afflict your souls. It is a statute forever" (Leviticus 16:29-31).*

In the Old Testament, the people of Israel brought a sin offering to atone for daily sins and passed their sins on to its head, confessing, "Lord, I have committed such and such sins. Please forgive me." Then, he cut the throat of the sin offering, gave the blood to the priest, and went home, convinced that he was now free of his sins. Thus, the sin offering died for the sinner, with the sin on its head. The sacrificial animal was killed instead of the sinner. In the Old Testament, the sin offering could be a goat, a lamb, a calf, or a bull, that is, one of the sacred animals that God had distinguished.

God, in His infinite mercy, allowed an animal's life to be

offered instead of a sinner having to die for his/her sins.

In this way in the Old Testament, sinners could atone for their sins through the sacrifice of atonement. The trespasses of the sinner were passed onto the sin offering by the laying on of hands, and its blood was given to the priest to expiate the sins of the sinner.

However, it was impossible to atone for sins everyday. As a result, God allowed the High Priest to expiate the sins of a whole year, every year on the tenth day of the seventh month, on behalf of all the people of Israel.

Then what was the role of the High Priest on the Day of Atonement? First, Aaron the High Priest laid his hands on the sin offering, confessing the sins of the people, "Lord, the people of Israel have committed such and such sins, murder, adultery, fornication, theft, false witness, blasphemy...."

Then, he cut the throat of the sin offering, took its blood, and sprinkled that blood seven times on the mercy seat inside the Holy Sanctuary. (In the Bible, the number 7 is considered to be the perfect number.)

It was his task to pass the yearly sins of the people onto the head of the sin offering on their behalf, and the sin offering was sacrificed vicariously.

Because God is just, to save all people from their sins, He allowed the sin offering to die in place of the people. Since God is truly merciful, He allowed the people to offer the life of a sacrificial animal in their stead. The High Priest then sprinkled the blood on the east side of the mercy seat and thus, atoned for all the sins of the people for the past year on the Day of Atonement, on the tenth day of the seventh month.

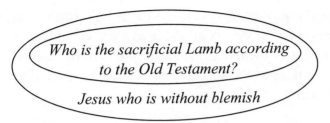

Who is the sacrificial Lamb according to the Old Testament?

Jesus who is without blemish

The High Priest had to offer two goats on the Day of Atonement for the people of Israel. One of them was called the scapegoat, which means 'to put out.' In the same way, the scapegoat of the New Testament is Jesus Christ. *"For God so loved the world that He gave His only begotten Son, that whoever believes in Him should not perish but have everlasting life" (John 3:16).*

God gave us His only Son as the sacrificial Lamb. As the sacrificial Lamb for all mankind, He was baptized by John the Baptist and became the Savior, the Messiah of the world. Jesus means 'the Savior' and Christ means 'the anointed King,' so Jesus Christ means 'the Son of God who came to save us all.'

Just as the yearly sins of the people were expiated on the Day of Atonement in the Old Testament, Jesus Christ, almost 2000 years ago, came to this world to be baptized and bled to death on the Cross to complete the gospel of the atonement for all our sins.

At this point, let us read a passage in Leviticus. *"And Aaron shall lay both his hands on the head of the live goat, confess over it all the iniquities of the children of Israel, and all their transgressions, concerning all their sins, putting them on the head of the goat, and shall send it away into the wilderness by the hand of a suitable man. The goat shall bear on itself all their iniquities to an uninhabited land; and he shall release the goat in the wilderness" (Leviticus 16:21-22).*

It is written that the sins of all Israelites were put on the head of the goat as it is also stated in Leviticus 1. *'All their transgressions'* refers to all the sins they committed in their hearts and with their flesh. And *'all their transgressions'* were put on the head of the sin offering by the laying on of the High Priest's hands.

By the Law of God, We Have to Have True Knowledge of All Our Sins

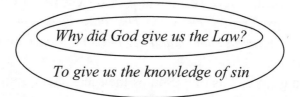

Why did God give us the Law?

To give us the knowledge of sin

The Law of God consists of 613 commandments. In fact, when we think about it, we do what He tells us not to do and don't do what He tells us to do.

Therefore, we are sinners. It is written in the Bible that God gave us those commandments in order for us to realize our sins (Romans 3:20). This means that He gave us His Law of commandments to teach us that we are sinners. He didn't give them to us because we are able to live by them, but for us to realize our sins.

He didn't give us His commandments for us to keep. You can't expect a dog to live like a human being. In the same way, we can never live up to the Law of God, but can only realize our sins through His Law of commandments.

God gave them to us because we are masses of sin, but we don't actually realize it. "You are murderers, fornicators, evildoers," God tells us paradoxically through the commandments. He told us not to kill, but we kill nevertheless in our hearts and sometimes, with our bodies.

However, because it is written in the Law that we should not kill, we know that we are murderers, saying, "Ah, I was wrong. I am a sinner because I did something I shouldn't have done. I have sinned."

To save the people of Israel from sin, God allowed Aaron to offer the sacrifice of atonement in the Old Testament, and it was Aaron who atoned for the people once a year.

In the Old Testament, two sin offerings had to be offered to God on the Day of Atonement. One was offered before God while the other was sent into the wilderness after the laying on of hands, taking with it all the yearly sins of the people. Before the goat was sent away into the wilderness by the hand of a suitable man, the High Priest laid his hands on the head of the live goat and confessed the sins of Israel. "Lord, the people have killed, fornicated, stolen, worshipped idols.... We have sinned before You."

The land of Palestine is a desert wilderness. The scapegoat was sent away into the endless wilderness and eventually died. When it was sent away, the people of Israel kept looking at it until it disappeared into the distance, and believed that their sins were gone with the scapegoat. The people earned peace of mind thus, and the scapegoat died in the wilderness for the yearly sins of all the people.

In this manner, God atoned for all our sins through the Lamb of God, Jesus Christ. All our sins were completely washed away through the baptism of Jesus and His blood on the Cross.

Jesus is God and our Savior. He is the Son of God who came to save all humankind from sin. He is the Creator who made us in His image and came down to this world to save us from sin.

Not only were the daily sins we commit with our flesh passed onto Jesus, but also all our future sins and the sins of our minds and flesh. Thus, He had to be baptized by John the Baptist to fulfill all the righteousness of God, the complete atonement for all the sins of the world.

Three years before Jesus was crucified, when He first began His public ministry, He took away all the sins of the world by being baptized by John the Baptist in the Jordan River. His salvation of humankind through the atonement for all our sins began with His baptism.

In the Jordan River, in a spot where it might be about waist deep, John the Baptist put his hands on Jesus' head and immersed Him in the water. This baptism was the same as the laying on of hands in the Old Testament and had the same effect of passing on all sins.

To be immersed in the water meant death, and the coming up from the water meant resurrection. Thus, by being baptized by John the Baptist, Jesus had fulfilled and revealed all three components of His mission: taking away all sins, crucifixion, and resurrection.

We can be saved only if we obey the words with which Jesus saved us from sin. God had decided to save us through Jesus, and the covenant that He had made in the Old Testament had been thus fulfilled. Through this act, Jesus walked to the Cross with all our sins on His head.

What kind of work is left to us since Jesus blotted out all our sins?

All we have to do is to have faith in the words of God.

In John 1:29, it is written, *"The next day John saw Jesus coming toward him, and said, 'Behold! The Lamb of God who takes away the sin of the world!'"* John the Baptist testified, *"Behold! The Lamb of God who takes away the sin of the world!"* All the sins of humankind were passed onto Jesus when He was baptized in the Jordan. Believe it! Then you will be blessed with the atonement for all your sins.

We have to have faith in the word of God. We have to put aside our own thoughts and stubbornness and obey the written Word of God. We must simply believe in the truth that Jesus took away all the sins of the world.

To say that Jesus took away all the sins of the world, and to say that He fulfilled the righteousness of God by atoning for our sins is exactly the same thing. The 'laying on of hands' and 'baptism' also mean the same thing.

Regardless of whether we say 'all,' 'everything,' or 'whole,' the meaning remains the same. The meaning of the word, 'the laying on of hands' in the Old Testament remains the same in the New Testament, except that the word 'baptism' is used instead.

It comes down to the simple truth that Jesus was both baptized and judged on the Cross to atone for all our sins. We can be saved when we believe in this original gospel.

When the Bible says that Jesus took away all 'the sin of the world' (John 1:29), what does the sin of the world mean? It means all the sins we were born with, that is, evil thoughts, thefts, fornications, covetousness, wickedness, blasphemy, pride, and foolishness that dwell in our minds. It also includes all the transgressions and trespasses we commit with the flesh and in the heart.

"For the wages of sin is death, but the gift of God is eternal life in Christ Jesus our God" (Romans 6:23). "And

without the shedding of blood there is no remission" (Hebrews 9:22). As it is said in these verses, all sins have to be paid for. Jesus Christ, to save all humankind from sin, offered His own life and paid the wages of sin for us once and for all.

Therefore, to be freed from all our sins, all we have to do is to believe in the original gospel—the baptism of Jesus and His blood, and His Divinity.

The Atonement for the Sins of Tomorrow

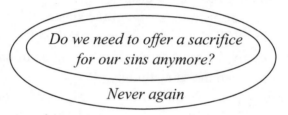

Do we need to offer a sacrifice for our sins anymore?

Never again

The sins of tomorrow, the day after tomorrow, and the sins that we commit until the day we die are also included in *'the sin of the world,'* just as the sins of today, yesterday, and the day before yesterday are also included in *'the sin of the world.'* The sins of people from birth to death are all part of *'the sin of the world,'* and the very sins of the world were absolutely passed onto Jesus through His baptism. All the sins we will commit until the day we die have already been taken away from us.

We need only to believe in this original gospel, the written words of God, and obey the truth to be saved. We should set aside our own thoughts to be redeemed of all our sins. You may well ask, "How could He take away the sins not yet committed?" Then, I would ask you in return, "Should Jesus come back to this world every time we sin and shed blood again and again?"

again and again?"

Within the gospel of being born again, there is the law of atonement for our sins. *"And without the shedding of blood there is no remission" (Hebrews 9:22).* When someone wanted to be redeemed of his sins in the days of the Old Testament, he had to pass on the sins by laying his hands on a sin offering, and the sin offering had to die for his sins.

In much the same way, the Son of God came down to this world to save all humankind. He was baptized to take away all our sins, bled on the Cross to pay the wages of our sins, and died on the Cross, saying, *"It is finished."* He was resurrected from the dead on the third day and now sits at the right hand of God. Thus, He has become our Savior forever.

To be completely remitted of our sins, we have to throw out all our fixed ideas and abandon the religious doctrine that tells us to redeem ourselves of our daily sins through prayers of repentance everyday. In order for the sins of humankind to be expiated, the lawful sacrifice had to be offered, once and for all. God in Heaven passed all the sins of the world onto His own Son through His baptism and had Him crucified for us. With His resurrection from death, our salvation was completed.

"But He was wounded for our transgressions, He was bruised for our iniquities. Surely He has borne our griefs and carried our sorrows; yet we esteemed Him stricken, smitten by God, and afflicted... and the Lord has laid on Him the iniquity of us all." In Isaiah 53, it is said that all the transgressions and iniquities of the world, of all humankind were passed onto Jesus Christ.

In the New Testament, in Ephesians 1:4, it is written, *"Just as He chose us in Him before the foundation of the world."* This tells us that He chose us in Him before the creation of the world. Before the world was even created, God in Christ. Whatever we may have thought before, we should now believe and obey the Word of God, the words of the water, the blood, and the Spirit.

God told us that His Lamb, Jesus Christ, took away the sins of the world and atoned for all humankind. In Hebrews 10, it is written, *"For the law, having a shadow of the good things to come, and not the very image of the things, can never with these same sacrifices, which they offer continually year by year, make those who approach perfect" (Hebrews 10:1).*

Here, it says that the same sacrifices, which they offer continually year by year, can never make them perfect. The Law is a shadow of the good things to come, and not the very image of the true things. Jesus Christ, the Messiah who was to come, made us perfect once and for all (just as the yearly sins of Israel were atoned once and for all) by being baptized and crucified to atone for all our sins.

Therefore, Jesus said in Hebrews 10, *"Then He said, 'Behold, I have come to do Your will, O God. He takes away the first that He may establish the second.' By that will we have been sanctified through the offering of the body of Jesus Christ once for all. And every priest stands ministering daily and offering repeatedly the same sacrifices, which can never take away sins. But this Man, after He had offered one sacrifice for sins forever, sat down at the right hand of God, from that time waiting till His enemies are made His footstool. For by one offering He has perfected forever those who are being sanctified. And the Holy Spirit also witnesses to us; for after He had said before, 'This is the covenant that I will make with them after those days, says the Lord: I will put My laws into their hearts, and their minds I will write them,' then He adds, 'Their sins and their lawless deeds I will remember no more.' Now where there is remission of these, there is no longer an offering for sin" (Hebrews 10:9-18).*

We believe that Jesus has saved us from all the sins of the world through His baptism and blood on the Cross.

The Salvation of Being Born Again of Water and the Spirit That Is Engraved in Our Hearts and Minds

Are we righteous just because we don't sin anymore?

No. We are righteous because Jesus took away all our sins and we believe in Him.

Do you all believe in His perfect salvation? —Amen— Do you obey with faith the words of God that Jesus Christ Himself was baptized and bled on the Cross to save us? We must have faith in His Word to be born again. We can be saved when we believe that Jesus Christ, through the gospel of remission, washed away all our sins, along with the sins of the world.

We can never become sinless by obeying the Law of God, but we can become perfect through our faith in His works. Jesus Christ took away all our sins through His baptism in the Jordan, suffered the judgment and was punished for all our sins on the Cross. By believing in this gospel with all our hearts, we can be redeemed of all our sins and become righteous. Do you believe this?

The baptism of Jesus, His crucifixion and resurrection are for the remission of all the sins of humankind and the law of salvation based on the infinite and unconditional love of God. God loves us as we are and He is just, so He made us righteous first. He made us righteous by passing all our sins onto Jesus through His baptism.

To wash away all our sins, He sent His only Son, Jesus, down to this world for us. He allowed Jesus to take away all the sins of the world through His baptism and then passed the judgment onto His Son for all our sins. He made us His righteous children through the salvation of the water and the blood, the agape of God.

It is written in Hebrews 10:16, *"I will put My laws into their hearts, and in their minds I will write them."*

In our hearts and minds, are we sinners before God or are we righteous? If we have faith in God's Word, we become righteous. Jesus Christ took away all our sins and was judged for them. Jesus Christ is our Savior. You may think, "Because we sin every day, how can we be righteous? We are definitely sinners." But when we believe in the Word of God, just as Christ Jesus obeyed the Father, we become righteous.

Of course, as I have said previously, we had sin in our hearts before we were born again. After we took the gospel of the remission of sins into our hearts, we were saved from all our sins. When we didn't know the gospel, we were sinners. But we became righteous when we started to believe in the salvation of Jesus, and became the righteous children of God. This is the faith of becoming righteous that the Apostle Paul talked about. The faith in the gospel of remission made us 'the righteous.'

Neither the Apostle Paul, nor Abraham, nor the ancestors of faith became righteous by their works, but rather by having faith in the Word of God, the words of His blessing of the remission of sins.

In Hebrews 10:18, *"Now where there is remission of these, there is no longer an offering for sin."* Just as it is written, God saved us so that we may not have to die for our sins. Do you believe in this? —Amen—

In Philippians 2, *"Let this mind be in you which was also in Christ Jesus, who, being in the form of God, did not consider it robbery to be equal with God, but made Himself of no reputation, taking the form of a servant, and coming in the likeness of men. And being found in appearance as a man, He humbled Himself and became obedient to the point of death, even the death of the Cross. Therefore God also has highly exalted Him and given Him the name which is above every name, that at the name of Jesus every knee should bow, of those in heaven, and of those on earth, and those under the earth, and that every tongue should confess that Jesus Christ is Lord, to the glory of God the Father"* (Philippians 2:5-11).

Jesus Christ, who is the radiance of His glory and the exact representation of His nature (Hebrews 1:3), did not pursue any grand reputation for Himself. Instead, He took upon Himself the form of a servant, and came in the likeness of a human being. He humbled Himself and became obedient to the point of death to save us.

Therefore, we praise Jesus, "He is our God, the Savior and King." The reason why we glorify God and praise Jesus is that Jesus obeyed the will of His Father to the end. If He hadn't obeyed, we wouldn't be glorifying the Son of God now. But because the Son of God obeyed the will of His Father to the point of death, all creation and all people on this earth glorify Him, and will do so forever.

Jesus Christ became the Lamb of God who took away the sins of the world, and it is written that He took them away through His baptism. Now, about 2000 years has passed since

He took away the sins of the world. You and I have been living in this world from our births, and all our sins are also included in the sins of the world.

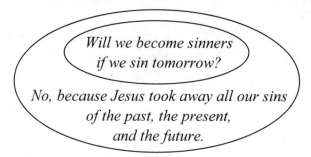

Will we become sinners
if we sin tomorrow?

No, because Jesus took away all our sins
of the past, the present,
and the future.

Without separating original sin from our own lifelong trespasses, haven't we sinned from the time we were born? —Yes, we have.—

Jesus knew that we would sin from the day we were born until the day we die, so He took away all our sins in advance. Can you see it now? If we were to live until 70, our sins would fill more than a hundred dump trucks. But Jesus took away all our sins at once with His baptism and carried them to the Cross with Him.

If Jesus had taken away only the original sin, we would all die and go to hell. Even if we felt that He couldn't have taken away all our sins, it would never change the fact that Jesus had blotted out all our sins.

How much sin can we commit in this world? All the sins we commit are included in the sins of the world.

When Jesus told John to baptize Him, it was exactly what He meant. Jesus testified Himself that He had taken away all our sins. God sent His servant before Jesus and had Jesus baptized by him. By being baptized by John, the representative of humankind, by lowering His head before him to be baptized, Jesus took away all the sins of all humankind.

All our sins from ages 20 to 30, from 30 to 40, and so on; even the sins of our children were included in the sins of the world, which Jesus took away through His baptism.

Who can say that there sin remains in this world? Jesus Christ took away the sins of the world, and we can all be saved when we believe in our hearts, without a shadow of a doubt, in what Jesus did to atone for our sins: His baptism and the shedding of His precious blood.

Most people live their turbulent lives wrapped up in their own thoughts, talking about their lives as if their lives were so important. But there are many who have led harder lives. Many people have lived turbulent lives. I also lived such a life before I was born again. How can you not understand or accept the gospel of remission, of the baptism of Jesus and His blood?

The Salvation of Sinners Has Been Completed

Why did Jesus wash Peter's feet?

Because He wanted Peter to have strong faith in the fact that He had already washed away all his future sins through His baptism.

Let us read John 19. *"And He, bearing His Cross, went out to a place called the Place of a Skull, which is called in Hebrew, Golgotha, where they crucified Him, and two others with Him, one on either side, and Jesus in the center. Now Pilate wrote a title and put it on the Cross. And the writing was: JESUS OF NAZARETH, THE KING OF THE JEWS. Then many of the Jews read this title, for the place where Jesus*

Then many of the Jews read this title, for the place where Jesus was crucified was near the city; and it was written in Hebrew, Greek, and Latin" (John 19:17-20).

Dear friends, Jesus Christ took on all the sins of the world and was sentenced to be crucified at the court of Pilate. Now let us think about this scene together.

From verse 28, *"After this, Jesus, knowing that all things were now accomplished, that the Scripture might be fulfilled,"* Jesus took away all our sins to fulfill the Scripture. *"And, He said, 'I thirst!' Now a vessel full of sour wine was sitting there; and they filled a sponge with sour wine, put it on hyssop, and put it to His mouth. So when Jesus had received the sour wine, He said, 'It is finished!' And bowing His head, He gave up His spirit" (John 19:28-30).*

Jesus said, *"It is finished!"* and then died on the Cross. After three days, He was resurrected from the dead and went up to heaven.

The baptism of Jesus by John the Baptist and His death on the Cross are indispensably linked with each other; one has no reason to exist without the other. Therefore, let us praise the Lord Jesus for saving us with His gospel of remission.

The flesh of humankind always follows the needs of the flesh, so we cannot help but sin with our flesh. Jesus Christ gave us His baptism and blood to save us from the sins of our flesh. He saved us from the sins of our flesh with His gospel.

Those who have complete remission of sins can enter the Kingdom of Heaven at any time by believing in Jesus, who was born in Bethlehem, was baptized in the Jordan, died on the Cross and was resurrected on the third day. We praise the Lord and glorify His name forever.

In the last chapter in John, Jesus went to Galilee after He was resurrected from the dead. He went to Peter and said to and Peter answered Him, *"Yes, Lord; You know that I love You."* Then Jesus told him, *"Feed My lambs."*

Peter realized everything, the gospel of the baptism of Jesus and His blood, the remission of sins. Now, believing in the gospel of the water and the blood that gave him the remission of all his sins and realizing why Jesus had washed his feet, his faith in Jesus became much stronger.

Let us read John 21:15 again. *"So when they had eaten breakfast, Jesus said to Simon Peter, 'Simon, son of Jonah, do you love Me more than these?' He said to Him, 'Yes, Lord; You know that I love You.' He said to him, 'Feed My lambs.'"* He could entrust His lambs to Peter because Peter was His disciple, who had been completely saved, and because Peter had become a righteous and perfect servant of God.

If Peter had become a sinner again by his daily sins, Jesus would not have told him to preach the gospel of the atonement for sins, because he, including the other disciples, could not help could not help but to sin everyday in the flesh. However, Jesus told them to preach the gospel that blotted out all their sins because they believed in the baptism of Jesus and His blood on the Cross, the gospel of the atonement for sins.

Lord, You Know That I Love You

Will you become 'a sinner' again when you sin again?

No. Jesus already took away all my future sins at the Jordan.

Let us think about the words of Jesus to Peter. *"Simon, son of Jonah, do you love Me more than these?" "Yes, Lord; You know that I love You."* His confession of love was true, arising as it did out of faith in the gospel of the atonement for all sins.

If Jesus hadn't taught Peter and the other disciples the gospel of the remission of sins by washing their feet, they wouldn't have been able to confess their love in that way.

Instead, when Jesus came to them and asked, "Do you love Me more than these?" Peter would have said, "Lord, I am merely an incomplete person. I am a sinner who cannot love You more than these things. Please leave me alone." And Peter would have run away, hiding himself from Jesus.

But let us think about Peter's answers. He was blessed with the gospel of the remission of sins, the baptism of Jesus and His blood that saved all humankind.

Therefore, Peter was able to say, *"Yes, Lord; You know that I love You."* This confession of love came out of his faith in the gospel of the remission of Jesus. Peter believed in the true gospel of the remission of sins, through which Jesus had taken away all the sins of the world. This included all the sins of the future, which people were bound to commit because of their deficiencies and weaknesses of the flesh.

Peter firmly believed in the gospel of the remission of sins, and because he also believed that Jesus was the Lamb of God, he was able to answer the Lord without hesitation. The salvation of Jesus came from the gospel of the remission of sins, and thus, Peter had been saved from all his daily sins as well. Peter believed in salvation through the gospel of the remission of all the world's sins.

Are you also like Peter? Can you love and trust in Jesus, who took away all our sins with His gospel of remission, with

His baptism and blood? How can you neither believe nor love Him? There is no other way.

If Jesus had only taken away the sins of the past or the present, and left the sins of the future to us, we wouldn't be able to praise Him as we do now. In addition to this, we would all surely go to hell. Therefore, we should all profess that believing in the gospel of the remission of sins has saved us.

The flesh is always prone to sin, so we constantly sin. Therefore, we must confess that believing in the gospel of the abundant atonement of sins that Jesus has given us, the gospel of the baptism and blood of Jesus, has saved us.

If we didn't believe in the gospel of the atonement of sins, which is the baptism and blood of Jesus, no believer would be saved from his/her lifelong sins. In addition, if we were redeemed of all our lifelong sins by confessing and repenting each time, we would probably be too lazy to stay righteous and would always have sin in our hearts.

If this were so, we would return to being a sinner and wouldn't love Jesus or get close to Him. Then, we also wouldn't be able to believe in the salvation of Jesus and follow Him to the end of our lives.

Jesus gave us the gospel of the remission of sins and saved those who believed. He has become the perfect Savior and washed away all our daily trespasses so that we may truly love Him.

We believers cannot help but love the gospel of the baptism and the blood of Jesus, the remission of our sins. All believers can love Jesus forever and become captives of the love of salvation through the gospel of the remission of sins that Jesus has given us.

Dearly beloved! If Jesus had left even a little sin behind, you wouldn't be able to believe in Jesus, nor would you be able to become the witness for the gospel of the remission of sins. You wouldn't be able to work as God's servant.

But, if you believe in the gospel of the remission of sins, you can be saved from all your sins. He allows you to be saved from all your sins when you realize the true gospel of remission, recorded in the Word of Jesus.

"Do You Love Me More Than These?"

What has made us love Jesus more than anything else?

His love for us through His baptism, which washed away all our sins, even all our future sins

God entrusted His lambs to His servants, who completely believed in the gospel of the remission of sins. Jesus asked three times, *"Simon, son of Jonah, do you love Me more than these?"* and Peter answered each time, *"Yes, Lord, You know that I love You."* Now, let us think about Peter's answers. We can see that this was not the expression of his will, but his faith in the gospel of the remission of sins.

When we love someone, and if that love is based on our wills, it can falter when we weaken. But if that love depended on the strength of God's love, then it would last forever. The Love of God, namely, the abundant atonement for all our sins, the salvation of the water of the baptism of Jesus and the Spirit, is like that.

Our faith in the gospel of the remission of sins must

become the foundation for our love and works for the Lord. If we loved Him only with our wills, we would stumble tomorrow and end up hating ourselves for our iniquities. However, Jesus washed away all our sins: original sin, our daily sins of the past, the sins of today and tomorrow, and all the sins throughout our whole lives. He has not left anyone out of His salvation.

All this is true. If our love and faiths depended on our wills and resolutions, we would fail in our faiths. But because our love and faiths depend on the gospel of remission Jesus has given us, we are already God's children, the righteous. Since we believe in the salvation of the water and the Spirit, we are without sin.

Due to the fact that our salvation came, not from the form of godliness in ourselves, but from the love of God and His law of true salvation by the remission of our sins, we are righteous no matter how incomplete or weak we are in life. We will enter the Kingdom of Heaven and praise God through all eternity. Do you believe this?

1 John 4:10 states, *"In this is love, not that we loved God, but that He loved us and sent His Son to be the propitiation for our sins."* Jesus saved us with the water and the Spirit, so we should have faith in the gospel of remission, the baptism of Jesus and His blood.

If God hadn't saved us with the gospel of the remission of sins, we could not have been saved, no matter how fervently we believed. But Jesus washed away all the sins we commit in our hearts and with our flesh.

In order for us to become righteous, we must be certain of our salvations through faith in the words of the water and the Spirit, the gospel of atonement. The gospel of the remission of all the sins of the world is composed of the baptism of Jesus and His blood. The gospel of remission is the content of the true faith, the true foundation of salvation, and the key to enter the Kingdom of God.

We Have to Discard the Faith of Our Own Wills

Where does true faith come from?

It comes from the love of the Lord, who has already washed away all our future sins.

The faith or love borne of one's own will is neither true love nor true faith. There are many in this world who first believe in Jesus with good wills, then later give up their faiths altogether because of the agony of sin in their hearts.

But we must realize that Jesus washed away all the sins of the world: not only the insignificant iniquities, but also the great sins that are committed through ignorance.

In John 13, in order to teach His disciples how all embracive and perpetually effective His salvation was, Jesus gathered His disciples together before He was crucified. While having dinner with His disciples, He rose and washed their feet to engrave the truth of His abundant salvation into their hearts. We should all know and believe in the gospel of remission, which Jesus taught the disciples by washing their feet.

But Peter firmly refused to let Jesus wash his feet at first. *"You shall never wash my feet!"* And this was the expression of the faith borne of his own will. But Jesus told him, *"What I am doing you do not understand now, but you will know after this."*

Now, with the gospel of the water and the Spirit, we can understand the words of the Bible that were beyond our comprehension. It is the Word of truth; the gospel of the water and the Spirit, the remission of sins, which lets the sinner become righteous by believing with all his/her heart.

Peter went fishing with the other disciples, just as they had done before they met Jesus. Then, Jesus appeared before them and called out to them. Jesus had prepared breakfast for them, and while eating breakfast, Peter realized the meaning of the words that Jesus had spoken before. *"What I am doing you do not understand now, but you will know after this."* He had finally realized what Jesus really meant by washing his feet before.

"The Lord washed away all my sins. All the sins I commit because of my weaknesses, including all the sins I will commit in the future as well." Peter gave up the faith borne of his own will and resolution, and began to stand firm on the baptism and blood of Jesus, the gospel of the remission of sins.

After breakfast, Jesus asked Peter, *"Do you love Me more than these?"* Now, fortified with faith in the love of Jesus, Peter confessed. *"Yes, Lord; You know that I love You."* Peter could reply because he had realized what Jesus had meant when He said, *"You will know after this."* He was able to confess his true faith, the faith in the baptism and blood of Jesus, the gospel of the remission of sins.

Afterwards, He Became a True Servant of God

After that experience, Peter and the other disciples preached the gospel until their dying breaths. Even Paul, who had mercilessly persecuted Christians, testified to the gospel during those hard days of the Roman Empire.

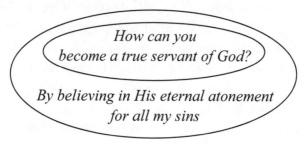

How can you become a true servant of God?

By believing in His eternal atonement for all my sins

Among the twelve disciples of Jesus, Judas sold Jesus and later hung himself. It was the Apostle Paul who took his place. The disciples had elected Matthias among themselves, but it was Paul whom God elected, so Paul became Jesus' Apostle and preached the gospel of the remission of sins with the other disciples.

Most of the disciples of Jesus died as martyrs. Even when they were threatened with death, they didn't deny their faiths, and went on preaching the original gospel.

They may have preached like this: "Jesus Christ washed away all the sins of your flesh with His baptism and blood, that is, with His gospel of the remission of sins. Jesus took away your sins with His baptism in the Jordan and bore the judgment for you on the Cross. Believe in the gospel of Jesus' baptism and His blood on the Cross, and be saved."

Hearing the original gospel and believing in it indeed saved many. It was the power of faith in the gospel of the baptism of Jesus, His blood, and the Spirit.

The disciples preached the gospel of the water and the Spirit, saying, "Jesus is God and the Savior." It is because they have testified to the gospel of the water and the Spirit that you and I can now hear the gospel of the baptism and blood of Jesus as our salvation, and be saved from sin. Because of

God's infinite love and Jesus' complete salvation, we have all become the disciples of Jesus.

Do you all believe? Jesus loved us so much that He gave us the gospel of the water and the Spirit, the remission of sins, and we have become righteous disciples of Jesus. In order to teach the true gospel of remission, Jesus washed His disciples' feet.

Jesus washed His disciples' feet to teach them and us that all the sins of the world, including all the sins we commit throughout our lives, were completely washed away when He was baptized and bled on the Cross. We thank Jesus for His love and the gospel of remission.

Jesus taught us two things by washing the feet of the disciples. First, it was to teach them, just as He had said, *"What I am doing you do not understand now, but you will know after this,"* that all our sins were washed away by the gospel of remission, the baptism of Jesus and His blood.

The second teaching was that as Jesus had lowered Himself to save the sinners and make them righteous, we, the born-again, should serve others by preaching the gospel of remission. It is right for us who came first, to serve those who come later.

The two reasons why Jesus washed the disciples' feet on the day of the Passover feast are clear and they still exist within His Church.

A disciple can never be higher than his teacher. Therefore, we preach the gospel to the world and serve it as if we were serving Jesus. We, who were previously saved, should serve those who come after us. To teach this, Jesus washed the disciples' feet. In addition, by washing Peter's feet, He showed us that He was the perfect Savior so that we may never be deceived by the devil again.

You can all be saved by believing in the gospel of the remission of sins, of the water and the Spirit. Jesus washed away all our sins with His baptism, crucifixion, and resurrection. Only those who believe in His gospel can be saved from the sins of the world forever.

Have Faith in the Gospel Which Washed Away All Our Daily Sins

We can cut off the deceptions of the devil by believing in the gospel of remission, the words of the water and the Spirit. People are easily deceived by the devil and the devil continuously whispers in their ears. Knowing that the flesh of people ceaselessly commit sins in the world, how can they ever be without sin? All people are sinners.

However, we know the answer. "Knowing that Jesus took away all the sins of our flesh with His baptism, how can a believer be with sin? Jesus paid in full all the wages of sin, so what wage is left for us to pay?"

If we do not believe in the gospel of the water and the blood, the words of the devil seem reasonable. But, if we have the gospel on our side, we can have unwavering faiths in the truth of God's Word.

We must have faith in the gospel of being born again of water and blood. True faith is to believe in the gospel of the baptism of Jesus, His blood on the Cross, His death and His resurrection.

Have you ever seen a picture of a model of the holy tabernacle? It is a small tent-house. The house is divided into two sections, the outer part is the holy place and the inner part is the Most Holy Sanctuary, in which the mercy seat is located.

There are a total of 60 pillars standing in the outer court of the holy tabernacle, and the holy place has 48 boards. We must picture the holy tabernacle in our minds in order to understand the meaning of the words of God.

What Was the Gate of the Court of the Tabernacle Made of?

What was the gate of the court of the tabernacle made of?

A screen woven of blue, purple and scarlet yarn and fine linen thread

The gate of the court of the tabernacle is described in Exodus 27:16, *"For the gate of the court there shall be a screen twenty cubits long, woven of blue and purple and scarlet yarn, and fine linen thread, made by a weaver. It shall have four pillars and four sockets."* The materials used for the gate of the court of the tabernacle were blue, purple, and scarlet yarn, and fine linen thread. It was intricately woven and very colorful.

God had ordered Moses to weave the gate colorfully with blue, purple, and scarlet yarn so that it would be easy for everyone to find the entrance. The gate woven with blue, purple, scarlet yarn, and fine linen thread was hung on four pillars.

These four materials symbolize the blueprint of God's salvation, by which He would save all those who believed in His Son, through the baptism and the blood of Jesus, and in His being God.

Each of the materials used to build the holy tabernacle has a specific meaning and it represents God's Word and His plans to save humankind through Jesus.

Now, how many different materials were used for the gate of the court of the holy tabernacle? Four different materials were used; blue, purple, scarlet yarn, and fine linen thread. These four are very significant in helping us strengthen our faiths in the gospel of being born again. If it were not important, this information wouldn't be recorded in the Bible with such great detail.

All the materials used for the gate of the court of the holy tabernacle imply significant meanings to our salvation. Therefore, God revealed these things to Moses and told him to do exactly as he was told.

What Do Blue, Purple, and Scarlet Yarn Mean within the Gospel of God?

What did all the materials used for the tabernacle symbolize?

The salvation of Jesus through His baptism and blood

Inside the holy tabernacle, blue, purple, and scarlet yarn, and fine linen thread were used again for the veil that was hung between the holy place and the Most Holy Place. The same materials were used for the robes of the High Priest, who could enter inside the Most Holy Place once a year.

Blue yarn symbolizes the baptism of Jesus. In 1 Peter 3:21, it is said, *"There is also an antitype which now saves us, namely baptism."* Peter confirmed the baptism of Jesus, through which He took on all the sins of the world in this verse, as the antitype of the salvation of atonement. All our sins were passed onto Jesus through His baptism. Therefore, blue yarn, the baptism of Jesus, is the most essential part of the Word of salvation.

Scarlet yarn symbolizes the blood of Jesus, and purple yarn symbolizes His Divinity—the status of Jesus as King and God. The three colors of yarn were necessary for our faiths in Jesus and His salvation.

The gorgeous outer garment worn by the High Priest was called an ephod, and the robe of ephod was also all blue. The High Priest wore a turban on his head, on which a plate of pure gold was engraved, *'HOLINESS TO THE LORD.'* The plate was fastened to the turban with a blue cord, too.

The Truth Represented by Blue Yarn

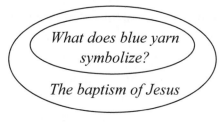

What does blue yarn symbolize?

The baptism of Jesus

I looked up the meaning of the blue yarn in the Bible. What does the Bible say about blue? We have to understand the blue yarn among the blue, purple, and scarlet yarns.

Blue yarn represents 'the water,' that is, the baptism of Jesus. Jesus Christ was baptized by John the Baptist to take on all the sins of the world (Matthew 3:15).

If Jesus had not taken away all the sins of the world with His baptism, we could not have become sanctified before God. Therefore, Jesus Christ had to come to this world and be baptized by John the Baptist in the Jordan River to take away all the sins of the world.

The reason why there had to be blue yarn in the gate of the court of the holy tabernacle was because we could not become sanctified without the baptism of Jesus.

Scarlet yarn represents His blood, the death of Jesus. Purple refers to Jesus' Godhead, thus Jesus' status as *"Only Potentate, the King of kings and Lord of lords" (1 Timothy 6:15).*

The truth is that scarlet yarn symbolizes the blood of Christ, who bled on the Cross to pay the wages of sin for all humankind. Jesus Christ came to this world in the flesh to take all the sins of humankind onto Himself through His baptism, and paid off all the wages of sin by sacrificing Himself on the Cross. The baptism and blood of Jesus is the true gospel of remission that is prophesied through the colors of yarn used for the holy tabernacle in the Old Testament.

The pillars of the tabernacle were made of acacia wood, the sockets were of bronze, and the bronze sockets were covered with bands of silver.

All sinners were judged for their sins because the wages of sin is death. Before someone could be blessed by God to earn a new life, he/she had to offer a sacrifice for his/her sins in the days of the Old Testament.

However, the baptism of Jesus in the New Testament, which is represented by the blue yarn of the holy tabernacle, had taken over all our sins. Jesus took our sins to the Cross, bled and was judged for them and in doing so, He saved all of us who have faith in the gospel of remission. He is the King of kings and the Holy God.

Beloved Christians, the baptism of Jesus was the salvation of Jesus, who saved us by taking away all our sins. Jesus, who is God, came down to the world in the flesh (the purple yarn); He was baptized to take on all the sins of the world (the blue yarn); He was crucified and bled on the Cross to accept judgment instead of us (the scarlet yarn). The baptism of Jesus undoubtedly teaches us that He had become the true Savior for all humankind.

We can also see it in the colors that were used for the gate of the holy tabernacle.

To embroider the cloth of the gate with blue, purple, and scarlet yarn in fine linen thread was to clearly tell us the truth of God's salvation. The fine linen thread here means that He saved all of us without exception from our sins. It was absolutely essential to the salvation of atonement.

We can see from the same materials used for the gate of the holy tabernacle that Jesus Christ did not haphazardly save us sinners, without planning. He, obeying God's carefully detailed plan, was baptized, crucified and resurrected from the dead to completely fulfill the salvation of humankind. With blue, purple, and scarlet yarn, the materials of the gospel of remission, Jesus saved all who believed in His salvation.

The Bronze Laver of The Old Testament Was a Shadow of the Baptism of The New Testament

Why did the priests wash their hands and feet before they entered the holy place?

Because they had to stand in front of God without any sin.

The laver was also made of bronze. Bronze represents the judgment Jesus suffered for us. The water basin symbolized the word of the gospel, which tells us that all our iniquities were washed away.

It shows us how the washing away of daily sins was carried out. The daily sins of all humankind can be washed away through faith in the words of the baptism of Jesus.

The altar of burnt offering represents the judgment. The water of Jesus, which is blue, is the gospel of the atonement for sins, in other words, the baptism of Jesus by John the Baptist (Matthew 3:15, 1 John 5:5-10). It is the word of testimony for the gospel of salvation through atonement.

In 1 John 5, it is written, *"And this is the victory that has overcome the world—our faith. And there are three that bear witness on earth: the Spirit, the water, the blood; and these three agree as one."* He also tells us that he who believes in the Son of God has the witness of the water, the blood, and the Spirit in him.

God allowed us to be sanctified through faith in the gospel of atonement and to enter the holy tabernacle. Therefore, we can now live in faith, be fed on the words of God, be blessed by Him, and live the life of the righteous. To become the people of God means to be saved through faith in the gospel of atonement and to live inside the holy tabernacle.

Many people today say that it is enough just to believe without thinking about the meaning of the blue, purple, and scarlet yarns of the gate of the holy tabernacle. If one believed in Jesus without knowing about these things, his/her faith would not be true because there would still be sin in his/her heart. Such a person would still have sin in his/her heart because of the disbelief in the truth of being born again through the gospel of atonement, of the water, the blood, and the Spirit.

If one was asked to evaluate someone one hardly knew, and if, to please the listener, he/she said, "Yes, I believe this person. Of course, I have never met him, but I believe him nevertheless." Do you think the listener would be pleased to hear that? Maybe some of you would behave like such in human affairs, but this is not the kind of trust God wants from us.

God wants us to believe in the gospel of the remission of sins, the salvation of Jesus through blue (Jesus' baptism), purple (Jesus' Deity), and scarlet (Jesus' blood) yarn. We should know, before having faith in Jesus, how He saved us from all sin.

When we believe in Jesus, we should know how He saved us from all our sins through the water (the baptism of Jesus), the blood (His death), and the Spirit (Jesus' being God).

When we truly understand, we can experience true and complete faiths. Our faiths would never be complete without knowing this truth. True faith comes only by understanding the testimony of the salvation of Jesus, the gospel of remission, and Jesus' being the true Savior of humankind.

What, then, would the faith that makes a mockery of Jesus

be like? Let us see.

The Faith That Makes a Mockery of Jesus

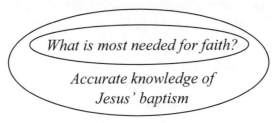

What is most needed for faith?

Accurate knowledge of Jesus' baptism

You have to realize that to believe in Jesus arbitrarily is to make a mockery of Him. If you think, "I find it hard to believe, but as He is God and the Son of God, I shall have to believe in Him anyhow," then you are making a mockery of Jesus. If you really want to be born again, you must believe in the baptism and blood of Jesus, the gospel of atonement.

To believe in Jesus without knowing the gospel of atonement is worse than not believing in Jesus at all. To preach the gospel of only the blood of Jesus is to work in vain without knowing the truth.

Jesus does not want anyone to go around preaching about believing in Him arbitrarily, or having faith in Him without reason. He wants us to believe in Him through knowing the gospel of atonement.

When we believe in Jesus, we have to admit that the gospel of atonement is the baptism and the blood of Jesus. When we believe in Jesus, we have to understand the gospel of atonement through His Word and know specifically how He washed away all our sins.

We also have to know what the blue, purple and scarlet yarn on the gate to the holy tabernacle implies. Then, we can have the true faith that will last eternally.

We Can Never Be Born Again without Believing in Jesus, the Realization of Blue, Purple, and Scarlet Yarn

What did the priests do before they entered the holy place?

They washed their hands and feet with the water from the bronze laver.

Our Lord Jesus saved us. We cannot but praise the Lord when we see how perfectly He saved us. We should look at the holy tabernacle. He gave us the words of the gospel of atonement through the blue, purple, and scarlet yarn of the holy tabernacle and saved us with them. We thank and praise the Lord.

Sinners could not enter the holy place without going through a terrible judgment. How could one enter the holy place without being judged for his/her sins? This would be impossible. If such a person entered the forbidden place, he/she would be killed right then and there. It would be severe damnation. A sinner could never enter the holy place and expect to live.

Our Lord saved us through the secret hidden in the gate to the holy tabernacle. With blue, purple and scarlet yarn, and fine linen thread, He saved us. He told us the secret of His salvation through these things.

Were you and I saved that way? If we do not believe in the words of the blue, purple, and scarlet yarn, there can be no salvation through the gospel of atonement. The color blue does not represent God; it symbolizes none other than the baptism of

Jesus. It is the baptism of Jesus who took away all our sins.

One can enter as far as the altar of burnt offering without believing in the blue yarn. However, he cannot enter the holy place where God resides.

Therefore, before we enter the gate to the holy tabernacle, we have to believe in the blue yarn (the baptism of Jesus), scarlet yarn (His blood on the Cross), and purple yarn (Jesus' being God and the Son of God). Only when we believe are we accepted by God and allowed to enter through the veil of the Most Holy Place.

Some enter the outer court of the tabernacle and think that they are inside. But this is not salvation. How far do we have to go to be saved? We have to be able to enter the Most Holy Place.

In order to enter the Most Holy Place, we have to pass the bronze basin. The bronze basin represents the baptism of Jesus, and we have to wash away all our daily sins with the baptism of Jesus and become sanctified to enter the holy place.

In the Old Testament, the priests had to wash themselves before they entered, and in the New Testament, Jesus washed His disciples' feet to symbolize the washing away of their lifelong trespasses.

The law of God says, *"For the wages of sin is death, but the gift of God is eternal life in Christ Jesus our Lord" (Romans 6:23).* God judges the sins of man without exception, but He passed them onto His Son and judged Him instead. This is the love of God, His salvation. True salvation is attained only when we believe in the gospel of atonement that contains the baptism, the blood, the death, and resurrection of Jesus.

In Order to Be Born Again, One Should Never Scorn the Biblical Truth, the Gospel of the Atonement for Sins

What is the only thing left for us to do?

It is to believe in the gospel, the written words of God.

I never scorn other people. When someone talks about something I am not familiar with, I ask him/her politely to explain it to me. But when I asked around about the implications of the holy tabernacle, nobody could tell me.

Then what could I do? I had to go back to the Bible. In the Bible, where is the holy tabernacle talked about? It is described in detail in Exodus. If one reads this Book carefully, one can understand its meaning through the written words of God.

Dear friends, you cannot be saved by recklessly believing in Jesus. You cannot be born again just by regularly attending church. We know what Jesus told Nicodemus. *"Most assuredly, I say to you, unless one is born of water and the Spirit, he cannot enter the kingdom of God...Are you the teacher of Israel, and do not know these things?" (John 3:5, 10)*

All those who believe in Jesus have to believe in the blue yarn (all the sins of the world were passed onto Jesus when He was baptized), scarlet yarn (the death of Jesus for all our sins), and purple yarn (Jesus is the Savior, God, and the Son of God).

We have to believe that Jesus is the Savior of all the sinners of the world. Without this faith, one can never be born again, nor can one enter the holy place of the Kingdom of God. One can't even live faithfully in this world without it.

Wouldn't it be so easy if one could be born again just by having faith in Jesus? —Yes— "♪*You have been saved. I have been saved. We have all been saved.*♪" How nice! But there are so many who believe in Jesus without being truly 'born again.'

We have to know the truth in the Bible as well as have faith in Jesus. We have to understand the gospel of the remission of sin in the Bible and the meaning of the blue, purple, and scarlet yarn in order to enter the holy tabernacle and be with God in the realm of faith. Inside the tabernacle of faith, we can live happily until the time when Jesus comes again to bring us to His Kingdom. It is essential for us to believe in Jesus the right way.

The Original Gospel Begets Sanctification with Blue Yarn

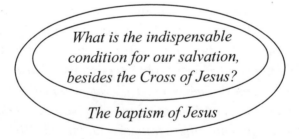

What is the indispensable condition for our salvation, besides the Cross of Jesus?

The baptism of Jesus

People to think that they can live perfectly without making mistakes. However, the harder they try to do good, the more they will soon discover their shortcomings. Human beings are so incomplete, so it is impossible for them not to sin. However, because Jesus saved us with the blue, purple, and scarlet yarn, the gospel of atonement, we can be sanctified and enter the holy place of God.

If God hadn't saved us with the blue, purple, and scarlet

yarn, we would never have been able to enter the holy place by ourselves. What is the reason for this? If only those who live perfectly by their flesh could enter the holy place, there would be none who would be qualified. When one believes in Jesus without knowing the true gospel, one only adds more sins to his/her heart.

Jesus saved us with His carefully planned salvation; the salvation of the blue, purple, and scarlet yarn, and fine linen thread. He washed away all our sins. Do you believe in this? —Yes— Do you have the truth of the gospel of remission in your heart and bear witness to it? —Yes—

Only when you bear witness to the gospel can you put on your forehead the golden plate that says *'HOLINESS TO THE LORD'* and join the *'royal priesthood' (1 Peter 2:9)*. Only then can you stand before people and tell them you are a servant of God, working as a royal priest.

The turban of the High Priest has a plate of gold and the plate is fastened with blue cord. Why blue? Because Jesus saved us with the gospel of remission, took away all our sins and made us sinless through His baptism. The baptism in the New Testament is equivalent to the laying on of hands in the Old Testament.

No matter how diligently and faithfully we believe in Jesus, we would not be able to earn the plate engraved with, *'HOLINESS TO THE LORD'* without recognizing the secret words of the blue, purple, and scarlet yarn.

How did we become righteous? It is written in Matthew 3:15, *"For thus it is fitting for us to fulfill all righteousness."* Jesus was baptized and saved us from all the sins of the world. Through His baptism, He took away all our sins, and we believers have become righteous.

How could we say that we are without sin if there hadn't

been the baptism of Jesus? Even if we believed in Jesus and cried out, thinking of His death on the Cross, all the tears in this world couldn't wash away all our sins. No. No matter how much we cried and repented, our sins would have remained within us.

'HOLINESS TO THE LORD.' Since He took away all our sins with His baptism and blood, the Lord allowed all the sins of us sinners to be passed onto Jesus, and because the word of salvation is recorded in the Bible, we have become righteous through our faiths, despite all our iniquities and weaknesses.

Therefore, we can now stand before God. We can now live as the righteous and preach the gospel to the world. *"♪I have been saved. You have been saved. We have all been saved.♪"* We have been saved according to God's merciful plan.

Without the word of the gospel of atonement in your heart, there is no salvation, no matter how hard you try. It is similar to a Korean popular song about unrequited love. *"♪Oh, my heart beats quickly without reason whenever I see her, every time I am near her. I must be in unrequited love.♪"* My heart beats quickly, but not hers. My love is never returned. Unfortunately, so many Christians still have an unrequited love toward God.

People tend to think that salvation comes in many different ways for many different people. They ask, "Why should it only come through the gospel of baptism?" But it could never be the complete salvation if it were not the gospel of the baptism of Jesus. It is the only way we can become righteous before God because it is the only way we can be completely cleansed of all our sins.

What Is the Salvation of Blue Yarn That Jesus Gave Us?

What has made us righteous?

The gospel of the blue, purple, and scarlet yarn

The salvation through the gospel of the blue, purple, and scarlet yarn is God's gift to all humankind. This gift has enabled us to enter the holy tabernacle and live in peace. It has made us righteous, enabled us to live within the church and be trained by the Holy Scriptures through the church.

Whenever we go before God to pray, the gospel blesses us with His love. This is why salvation is so precious to us. Jesus tells us to build a house of faith 'on the rock.' The rock is the gospel of His baptism. We should all be saved, live with salvation, go to Heaven, earn everlasting life, and become the children of God.

Dear friends, because of the gospel of atonement, we are able to enter the holy tabernacle with faith. Because of the washing away of all our sins (the baptism of Jesus) and the judgment on the Cross, we have been saved by having faith in the gospel of the baptism of Jesus.

The abundant atonement for all our sins, the baptism and the blood of Jesus, is the gospel that washed away all our sins. Do you believe this? The true gospel is the heavenly gospel of atonement that completely washed away all our sins.

We have been born again by believing in the gospel of atonement. Jesus has given us the gospel of atonement, which washed away all our daily sins and even all future sins. Praise the Lord. Hallelujah!

The gospel of the water and the Spirit (the gospel of the water and the blood) is the true gospel accomplished and preached by Jesus Christ. This book was written to reveal the secret of the gospel of Jesus, the gospel of the water and the Spirit.

Because many people believe in Jesus without knowing the complete truth, they are now only boasting themselves to be the fundamentalists or the religious pluralists in the world of Christian theology (the so-called philosophical theology); in short, they live in heresy and confusion. Therefore, we should go back and believe in the true gospel. It is not yet too late.

I will go into more detail in the second book for those who have questions about the gospel of being born again of water and the Spirit. ⊠

APPENDIX 1

Testimonies of Salvation

Testimonies of Salvation

I had agonized over my sins

Brother Jae-dong Park, Korea

"But Jesus answered and said to him, 'Permit it to be so now, for thus it is fitting for us to fulfill all righteousness'" *(Matthew 3:15).*

The one who was destined to hell for his sins has been saved. Glory be to God!

"Stand now with your enchantments and the multitude of your sorceries" (Isaiah 47:12). I did just that.

I was born into a conservative family to a mother who was a faithful Buddhist. As I was growing up, I participated in the Buddhist camps and memorized Buddhist scriptures and attended temple eagerly. I thought scorn of the superstitious Buddhism that most women followed, and tried to find something else to give meaning to my life. But, still I felt the weight of sin in my heart, and so tried to correct my behavior, winning praise from the people around me.

When I was going to college in Sokcho-City, I met a friend who was a Christian. That was the turning point in my life. God had planned this meeting. Later I found out that the friend, just as I used to, had thrown himself into religious rituals with enthusiasm but hadn't found any satisfaction in his life; it made me feel very sorry for him. In church, I realized that my forced good attitude itself was a sin.

"For from within, out of the heart of a man, proceed evil

thoughts, adulteries, fornications, murders, thefts, covetousness, wickedness, deceit, licentiousness, an evil eye, blasphemy, pride, foolishness" (Mark 7:21-22).

I realized that I could not produce true goodness because my mind was full of evil things, and my difficulty with sin had not been solved. I was heading toward hell. From then on I agonized over my sins and decided to ask Rev. Samuel Kim for help. I learned from him that Jesus was the One *"who took away the sin of the world" (John 1:29)* and that He had taken my sins and paid for them too. It greatly relieved me, and my wretched mind seemed to enter the rest that came from Heaven.

Later I met Rev. Paul Jong and learned how Jesus washed away all our sins and how the people of Israel offered sacrifices in the Old Testament. In addition, I also realized why Jesus, who was conceived of the Holy Spirit (Matthew 1:20), had to be cursed and hung on a tree (Galatians 3:13). *"Permit it to be so now, for thus it is fitting for us to fulfill all righteousness" (Matthew 3:15).* John the Baptist, as the last High Priest, baptized and passed all sins onto Jesus, the Lamb of God without blemish. Then Jesus paid the wages of all our sins on the Cross. This was the true gospel that awakened me and made me righteous. I, who once was a sinner, have become righteous.

"Old things have passed away; behold, all things have become new" (2 Corinthians 5:17). It was the same for me. I repented of my life (Acts 11:18) and was baptized into Christ, and there will be no condemnation for me (Romans 8:1). I am basking in His Grace and I thank God for saving me. May all those who are agonizing over sin and seeking Jesus find the gospel of redemption in Him!

Hallelujah. ✉

From superstition to true faith in God

Sister Sung-neo Kim, Korea

I was married at 19, and my husband's family was very poor. Since then I have never been affluent, nor was I ever loved by my husband. I had always envied women who had loving husbands and enjoyed riches. My husband's family believed in mountain gods, and my father-in-law was a fortuneteller. My husband was enlisted in the army 3 days after our marriage, and my brother-in-law became mentally ill at the age of 22. Moreover, my mother-in-law became blind around the age of 50. Those days were really terrible for me.

Since I was without learning and didn't have beautiful looks nor a cultivated mind or intellect, I thought it was my destiny to live like that for all my life. My mother-in-law longed to have an operation, but I never took her to a hospital and couldn't be bothered to buy any medication for her. I just hoped that she would get sick and die shortly.

I am now 54 years old and my mother-in-law died two years ago. There is a saying that it is bad luck to put the pillow of the deceased in the coffin, but I didn't know it at the time and buried her with her pillow.

Since then she has often appeared in my dreams, and I am sorry that I put her pillow in the coffin and that I was so harsh to her when she was alive. Other people seem nice to their in-laws, but I couldn't keep myself from hating her. I was tormented with nightmares and a stricken conscience.

I have a son and four daughters, and I was afraid that something bad would happen to my only son. When I told them about my dreams, my neighbors advised me that the bad spirit should be exorcised. I visited shamans and went to temples to bow endlessly and beg for relief but it was no use. I felt like ending my life to escape from my conscience.

If I had not found Jesus nor been redeemed, I wouldn't be alive today. One day I ran away from my house and went to my daughters' houses in turn to rest and take some herbal medicine. That was when God showed me the way to life. One of my daughters is a born-again Christian, and she invited her pastor's wife for me. She came with some other women and talked to me.

I knew nothing about God. But when they told me that Jesus had taken away all my sins, I decided to believe in His Word. I used to tell my daughters not to go to church because I thought that might bring bad luck to have two gods under one roof. But I thought things couldn't get any worse than this and I didn't want to die as a sinner.

The pastor's wife told me that all people are born sinners but that God had taken away all our sins through Jesus and we would not be sinners anymore if we believed in Jesus. So I started to attend church regularly and tried to listen to the Word, but I couldn't understand much of what was said. But as time went on, all His words started to make sense to me. I realized that I was born as a sinner and I cannot help being a sinner because of original sin. I also found out that the evil thoughts in my mind were also sins before God.

Offering sacrifices in the Old Testament was His way of showing us the good things to come. And Jesus, as it was done by laying hands on the head of sacrificial animal in the Old Testament, was baptized by John and all my sins were passed onto Him in the Jordan. He took away all my sins and bled on the Cross to pay for them.

I was finally convinced that I was without sin, and no one

could condemn me. And I could sleep in peace from then on.

"There is therefore now no condemnation to those who are in Christ" (Romans 8:1). I had suffered so much with sin in my heart and now the sin is gone. I no longer have nightmares.

I cannot write well of my feelings since I do not know how to read well but I can talk to anyone about how Jesus took away all the sins from my heart. I pray that Jesus will save my husband and other family members as He saved me. And I hope this testimony will help others to find redemption in Jesus.

I thank God for saving me and I am so happy to be able to spread the gospel to many people. Now I don't envy rich or smart people anymore. ✉

By the true gospel preached in Moscow

Sister Belova Lyssa
Moscow, Russia

I would like to say hello to all the ministers in Korea in the name of Jesus and share with you a joyous event that completely changed my life.

In a seminar held in Moscow a couple of years ago, I heard the amazing words of God. When I participated in a training seminar in Korea the next year, I heard so many teachings about the Word of God, especially about being born again of water and the Spirit. What a joy it is to see so clearly that I have become truly free from all my sins!

It has been 6 years since I started to believe in Jesus. Prior to being "truly born again," I was taught that I was a great sinner and that I had to repent continuously. I prayed and repented every day over and over. I had received water baptism, but I was still not born again. I recognized that I was a sinner and that I had so much sin in my heart. I had to continually ask for God's forgiveness. I was always tormented by my sins. But I truly believed that God would not leave me in this sorrow and that He would somehow save me in the end.

God then led me to a servant who had been born again. Through him I was able to hear the most precious gospel in this world, the only true gospel of salvation. I learned that Jesus had washed away all my sins with His baptism and the Cross and that now I was without sin.

Now I am not a sinner anymore, and my heart is filled with joy. Now, instead of the prayers of repentance, I offer my great thanks to God every day, and my life has become so peaceful and joyous. I know now that there is no other gospel, no other faith as true as this one. I only pray that my faith will become stronger. I offer praise to God every day and I believe that there is no faith more precious than this.

I am at peace knowing that I will enter the Kingdom of Heaven when my life comes to an end. I now work for God and am preaching the gospel to others around me. I live in constant joy, sharing God's love with all the people of the world. ✉

Now, I have strong faith in Christ

Peter Chris, Teenagers for Christ, Nigeria

What I understand from this book, which is the right understanding of God's righteousness, is that the baptism of Jesus and the Cross. Both of them have to go together to bring the complete requirement for our salvation. The baptism of Jesus (water), which was received from John the Baptist who represent the whole of mankind, took the sin of all mankind on His head by going through the baptism (in form of laying on of hands), and then taking them to the Cross to get judgment for them all since taking the sins upon Himself. So if I didn't accept His baptism, which was what lead Him to the Cross, my salvation cannot be complete, no matter how perfect the victory of Christ on the Cross would be.

I still sin despite the fact that I have received Christ, but I am not a sinner for Christ who knows no sin became a sinner so that we will become the righteousness of God. From your book, I now have a strong faith in the work of salvation of Christ through His baptism and the Cross (water and blood), which had paid off all my past, present and future sin. God has washed away all my sins and judged them through Christ.

As a born-again Christian, I want to do my best to avoid anything that will lead us to sin. We should realize that Christ has paid all sins for us but we shall not delight in sin for if we do we are making mockery of His saving grace. ✉

Jesus took my sins on Himself

Pastor Timothy Katola, Kenya

God bless Rev. Paul C. Jong for bringing the true gospel more clearly to the readers of his book, "Have You Truly Been Born Again of Water and the Spirit." After I read this book a few weeks ago, the message of redemption through the death of our Savior Jesus Christ became more vivid in my life. The truth of His baptism, which passed all sins on to Jesus by John the Baptist at the Jordan River, gives every human being the assurance that all burden of sin is wiped out from our lives, once we believe the gospel.

John the Baptist was an antitype of Aaron the High Priest of the Old Testament, who sacrificed for the sins of the Israelites. Aaron offered sacrifices to God pleading for the forgiveness of sins committed by the Israelites. He passed all the sins of Israelites on to the scapegoat by laying his hands on the head of it. Likewise, Jesus at His baptism took all our sins when John the Baptist laid his hands on Jesus. The high priests had to offer scapegoats every year, *"but in those sacrifices there is a reminder of sins every year. For it is not possible that the blood of bulls and goats could take away sins" (Hebrews 10:3-4).* However, Jesus Christ did it once and for all for all humanity. Once we believe in the Lord Jesus Christ, we receive the remission of all our sins once and for all.

Paul C. Jong shows us clearly how our sins were put on Jesus and that sin should no longer be a problem in our lives. I am not now a sinner any more because I am forgiven after JESUS TOOK MY SINS ON HIMSELF through His baptism and died in my place.

Everyone's greatest problem today is freedom from his/her sinful nature. This book shows us clearly how we can live a life without sin and condemnation as we believe in the true Gospel of Jesus. Thank God for His revelation on His servant Paul C. Jong. ✉

WOW! Amazing!

Missionary Brucilla Johnson, USA

I bring you greetings and glad tidings in the precious wonderful name of our Lord and Savior, Jesus Christ. This is in reply of the question you e-mailed to me a few days ago: "Why did John the Baptist lay his hands on Jesus in the Jordan River?"

It was the Law of Atonement in the Old Testament (OT). It was the command of God for Moses to ordain his brother, Aaron, the first High Priest, to lay hands on the head of a sacrificial animal (goat), and confess the horrific sins of the children of Israel and their transgressions. (Isaiah 53:3-5). Afterwards, the goat would bear and carry the iniquities and transgressions of the Israelites upon itself and send it away by a suitable man who was to release the goat into the wilderness. (Leviticus 16:21-22.)

John the Baptist laid his hands on Jesus head in the same like manner shortly before His public ministry. In order for Jesus to take away all the sins and transgressions of the world, He was willing and humbled to be baptized by John in this manner.

He bored all our sins and transgressions upon His head and shoulders (the High Priest and goat; Isaiah 53:3-5, Matthew 3:13-17).

The baptism (immersion of water), is this, Jesus took or bore all the sins of the world upon Himself was now to be purged, cleansed, washed and purified by the baptism ritual (John 1:29).

The Bible states like this. *"We fall down, but we get up"*

(Psalms 37:23-24), "All have sinned and have come short to the glory of God" (Romans 3:23). "No, there is none that doeth good. No, not one" (Romans 3:10-12).

Oh! But praise God, Hallelujah! Glory be to God, *"For by grace we have been saved through faith." (Ephesians 2:8, 1 John 1:9).* The Lamb of God has bore and taken the wages of sin in this world upon Himself through His baptism and death on the Cross (John 1:29).

I am without sin having been saved by the grace of Jesus Christ through faith washed and cleansed by Jesus Christ, through both His Baptism and the Blood of the Lamb Of God.

Now, we should "Return to the Gospel of the Water and the Spirit." To return to the Gospel of the Water and the Spirit means to come with a contrite spirit and a representative heart and confession of the mouth. And the Lord Jesus will forgive us of our sins and heal us from all sicknesses, diseases and unrighteousness (1 John 1:9, 2 Chronicles 7:14, 3 John 2) with the true gospel of the water and the Spirit. To Return to the Gospel of the Water and the Spirit also means to make a "true confession of sin" and be renewed by the transforming of the mind by the Spirit Of God and be ye "Baptized" with the Holy Spirit (Acts 1:5).

I am so elated and joyous in the readings of these books that has enlightened and given me a deeper understanding in His word. These awesome, powerful tools have also given me knowledge and a word I really did not know and was not aware of. WOW! Amazing! ⊠

I was a hopeless sinner

Mrs. Alderman, USA

First of all, God sent His servant John the Baptist to baptize His Son so that John could help prepare the way for Salvation. John the Baptist laid his hands on Jesus in the Jordan River. It was one Man's righteous act, which took away all the sins of humankind. Jesus took away all the sins of this world by being baptized. Jesus gave His life at the Cross for the wages of sin. He paid the wages of sin with His death on the Cross.

Our sins were passed onto Jesus and that He was judged instead of us in order to save mankind. Jesus had to take away our sins and die for them. A person is in sin if they do not believe in the baptism of Jesus Christ and the Cross. So it is a sin not to accept the Word of God and to deviate from the truth to false theories. It is a sin if one does not believe in the written Word that Jesus was baptized and died on the Cross and was resurrected to free us from our sins.

By repentance and acknowledge our selves as complete sinners and to believe Jesus the Son of God, as Our Savior who saved us from all sins, we can be free from sin absolutely. Therefore we must believe in the baptism and the blood of Jesus that cleansed us of all sins.

I was a hopeless sinner before I believed in Jesus' baptism! If Jesus Christ had not been baptized by John the Baptist, I could not but remain as a sinner and be lost. ✉

I can now stand before God

Pastor Steven Icke, England

In the Old Testament the High Priest laid his hands on the head of the offerings to pass on the sin (Leviticus 16:3-4). The laying on of hands was an essential part of the Day of Atonement. If it had not done so, offering the sacrifice couldn't have been carried out because atonement for sin could not be accomplished without the laying on of hands, thus passing the yearly sins of Israel on to the sin offering.

In Leviticus 16:21, *"And Aaron shall lay both his hands on the head of the live goat, confess over it all the iniquities of the children of Israel, and all their transgressions, concerning all their sins, putting them on the head of the goat, and shall send it away into the wilderness by the hand of a suitable man."*

He took two goats as sin offerings and a ram as a burnt offering from the people. Then he presented two goats before the Lord at the door of the tabernacle and cast lots to select the one for 'the Lord' and the other to act as 'the scapegoat.' The one for the Lord was offered as a sin offering, and the scapegoat was offered alive before the Lord to atone for the yearly sins of the people of Israel and then put out into the wilderness (Leviticus 16:7-10).

The sins of Israel had to be passed on to the scapegoat by the laying on of hands. Then the scapegoat, which took on itself all the sins of Israel, was put out into the wilderness for peace between people and God. Thus the yearly sins of Israel were washed away. In the same way in the New Testament, Jesus Christ was baptized (the laying on of hands in the Old

Testament) by John the Baptist who was the last descendant of the High Priest Aaron, and took away all the sins of the world as the sacrificial Lamb to fulfill the salvation of God (Leviticus 20:22, Matthew 3:15, John 1:29, 36).

In the Old Testament, before the casting of lots, Aaron killed the young bull as a sin offering for himself and his house (Leviticus 16:11). Then he took a censer full of burning coals of fire from the altar before the Lord with his hands full of sweet incense beaten fine and took it beyond the veil. Then he put the incense on the fire before the Lord so that the cloud of incense might hover over the mercy seat. He also took some of the blood of the bull and sprinkled it with his finger on and before the mercy seat seven times (Leviticus 16:12-19).

On the Day of Atonement, the laying of Aaron's hands on the head of the offering could not be omitted. Aaron laid hands on the goat and passed all the sins and all the iniquities of Israel on to his head. Then a suitable man took the goat into the wilderness and sent it forth. The scapegoat wandered in the wilderness with the sins of Israel and died for them in the end. This was the sacrifice of atonement in the Old Testament.

It is the same in the New Testament except it was Jesus Christ, as the scapegoat, who took away all the sins of the world upon Himself through His baptism and bled and died on the Cross for us.

Therefore now, the salvation from all sins cannot be brought without the baptism and crucifixion of the heavenly High Priest, Jesus Christ. This is the fulfillment of salvation of being born again of water and the Spirit.

Jesus was the One *"who took away the sin of the world" (John 1:29)* and that He had taken my sins and paid for them too. Jesus washed away all our sins just like how the people of Israel offered sacrifices in the Old Testament. This was why

Jesus, who was conceived of the Holy Spirit (Matthew 1:20), had to be cursed and hung on a tree (Galatians 3:13). *"Permit it to be so now, for thus it is fitting for us to fulfill all righteousness" (Matthew 3:15).*

John the Baptist, as the last High Priest, baptized and passed all sins on to Jesus, the Lamb of God without blemish. Then Jesus paid for the sins on the Cross. This is the true gospel that awakened me and made me righteous. I, who once was a sinner, have become righteous.

"Old things have passed away; behold, all things have become new" (2 Corinthians 5:17). I repented of my life (Acts 11:18) and was baptized into Christ, and there will be no condemnation for me (Romans 8:1). I am basking in His Grace and I thank God for saving me. So even though I my sin I can turn to Jesus baptism know that Jesus has already paid my price and through His Grace and mercy receive forgiveness. PRAISE GOD!!!

Now, I am without sin, even though I still cannot but commit sins in my every day life. It is written, *"The wages of sin is death" (Romans 6:23).* I realized that I could never stand before God with all my sins, and my heart being heavy, however, God LOVES me. He sent his Son to redeem me. *"Behold, the Lamb of God who takes away the sin of the world!" (John 1:29)* I realized that the sin of the world means all sins, including my own. He not only took away the sins of yesterday and today, but also the sins of tomorrow. Jesus took away all the sins of the world when He was baptized.

"But Jesus answered and said to him, 'Permit it to be so now, for thus it is fitting for us to fulfill all righteousness.' Then he allowed Him" (Matthew 3:15).

I could finally believe that all my sins had been passed on to Jesus when He was baptized by John the Baptist and that all my sins were paid off when He died at the Cross. *"For the life of the flesh is in the blood, and I have given it to you upon the altar to make atonement for your souls; for it is the blood that makes atonement for the soul" (Leviticus 17:11).* Jesus didn't just die but said, *"It is finished!" (John 19:30)* His side was then pierced and immediately blood and water came out (John 19:34), bringing down the wall of sin that separates God and humankind. I can now stand before God now that I am truly redeemed. ⊠

Now I fully believe the gospel of the water and the Spirit

Brother Godson, India

In the Holy Bible we can find clear explanation about the baptism of Jesus. John 3:5 says, *"Unless one is born of water and the Spirit, he cannot enter the kingdom of God."* The water mentioned here is the baptism of Jesus, and the above verse shows us that it constitutes the only way for us to enter the Kingdom of God. Therefore, without having faith in the baptism of Jesus, we cannot be saved. And the Apostle Peter declared it as *"an antitype which now saves us" (1 Peter 3:21).*

We cannot be redeemed before God just by believing in Jesus' death on the Cross. In the Old Testament, if the Israelites had offered the sacrifice without laying their hands on the sacrifice, it wouldn't have been correct. And in the same way John the Baptist, as the representative of all human beings, put his hands upon Jesus when he baptized Him, which makes the sense that all our sins were passed on to Jesus.

Now it is clear to us that Jesus had fulfilled God's righteousness for all men through His baptism justly and fittingly. So, John the Baptist testified the next day he baptized Jesus, *"Behold the lamb of God who takes away the sins of the world" (John 1:29).* With all the sins of the mankind on His shoulders Jesus walked towards the Cross and took the judgment for all the sins He had taken on Himself through His baptism. Then He died on the Cross, saying, *"It is finished!" (John 19:30)*

Jesus Christ washed away all our sins even before we

were born. He took them all away. The sins that we will commit tomorrow are also included in the sins of the world. And all the sins of the world were passed on to Jesus 2000 years ago. He has not left even one sin behind. The gospel tells us to believe whole-heartedly that Jesus took away all our past and future sins all at once and paid for all of them.

"For as many of you as were baptized into Christ have put on Christ" (Galatians 3:27). Being baptized into Christ means that we are in union with Christ by our faith in His baptism. When Jesus was baptized, our sins were passed on to Him through John the Baptist and our sins were washed away, in other words, we are with no sin now. We became righteous from the very moment when we received the baptism of Jesus into our heart.

Nowadays, most people are not sure if they are forgiven for their sins or not. Some people spend their entire life in this dilemma. However, if we subject our selves to the true gospel, we can confidently say that we are not with sin now.

Jesus said that He sanctified us once for all. If we repent everyday, we might as well go back to the time of The Old Testament. Then we will never become righteous. Even if we believe in God, we cannot live without sinning. And in the mean time we could never be sanctified by repentance. We sin ceaselessly each day. So, it is impossible for us to completely repent of all our sins.

In the Book of Hebrews, we can find that our debt was paid at once. Therefore Jesus was baptized once and offered Himself on the Cross once so that we might become sanctified all at one time. We were not redeemed whenever we repent, rather we were redeemed from our sins once for all. *"By that will we have been sanctified through the offering of the body of Jesus Christ once for all" (Hebrews 10:10).* And finally the thing we got to do is to just to believe His baptism and crucifixion.

Now I fully believe the gospel of the water and the Spirit, which I believe that it is the true gospel. I promise to do all the work faithfully which you give because I love Jesus more than any thing and this is the only thing I could do for Him. ✉

APPENDIX 2

Supplementary Explanation

Supplementary
Explanation

• Ransom

The release of property or a person in return for payment of a demanded price. The price or payment of money demanded or paid for such release. Used most often as the positive representation of redemption (ex: Exodus 21:30, 'sum of money'; Numbers 35:31-32, Isaiah 43:3, 'ransom'). In the New Testament, Matthew 20:28 and Mark 10:45 describe ransom as the "payment of money."

• Atone, Atonement

The ritual of passing all the sins of humanity onto Jesus. In the Old Testament, atonement was the passing on of sin to a sacrifice by the laying on of hands on its head. In the New Testament, it means the baptism of Jesus by John the Baptist. In Hebrew and Greek, this word means the passing of sin onto Jesus Christ so that sinners may enter the right relationship with God. The New Testament illustrates the offering for atonement well: the baptism of Jesus and His death on the Cross.

In the Old Testament: The word *'atonement'* is used almost 100 times in the Old Testament and it is always expressed as (ex. Leviticus 23:27, 25:9, Numbers 5:8) *'kaphar'* in Hebrew (usually written as *'make an atonement'*).

Atonement is a translation of a Hebrew word signifying the passing on of sins by the laying on of hands on the head of a live goat and confessing over it all the iniquities of the Israelites (Leviticus 16:20).

In the New Testament: Atonement is related to the Aramaic *'kpr'* which means to cover. This means the baptism of redemption of Jesus in the New Testament. Jesus came to this world and was baptized at the age of 30 to fulfill the salvation of all humanity.

• The Biblical atonement

A. In the Old Testament, atonement was usually given through the sacrifice of an animal (ex. Exodus 30:10, Leviticus 1:3-5, 4:20-21, 16:6-22).

B. In the New Testament, the concept of the sacrifice of atonement of the Old Testament was basically maintained, but the redemption of all humankind could be fulfilled only by offering the body of Jesus Christ, the Son of God. The Apostle Paul said Jesus Christ died for our sins (1 Corinthians 15:3).

The word atonement was not only used to refer to the death of Christ to expiate original sin, but to take away all the sins of all human beings. After the baptism through which the sins of the world were passed onto Jesus (Matthew 3:15), He saved humankind by bleeding on the Cross (Leviticus 1:1-5, John 19:30).

The Apostle Paul explains in 2 Corinthians 5:14 that *'One died for all,'* then, in the following verse 21, he stated it was *'for us,'* and again in Galatians 3:13, *'having become a curse for us.'* Only a few verses in the New Testament refer to Jesus as the Sacrifice (ex. Ephesians 5:2): John 1:29, 36

('Lamb'—John the Baptist) and 1 Corinthians 5:7 ('our Passover'—the Apostle Paul).

However, Paul specified that the baptism of Jesus in the Jordan was the atonement for all the sins of the world. He explains in Romans 6 that all the sins of the world were passed onto Jesus through His baptism by John the Baptist.

He goes on to explain that the crucifixion of Jesus was the judgment and compensation for sin, and that the sacrifice of atonement was offered for the souls of all people.

The death of Jesus was the realization of God's plan, implied in the sacrifice of atonement in the Old Testament. The laying on of hands in the Old Testament and the baptism of Jesus in the New Testament are in accordance with the Law of God (Isaiah 53:10, Matthew 3:13-17, Hebrews 7:1-10, 18, 1 Peter 3:21).

The New Testament does not end with the baptism and the death of Jesus, but goes on to tell us that the fulfillment of salvation is our being baptized into Christ, which enables our old selves to die with Him (Romans 6:3-7, Galatians 2:19-20).

It tells us that John the Baptist baptized Jesus Christ to take away all the sins of the world and that as a result, He was crucified. Jesus Christ, through His baptism and blood, not only washed away the sins of the world, but also saved us from the power of Satan and returned us to the power of God by accepting punishment and enduring the pain in the place of mankind.

Therefore, the redemption of Jesus solved the problem of sin that was blocking people from being close to God. This momentous event restored peace and harmony between people and God, bringing salvation, joy (Romans 5:11), life (Romans 5:17-18), and redemption (Matthew 3:15, John 1:29, Hebrews 10:1-20, Ephesians 1:7, Colossians 1:14) at the same time.

• The Day of Atonement

In Hebrew, this concept means the day of *'covering,'* or *'reconciliation.'* The most important day for the Jews was the Day of Atonement on the tenth day of the seventh month (Leviticus 23:27, 25:9). We can see in Leviticus 16 that even the High Priest could not enter the Most Holy Place except for the specified rituals on that day.

The Most Holy Place itself needed atonement as well as the people of Israel; thus, the High Priest had to offer the sacrifice in order to pass on sins by laying his hands on the head of the sacrifice. The Israelites thought about the holiness of God and their sins on the Day of Atonement.

At that time, as many as 15 offerings (including the scapegoat), 12 burnt offerings and 3 offerings of atonement were sacrificed to God (Leviticus 16:5-29, Numbers 29:7-11). If we count *'the other lamb'* mentioned in Numbers 28:8, there are 13 burnt offerings and 4 offerings of atonement.

The day when the Israelites used to atone for the year's sins was the tenth day of the seventh month. By the same token, the Day of Atonement for the whole world was the day Jesus was baptized by John the Baptist. It was actually the Day of Atonement for all mankind. It was the day God washed away all the sins of the world (Matthew 3:13-17). It was the Day of Atonement on which God *"for thus... fulfilled all righteousness"*.

• The sacrifice of atonement

In the Old Testament: Just like the other sacrifices, the sacrifice of sanctification for all Israelites was offered in the tabernacle. The High Priest cleaned himself and put on the holy linen garments instead of the usual formal dress for rituals, selected a young bull as a sin offering and a ram as a burnt offering for himself and his house (Leviticus 16:3-4). The High Priest laid his hands on the head of the offerings to pass on the yearly sins of his people.

The laying on of hands was an essential part of the Day of Atonement. If it had not been performed, offering the sacrifice couldn't have been carried out because the atonement for sin could not be accomplished without the laying on of hands, thus passing the yearly sins of the Israelites onto the sin offering.

In Leviticus 16:21, *"And Aaron shall lay both his hands on the head of the live goat, confess over it all the iniquities of the children of Israel, and all their transgressions, concerning all their sins, putting them on the head of the goat, and shall send it away into the wilderness by the hand of a suitable man."*

He took two goats as sin offerings and a ram as a burnt offering from the people (Leviticus 16:5). Then, he presented two goats before the Lord at the door of the tabernacle and cast lots to select the one for *'the Lord'* and the other to be the *'scapegoat.'*

The one for the Lord was offered as a sin offering, and the scapegoat was offered alive before the Lord to atone for the yearly sins of the people of Israel and then put out into the wilderness (Leviticus 16:7-10).

The sins of Israel had to be passed onto the scapegoat by the laying on of the hands of the High Priest. Then, the scapegoat, which took on itself all the sins of Israel, was put out into the wilderness for reconciliation between the people and God. Thus the yearly sins of Israel were washed away.

In the New Testament: In the same way, Jesus Christ

was baptized by John the Baptist (the laying on of hands in the Old Testament) and took away all the sins of the world as the sacrificial Lamb to fulfill the salvation of God (Leviticus 20:22, Matthew 3:15, John 1:29, 36).

In the Old Testament, before the casting of lots, Aaron killed the young bull as a sin offering for himself and his house (Leviticus 16:11). Then, he took a censer full of burning coals of fire from the altar before the Lord with his hands full of sweet incense, beaten fine, and took it beyond the veil. He then put the incense on the fire before the Lord so that the cloud of incense might hover over the mercy seat. He also took some of the blood of the bull and sprinkled it with his finger on and before the mercy seat seven times (Leviticus 16:12-19).

On the Day of Atonement, the laying of Aaron's hands on the head of the offering could not be omitted. Aaron laid hands on the head of the goat and passed all the sins and all the iniquities of Israel on to his head. Then, a suitable man took the goat into the wilderness and sent it forth. The scapegoat wandered in the wilderness with the sins of Israel and died for them in the end. This was the typical sacrifice of atonement in the Old Testament.

It is the same in the New Testament except the scapegoat was substituted by Jesus Christ, who took away all the sins of the world upon Himself through His baptism, bled and died on the Cross for us all.

Therefore now, the salvation from all sins cannot be brought without the baptism and crucifixion of Jesus Christ, the heavenly High Priest. This is the fulfillment of salvation of being born again of water and the Spirit.

• The laying on of hands, the ordination

This was a God given method for the passing of sin onto the sin offering in the Old Testament (Leviticus 4:29, 16:21). In the days of the Old Testament, God allowed people to atone for their sins by laying hands on the heads of the sin offerings inside the tabernacle. It was to reveal the baptism of Jesus to come in the New Testament.

• Baptism

Baptism means ① to be washed ② to be buried (to be immersed) and in spiritual meaning, ③ to pass on sin by laying on of hands, as ministered in the Old Testament days.

In the New Testament, the baptism of Jesus by John the Baptist was to wash away all the sins of the world. *'The baptism of Jesus'* has the meaning of taking away the sins of all mankind, to wash away the sins of the world.

Jesus was baptized by John the Baptist, the representative of all human beings and the High Priest of the lineage of Aaron, and took all the sins of the world upon Himself. This was the purpose of His baptism.

The spiritual meaning of the word *'baptism'* is *'to pass on, to be buried.'* So, "the baptism of Jesus" means that all sins were passed onto Jesus and that He was judged instead of us. In order to save mankind, Jesus had to take away our sins with His baptism and die for them.

Thus, His death is also the death of you and me, all the sinners of the world, and His resurrection is the resurrection of all people. His sacrifice is the salvation of sinners, and His baptism is the very witness to washing away all the sins of humankind.

The Bible tells us, *"There is also an antitype which now saves us, namely baptism" (1 Peter 3:21).* The baptism of Jesus is the righteous way of saving all humanity by washing away our sins.

• Sin

Everything that is opposed to God is sin. This refers to all sins, including the original sin and trespasses that we commit throughout our whole lives.

Sin is *'hamartia'* in Greek. And its verbal form is *'hamartano,'* which means 'to miss the mark.' Hence, one of the most serious sins is to incorrectly believe in Jesus, and thus lack the ability to be saved. To neither know nor believe in the truth is to commit the sin of disobedience and to blaspheme against God.

If we truly do not want to commit such a sin before God, we have to understand His words correctly and realize the truth that Jesus has become our Savior.

We should believe in the baptism of Jesus and His Cross through the words of God. It is a sin not to accept the Word of God, to deviate from the truth, and to believe in false theories.

The Bible tells us that the most serious sin, 'the sin leading to death' (1 John 5:16), is not to believe that God washed away all the sins of the world. We have to believe in the birth of Jesus, in His washing away of sin through His baptism, and in giving us life with His blood on the Cross. It is a sin if one does not believe in the written words that Jesus was baptized, died on the Cross and was resurrected to free us from all our sins.

• **Repentance**

When one who has drifted away from God realizes his/her sins and thanks Jesus for washing them away and comes back to God, this is called repentance.

All of us are lumps of sin. True repentance is to admit the following truth: that we are sinners before God, and that we cannot but sin all our lives and go to hell when we die; that we have to accept Jesus as our Savior by believing that He came to this world to save sinners like us, and that He took away all sins (through His baptism), died and was resurrected to save us. True repentance is to give up our own thoughts and return to God (Acts 2:38).

Repentance is to admit our sins and turn back to the Word of God, to accept the salvation of the water and the blood with all our hearts (1 John 5:6).

True repentance is to admit ourselves as complete sinners and to believe in Jesus, the Son of God, as our Savior who saved us from all our sins. In order to be saved and be washed of all sins, we must stop trying to be sanctified through our own works, and admit that we are complete sinners before God and His Laws. We then have to accept the truth of His salvation, the gospel of the water and the Spirit, which Jesus gave us with His baptism and blood.

A sinner has to give up all his/her own thoughts and will and return to Jesus completely. We will be saved when we come to believe that the baptism of Jesus was to take all our sins onto Himself.

In other words, the baptism of Jesus, His crucifixion, and His resurrection have fulfilled God's righteousness, His salvation of all sinners. Jesus came in the flesh, was baptized and crucified to wash away all our sins. Having complete faith in all these and believing that Jesus was resurrected to become the Savior of all those who believe in Him is true repentance and genuine faith.

• Salvation

Salvation in Christianity means 'deliverance from the power or penalty of sin.' We receive salvation when we admit that we cannot but go to hell for our sins and believe that Jesus saved us from all our sins through His birth, baptism and the blood on the Cross.

Those who become sinless by believing in the salvation of Jesus, the baptism and blood of Jesus, are called 'the saved, the born-again, and the righteous.'

We can apply the word *'salvation'* to those who have been saved from all their sins, including the original sin and their daily sins, by believing in Jesus. Just as a drowning man is saved, one who is drowning in the sin of the world can be saved by believing in Jesus as his/her Savior, by believing in His baptism and blood, the words of the spiritual truth.

• Born again

It means *'to be born the second time.'* A sinner is born again and becomes righteous when he/she is saved spiritually by believing in the baptism of Jesus and His Cross.

We can spiritually be born again by believing in the baptism and the blood of Jesus. The born-again are those who have been washed of all their sins and *"who eagerly wait for Him He will appear a second time, apart from sin, for salvation" (Hebrews 9:28).*

• The remission of sins

This important concept is also known as the forgiveness of sins. Sins are forgiven when we become cleansed of all sins once and for all through the gospel of the water and the Spirit. The faith in the gospel of the water and the Spirit is to believe in a series of truths: Jesus Christ's divinity, the incarnation of the Son of God, His baptism and crucifixion for the salvation of us all, and His resurrection.

The redemption Jesus gave us can be ours through the faith in His baptism and blood. As prophesied in the Old Testament, Jesus Himself saved all people from sin. The redemption in the Bible points to the washing away of sins through faith in the baptism of Jesus and His blood. All sins were passed onto Jesus, so there is no longer any sin in the hearts of humankind.

We can call ourselves the redeemed and the righteous only after passing all our sins onto Jesus through faith in His baptism.

• Jesus Christ

JESUS: *'The Savior who saved all people from their sins and the punishment for those sins.'* Jesus refers to the Savior, the One who has saved all people from their sins.

CHRIST: *'The Anointed.'* There were three kinds of persons in vocational posts who had to be anointed before God: ① kings, ② prophets and ③ priests. Jesus fulfilled all of them.

Jesus Christ was all of these. He did the work of all of these. We have to believe in Jesus as the King, the Prophet, and the Priest who brought us redemption and salvation. Thus, we come to call Him *'Jesus Christ.'* He was the heavenly High Priest who saved us from all the sins of the world with His baptism and blood.

Therefore, He is the King of all who believe in Him. He makes us realize our sins when we come before Him. He taught us that we are sinners from the time of our ancestors; that as the descendants of sinners, we were born sinners, and as a result, we are under the judgment of God.

He also taught us that we are washed of our sins through His baptism and blood. He did all these works for us sinners.

• Why did the Son of God become a man?

He became a man to be the Savior and save all sinners from sin and the judgment of hellfire.

• Who is Jesus?

As stated in Genesis 1:3 and John 1:1-3, He is the Creator, the true God, the God of all the universe who saved all sinners from the sins of the world *(Philippians 2:6, "Who, being in the form of God," John 1:2-3, "He was in the beginning with God. All things were made through Him, and without Him nothing was made that was made.")* Jesus is the God of creation, the Master of the universe.

However, many people fail to be saved by not believing in

the love and salvation of Jesus, who came down to this world in the flesh. But many others have received salvation, become God's people, and gained everlasting life by believing in Him. They have become the righteous.

• What are the Laws established by God?

God is the Planner, the only true God, and the Absolute Being. Therefore, He set up the Law in the world for the following purposes:

① He gave sinners His Law and Commandments to save them from their sins. *"By the law is the knowledge of sin" (Romans 3:20).*

② The second law is the Law of Faith that saves sinners. It is 'the law of the Spirit of life' (Romans 8:2) that grants access to salvation through faith in Jesus Christ, our Savior (Romans 5:1-2). Jesus came down to this world to fulfill this Law. He was baptized, bled on the Cross and was then resurrected. Jesus set up the law of salvation to save all the sinners of the world.

God established the Law of faith for those who believe in the salvation of the water and the Spirit. Anyone who wants to be saved and become a child of God has to believe in the Law of faith God ordained. It is the only way to salvation. Thus, He allowed the access to Heaven to those who believe in the spiritual salvation of the truth according to this Law.

• God's Law: the Ten Commandments

There are 613 articles of laws in God's Law concerning

everyday life. But the gist of it is the Ten Commandments, which we have to keep before God. There are orders and prohibitions such as "Do this" and "Don't do that." These are the guidelines to live by, and the Commandments of God were given to us so that we might realize our sins. Through the written commandments of God, we can recognize how much we disobey Him (Romans 3:19-20).

The reason God gave us His commandments was to make us realize our sins. We can never keep all His commandments, so we must humbly accept the fact that we are sinners before we believe in Jesus. We are all sinners and God knows that we can never live according to His Law. So, He came down to this world as a man, was baptized and judged on the Cross. Trying to live by His commandments is the sin of arrogance. We shouldn't do that.

The Law shows us how perfect and holy God is, as well as how weak we human beings truly are. In other words, the holiness and perfection of God is revealed in the Law of God.

• Do we have to believe in Jesus?

Yes, we have to, because He is our Lord, the most righteous and because it is His will. *"For there is no other name under heaven given among men by which we must be saved" (Acts 4:12).* There is no other Savior. Jesus is our only Savior. We can be redeemed and born again only by believing in Him. Because we can only enter Heaven and live forever by believing in Him, we must have faith in Him.

• Can we Christians still be sinners?

No. The Apostle Paul said in 1 Timothy 1:15 that he was one of the *"sinners of whom I am chief,"* recalling the days before he met Jesus. In Christian communities today, there are many who think that they are sinners even after they believe in Jesus. But it is not true.

We are all sinners before we believe in Jesus. However, once we believe in Jesus correctly according to His Word, we become righteous immediately. The Apostle Paul remembered the time before he knew Jesus and confessed that he was the chief of all sinners.

Paul, when he was called Saul, met Jesus on the road to Damascus and realized that Jesus was his Savior, so he believed in and thanked Him. Then, for the rest of his life, he witnessed that the righteousness of God, the baptism of Jesus, had taken away the sins of the world and that He had to die to blot out the world's sins.

In other words, he became a servant of God who preached the gospel of the water and the Spirit. However, most Christians still think that the Apostle Paul was a sinner even after he met Jesus. They misunderstand this passage from the viewpoint of Christian sinners, who are not yet born again.

The truth, however, is that he was no longer a sinner after he met Jesus, but one who could face Jesus whenever he wanted. He had devoted the rest of his life to preaching the gospel of salvation, the redemption of the baptism and the blood of Jesus. Even after he passed away, his Epistles are left to us in the Bible, testifying that the gospel of the water and the Spirit was the true gospel from the early church. Hence, the confession of the Apostle Paul in 1 Timothy 1:15 was a recollection of his old days and a thanksgiving to the Lord as well.

Was he a sinner after he believed in Jesus? No. He was a sinner before he was born again. At the moment he believed in Jesus as his Savior, the moment he realized that the sins of the world were passed onto Jesus through His baptism, the moment he believed in His atoning blood of the Cross, he became righteous.

The reason he called himself the chief of all sinners was because he was remembering the time he had persecuted the followers of Jesus and thanked God for saving him, the most hopeless sinner.

Who can call him still a sinner? Who can call someone a sinner if he/she became righteous by believing in the baptism and blood of Jesus as his/her salvation? Only those unaware of the truth of the redemption of Jesus can do that.

The Apostle Paul became righteous by believing in salvation through Jesus and from that time on, as a servant of God, preached the gospel of becoming righteous by believing in Jesus Christ to everyone, the Son of God as the Savior. From then on, the Apostle Paul was not a sinner, but a righteous servant of God, a true servant who preached the gospel to the sinners of the whole world.

Can a sinner preach to others? It would never work. How can one preach to others what he himself does not have! When a person has not been saved, how can the person save others!

If a man was drowning and tried to help another drowning man near by, both would end up under water. How can a sinner save others? He/she would only take them down to hell with him/her. How can a sick man care for another sick person successfully? How can one deceived by Satan save another?

The Apostle Paul was a sinner, but became righteous when he believed in the baptism and blood of Jesus and was saved from sin. Therefore, he could become a servant of God and preach the gospel to the sinners of the world. He saved many sinners with the righteousness of God. He himself was no longer a sinner from then on.

He was born again and lived not in the righteousness of the law, but in the righteousness of God. He became a servant and preacher of the righteousness of God, and he wined countless souls to God. He was not a preacher of his own enthusiasm or the righteousness of the Law, but the righteousness of God.

Was he a sinner to the end? No. He was righteous. As a righteous man, he became the apostle of the truth of God. Do not call him a sinner because it would be an insult to God as well as a clear misunderstanding of the truth. He was righteous. We should never insult him or Jesus by thinking otherwise.

If we say he was still a sinner after he met Jesus, it is calling Jesus a liar. Jesus made him righteous, and it was Jesus who made him a servant of His righteousness.

• Can prayers of repentance wash our sins away?

Prayers of repentance can never wash our sins away because redemption can never come through our own works. Rather, in order to be completely and permanently washed of our sins, we have to believe in the baptism and blood of Jesus, and that Jesus is God. True redemption is given to those who believe Jesus washed away our sins by being baptized and bleeding on the Cross to give us new lives.

Then can we wash away daily sins by offering prayers of repentance? No. All the sins we commit in our lives were already washed away almost 2000 years ago, when Jesus took them away with His baptism. We were permanently cleansed of all our sins with the baptism of Jesus and the shedding of His blood on the Cross. He became the sacrificial Lamb for us believers, washed away all our sins, and paid for them all with His baptism and blood on the Cross.

Even the sins we commit after believing in Jesus are washed away by faith in the spring of salvation of baptism, the truth of redemption; Jesus has already become our Savior and has taken away all the sins we commit until the day of our deaths. Jesus came to this world and was baptized *"for thus"* *(Matthew 3:15),* fulfilling all righteousness by taking away all our sins. The Son of God took charge of our sins by being baptized.

The baptism of Jesus has the meaning of *"to be washed."* Because all our sins were passed onto Jesus when He was baptized, we are completely washed of our sins and it has set us free from all our sins.

Baptism also means *'to be immersed, to be buried.'* Since all our sins were passed onto Jesus, He had to die for us sinners. Those who believe that all sins were passed onto Jesus through His baptism become sinless forever.

True faith is to believe with all our hearts that all our sins, even the sins we commit now and in future, were passed onto Jesus about 2000 years ago, when He received baptism from John, and *'for thus'* fulfilled all the righteousness of God.

If He had not already washed away our sins a long time ago with His baptism, there would now be no way for us to wash away our own sins. Remember that Jesus washed all our sins away a long time ago.

True faith and spiritual salvation today means bringing our sins before Jesus to make sure that they have already been washed away, saying, 'You have washed away these sins too, haven't You?' It also means to believe in Him and thank Him. That is why He came to earth, was baptized, died on the Cross and was then resurrected on the third day; thus becoming our Savior.

Blessed are those who have washed away their sins by believing in the baptism of Jesus, which washed away all our sins. This is the truth of being washed of daily sins. True faith is to believe in Jesus, who took away all the sins of the world through His baptism.

- **Romans 8:30 states, *"Moreover whom He predestined, these He also called; whom He called, these He also justified; and whom He justified, these He also glorified."* Then, does this passage support the doctrine of incremental sanctification?**

This passage is does not teach about incremental sanctification. Many theologians and false preachers have taught, "Those who believe in Jesus will change gradually and will become completely sanctified in the flesh and the spirit," and many have believed it.

But as a matter of fact, Christians who have not yet been born again find themselves becoming more and more stubborn. The sin in their hearts grow as they get older. How can our sanctification depend on time? The words 'incremental sanctification' are the ones that God hates the most and the ones the devil loves to use.

We can only become righteous when we have no way out from sin by ourselves. Because Jesus washed away all our sins with His baptism and sacrificed Himself to pay for them

Himself, we owe our righteousness solely to the baptism and blood of Jesus. We become righteous through faith in the fact that Jesus took all our sins onto Himself.

The word *'sanctification'* means *'to become holy.'* Trying to become sanctified by oneself is not to believe in the truth, but to be persuaded by one's own weak flesh.

Hope for gradual sanctification also comes from our own spiritual desires. Each religion has its own word of sanctification, but we who believe in Jesus should never place importance on the word itself.

We do not become sanctified gradually by believing in Jesus; we become righteous once and for all by believing in the baptism and blood of Jesus, the gospel of spiritual circumcision. The truly righteous are those who have been born of the faith in the gospel of the baptism and the blood of Jesus.

• Can confessing our sins make them disappear?

No. Sins do not disappear with confession, but with faith in the gospel of the water and the Spirit. Our sins can disappear only when we believe in the baptism and the blood of Jesus, which cleansed us of all sins. This is the gospel of the spiritual salvation of Jesus, who washed away all our sins with His baptism in the Jordan.

The confession of sins is the only evidence for someone to recognize the Law of God, but redemption is given to us only when we believe in the baptism and the Cross of Jesus.

The water of His baptism and the blood of Christ is the truth of Heaven that saved all people from sin, and our salvations do not depend on the confession of sins, but on believing that Jesus took the sins from all human beings with

His baptism. The crucifixion of Jesus was the punishment for all those sins He took away from us sinners.

Therefore, our true salvation is in the baptism in the Jordan and the blood on the Cross. The reason we were cleansed of all our sins is because we believe in Jesus, who washed away all our sins.

Those who preach that we can be redeemed by confessing our sins are ignoring the true salvation of God.

Therefore, we must believe in the baptism and the blood of Jesus, the salvation of God. Do not ever say that the sins of mankind can be forgiven by confessing them to God.

Know that our sins will put us into hell, but believing in Jesus, His baptism and blood, which redeems us and lets us become righteous before God, can wash our sins away. It is the only way we can be saved from all our sins. Let us all become aware that we have been washed of our sins all at once by believing in the words of truth, the water and the blood of Jesus (1 John 5:4-8).

Sins are not blotted out every time we confess. If you insist on relying on confession, you will end up in hell. Let us believe in the true gospel so that the sins in our hearts can be washed away. Believe with your heart, not only with your head, and be free of your sins forever.

• What is the true gospel?

The true gospel is the one that enables us to be free of our sins completely, once and for all when we believe in it. The power of the gospel of God is that of dynamite.

The gospel of God is that, "Jesus Christ settled the debt for the debtor (sinner), who cannot possibly settle his own debt." The reason for calling this gospel 'dynamite' is because when we had to die for our sins and go to hell to be judged, the Son of God became the sacrificial offering for us in order to blot out all our sins.

He came to this world and took on all the sins of the world through His baptism in the Jordan and washed away all our sins forever.

He paid the wages of our sins by taking away all our sins with His baptism in the Jordan and by dying on the Cross. Jesus blew up all the sins of the world like dynamite with His baptism and blood. This is the true gospel.

The true gospel is that Jesus came to this world and by being baptized and bleeding on the Cross, saved all those who believe in Him.

As it is written in 1 John 5:6, *"This is He who came by water and blood—Jesus Christ; not only by water, but by water, and blood. And it is the Spirit who bears witness, because the Spirit is the truth."*

• Why did Jesus sacrifice Himself on the Cross?

The sacrifice of Jesus was for our sins that had been taken away through His baptism. He gave us His flesh to pay for our sins so that we could be set free from the punishment for all our sins.

What we have to know is that Jesus was baptized in the Jordan to take away all our sins. We have to believe that Jesus died on the Cross for this reason.

If Jesus had not been baptized before He was crucified and if He Had not died on the Cross, all our sins would have remained. Therefore, we must believe in both the baptism and the blood of Jesus. Because Jesus is the Son of God, the sacrificial Lamb, He was sacrificed to blot out all our sins.

We should all believe that Jesus is the Son of God, that He was baptized to take away all the sins of the world, and that He was crucified for our sins. Jesus was baptized to take away all our sins, then was crucified so that we, the sinners, could be saved from all our sins and be free of punishment.

• Who is John the Baptist who baptized Jesus?

God gave Israel His Law through Moses as well as the sacrificial system so that they could attain atonement for their sins and iniquities. He ordained Aaron, the elder brother of Moses, as the High Priest and had him offer the sacrifice of atonement on the tenth day of the seventh month, the Day of Atonement, so that the yearly sins of Israel could be washed away (Leviticus 16).

God specified that the sacrifice of the Day of Atonement could only be offered by Aaron and the succeeding High Priests among his descendants. God opened the way for Israelites to atone for all their sins through the laying on of Aaron's hands on the head of the scapegoat. This is the law of atonement God established for them.

By this shadow, He let it be known clearly that Jesus was the Savior of mankind. In the age of the New Testament, God sent John the Baptist, a descendant of Aaron (1 Chronicles 24:10, Luke 1:5) and the last High Priest of the Old Testament (Matthew 11:11-13). John the Baptist, as the God-sent prophet, representative and High Priest of humankind, baptized Jesus in order to pass all the sins of humankind onto Him, the Son of God, who came to save sinners.

All people are blessed indeed to be able to pass their sins onto Jesus through John the Baptist. The role of John was to be the High Priest who represented humankind and the servant of God who passed all our sins onto Jesus.

John the Baptist was the representative and the High Priest of humankind sent by God, and the messenger who was sent 6 months prior to Jesus. On the other hand, Jesus was the Lamb of God who took away all the sins of the world while John the Baptist was the last High Priest who passed the sins of the world onto Jesus through baptism. John the Baptist was a servant of God.

• The Jordan River, where Jesus was baptized

The Jordan River rapidly flows into the Dead Sea. The surface of the Dead Sea is about 400 meters lower than sea level. Therefore, the water in the Dead Sea cannot flow anywhere; it is locked in the Dead Sea.

The salinity of the Dead Sea is 10 times higher than the other ordinary seas, and no living thing exists there. Thus, it is called the Dead Sea. Jesus was baptized by John the Baptist in the river of death (the Jordan River). This represents that all human beings, except those without sin in their hearts, face eternal damnation for their sins in the end.

Therefore, the Jordan River is the river of washing away sins, the river where sinners die. In short, it is the river of redemption where all the sins of the world were washed away through His baptism, the passing of sins on to Jesus.

• What was the sacrifice of atonement for daily sins in the Old Testament?

There was the sacrifice of atonement for a day's sin. In order to atone for a day's sin, a man had to bring a lamb, a sheep, a bull or a dove into the tabernacle and lay his hands on the sacrifice to pass his sins onto the sacrifice. This was the sacrifice of atonement for a day's sins as given in the Law of God (Leviticus 3:1-11).

• What was the sacrifice of atonement for a year's sins in the Old Testament?

It was the sacrifice of atonement for a year's worth of Israel's sins all at once. The High Priest laid his hands on the head of a goat and passed on a year's sins of all the people of Israel all at once (Leviticus 16:1-34).

Jesus Christ completed the sacrifices for a day's sin and a year's sins when He became the Lamb of God to take all sin onto His head through His baptism.

• What was the sacrifice for permanent atonement?

It was the atonement for all the sins of the world all at once by believing in Jesus. Since Jesus is the Son of God and our Lord who lives forever, He can take away all the sins of the world forever. How did He take away our sins forever?

He did it

① by being born in the flesh of a man,

② by being baptized by John the Baptist at the Jordan,

③ by being crucified on the Cross to take all the judgment in our stead,

The Son of God came to this world in the flesh of a man and was baptized to take away all the sins of the world through John the Baptist. He then bled on the Cross to save humankind from all their sins forever (Leviticus 16:6-22, Matthew 3:13-17, John 1:29, Hebrews 9:12, 10:1-18).

• Is the remission of sins given all at once or gradually?

It is given all at once because Jesus took away our sins once and for all by being baptized once and received the judgment all at once. He said, as recorded in Matthew 3:15, *"Permit it to be so now, for thus it is fitting for us to fulfill all righteousness."*

In John 1:29, John the Baptist said, *"Behold! The Lamb of God who takes away the sin of the world!"* and in John 19:30, Jesus said, *"It is finished."*

In Hebrews 10:9-18, *"Then He said, 'Behold, I have come to do Your will, O God.' He takes away the first that He may establish the second. By that will we have been sanctified through the offering of the body of Jesus Christ once for all. And every priest stands ministering daily and offering repeatedly the same sacrifices, which can never take away sins. But this Man, after He had offered one sacrifice for sins forever, sat down at the right hand of God, from that time waiting till His enemies are made His footstool. For by one offering He has perfected forever those who are being sanctified. And the Holy Spirit also witnesses to us; for after*

He had said before, 'This is the covenant that I will make with them after those days, says the Lord: I will put My laws into their hearts, and in their minds I will write them,' then He adds, 'Their sins and their lawless deeds I will remember no more.' Now where there is remission of these, there is no longer an offering for sin."

The baptism and the blood of Jesus blotted out all the sins of the world all at once.

• What is the wages of sin?

The wages of sin is death. Regardless of what it is, every sin has to be judged before God, and the judgment for even a single sin is death. In order to atone for sins, the people of Israel had to offer a sheep without blemish before God. But such sacrifices could not possibly cleanse all their sins forever, *"For it is not possible that the blood of bulls and goats could take away sins" (Hebrews 10:4).*

Therefore, God prepared the Lamb to deliver all people from their sins. Each sacrificial animal had to be subjected to the laying on of hands to take away all sin and then died instead of them.

In the New Testament, Jesus took away all our sins through His baptism in the Jordan as the Lamb of God and died for us. *"The wages of sin is death, but the gift of God is eternal life in Christ Jesus our Lord" (Romans 6:23).*

The wages of sin is death, but Jesus expressed His love by dying on behalf of us and making a gift of eternal life for all the sinners of the world.

• Why did Jesus have to die on the Cross?

The death of Jesus was the payment for all the sins of the world that had been taken away through His baptism. People were facing eternal deaths of hellfire for their sins, but because Jesus loved us, He accepted baptism, which passed all our sins on to Him, and died on the Cross to save us.

He sacrificed Himself to save us from sin and from the curse of hell. His death was the payment for the sins of humankind. He was baptized to take away all the sins of the world and gave Himself to judgment on the Cross in order to save all of us from sin, death, judgment and damnation.

The death of Jesus was for the sins of the world that He took onto Himself at the Jordan so that He could receive judgment for the sins of humankind. He died on the Cross and was resurrected to let us live again as the righteous.

• What do we get when we believe in Jesus?

① We receive the remission of all our sins and become righteous (Romans 8:1-2).

② We receive His Spirit and everlasting life (Acts 2:38, 1 John 5:11-12).

③ We receive the right to become the children of God (John 1:12).

④ We receive the privilege to enter the Kingdom of God, the Kingdom of Heaven (Revelation chap. 21-22).

⑤ We receive all the blessings of God (Ephesians 1:3-23).

• Why do we have to believe in Jesus?

We have to believe in Jesus:
① to fulfill the will of God
② to be saved from all our sins
③ to enter the Kingdom of Heaven so that we may live forever with the Lord.

We are all sinners who would fall into hell without faith in Jesus Christ, our Savior. Only Jesus is our Savior who can rescue us from hell. We have to believe in Jesus because only He is the true Savior.

• Where do the people who believe in Jesus and are redeemed of all their sins end up? —In Heaven.—

• Where do those who neither believe in Jesus nor are redeemed finally end up? —In hell for all their sins; the lake, which burns with fire and brimstone (Revelation 21:8).—

• Who are the sheep of God? —Those who receive the remission of sins by believing in the baptism and the blood of Jesus.—

And *"other sheep which are not of this fold" (John 10:16)* are goats because they arbitrarily believe in what they understand by instinct, because they are still sinners while the ones who believe in the baptism and the blood of Jesus are saved all at once and become God's sheep.

• What is the true church of God?

The church of God is where the righteous, those who are redeemed and sanctified in Christ by believing in the baptism and blood of Jesus, gather together and worship God (1 Corinthians 1:2). The true church of God, as recorded in

Ephesians 4:5, is a place where all members believe in *"one Lord, one faith, one baptism; one God and the Father of all."*

• Who is a heretic in the Bible?

A heretic is one who has sin in his/her heart while believing in Jesus. In Titus 3:11, it says, *"Such a person is warped and sinning, being self-condemned."*

Jesus took all our sins with His baptism, but a heretic doesn't believe in this blessed gospel of the water (the baptism of Jesus, the baptism of redemption), which is the gracious present of God, but rather condemns himself/herself as a sinner while rejecting the perfect salvation.

The Bible defines these kinds of people as 'heretics,' who believe in Jesus yet condemn themselves as sinners (Titus 3:11). You must wonder if you yourself are a heretic or not. If you believe in Jesus, but still call yourself a sinner, then you do not know the spiritual truth of the gospel of the water and the Spirit.

If you believe in Jesus, but still consider yourself a hopeless sinner, then you are a heretic. It means that you think the true gospel of the water and the Spirit is too impotent to blot out all your sins and make you His child. If you are one of those people, namely, a heretic who confesses your sins everyday before God for forgiveness and admits that you are still a sinner, then you must seriously reconsider your faith.

How can you still be a sinner when Jesus has taken all your sins away? Why do you keep trying to repay the debt when it was already taken care of by Jesus as a gift to you? If you insist on repaying the debt yourself, you are a heretic because your faith is different from that God has given. Any

Christian who believes in Jesus, but is not born again, is a heretic. You must know the truth. God took away all the sins of the world, and if you ignore His salvation, you are a heretic.

A heretic is one who calls himself/herself a sinner, in other words, a self-condemned one. Do you think it possible that the Holy God would admit a sinner as His child? If you call yourself a sinner while you believe in Holy God, you are a heretic. In order not to become a heretic, you have to believe in both the baptism of Jesus and His blood on the Cross as a set of truth.

You can be saved only when you believe in both at the same time: the baptism of Jesus and His blood. ✉

APPENDIX 3

Questions & Answers

Questions & Answers

Question 1: I have been reading the books you were kind enough to send me and find some of your concepts on the baptism of Jesus interesting. Can you tell me what you teach about the relationship of our baptism to the baptism, death and resurrection of Jesus Christ?

Answer: First of all, we should pay attention to the *"doctrines of baptisms"* as written in Hebrews 6:2. According to the Bible, there are three different baptisms; the baptism of John the Baptist for repentance, the baptism Jesus received from John the Baptist, and our water baptism as a ritual.

The baptism that we receive is a confession of our faiths in the baptism of Jesus. That is to say, we are baptized in order to confess our faiths that we believe Jesus was baptized to take away all our sins and also died on the Cross to atone for them. Now you can understand Matthew 3:15 where it says, *"Permit it to be so now, for thus it is fitting for us to fulfill all righteousness."* Here, *"for thus"* means that Jesus Himself bore all the sins of the world by being baptized by John the Baptist, the representative of all humankind.

It was the profound plan of God to save us from the inevitable trap of sin. The Lord God *"has laid on Him the iniquity of us all" (Isaiah 53:6)* and has granted us His righteousness. *"Righteousness"* here means *"dikaiosune"* in Greek, which also signifies "fairness and justice." It tells us that Jesus bore the iniquity of all humankind in the most fair and just way by being baptized in the form of the laying on of hands.

We have been saved by our strong faiths in the baptism, the death on the Cross, and the resurrection of Jesus. The power of the spiritual circumcision (Romans 2:29) of His baptism, which cut off all our sins from our hearts, has washed away the sins in our hearts. Therefore, the Apostle Peter said to the people, *"Repent, and let every one of you be baptized in the name of Jesus Christ for the remission of sins; and you shall receive the gift of the Holy Spirit" (Acts 2:38)* on the Day of Pentecost.

All sinners should obtain the forgiveness of sins in their hearts by believing in the name of Jesus. What's the meaning of His name? *"You shall call His name JESUS, for He will save His people from their sins" (Matthew 1:21).* The name Jesus means 'the Savior' who saves His people from all their sins. How did He save us from all our sins? Jesus has saved us from all our sins through His baptism and death on the Cross.

When the Apostles of Jesus Christ preached the gospel, they ensured a clear understanding of the baptism of Jesus and the Cross, so they taught the true gospel, and then baptized those who believed in it. Accordingly, we're baptized to confess outwardly that we believe in the baptism and the death of Jesus deep in our minds. When we're baptized, we confess, "Thank you, Lord. You bore all my sins through Your baptism, died for me and rose again to save me. I believe in Your gospel." We are baptized in water by ministers as a symbol of our faith in Jesus' baptism and His death on the Cross, just as He was baptized by John the Baptist. Thus, the saints in the early church were baptized as proof of their beliefs, after they confessed their faith in the gospel and had redemption, the forgiveness of sins.

The ritual of baptism is not a necessary condition to be saved. Even though it is very important to clarify our faiths, our water baptisms have nothing to do with our salvations. We can only be saved by believing in the gospel of the water and the blood. The Bible states that we are baptized into Jesus Christ (Romans 6:3, Galatians 3:27) when we believe in His baptism.

Then, how could we be *"baptized into Him"*? It is possible only when we believe in His baptism since the flesh, our old selves, could be united with Jesus and crucified with Him only by our faith in His baptism. Consequently, since Jesus bore all our sins by His baptism, His death was the judgment for our iniquities. Therefore, we also died on the Cross with Him. In other words, our flesh, which cannot but commit sins until death, died to sin and we have been saved from all our iniquities in union with Jesus through His baptism.

Those who are united with Jesus through His baptism and death can also be united with His resurrection. His resurrection is not only our resurrection from our deaths to sin, but it also allows us to be born again as the children of God and the consecrated, who are pure and sinless in front Him.

If we had not passed our sins onto Him by distrusting His baptism, His death and resurrection might have been meaningless, having nothing to do with our salvation. Those who have laid all their sins on Him with faith are united with His death on the Cross, allowing them to be born again as the righteous. However, those who have not laid their sins on Him by not believing in His baptism, have no relationship with His death and resurrection whatsoever.

The baptism of the believers is trustworthy just as we can admit a husband and wife as a legal couple through a wedding ceremony. The baptism of the saints is an outward proclamation of such an inward belief. When we proclaim our belief in His baptism and the Cross in front of God, saints, and the world, our belief becomes more immutable.

Having misunderstood the true meaning of the baptism that Jesus has received by John Baptist, we should not believe that we could be saved if we do not believe in His baptism and its significance. It's simply a cunning trick of the devil. We can receive the remission of sins and be welcomed to Heaven by truly believing in the baptism of Jesus in our hearts instead of believing in our own baptisms.

Question 2: **How can I say, "I'm righteous" when I am sinning everyday?**

Answer: We, as human beings, commit sins from the very moment we're born until we die. As a matter of fact, this is due to our fundamental natures; that we sin from the beginning. So, the Bible says, *"There is none righteous, no, not one" (Romans 3:10)*. That is why the Apostle Paul confessed in front of God that *"This is a faithful saying and worthy of all acceptance, that Christ Jesus came into the world to save sinners, of whom I am chief" (1 Timothy 1:15)*.

"But now the righteousness of God apart from the law is revealed, being witnessed by the Law and the Prophets, even the righteousness of God, through faith in Jesus Christ, to all and on all who believe. For there is no difference; for all have sinned and fall short of the glory of God, being justified freely by His grace through the redemption that is in Christ Jesus" (Romans 3:21-24).

This *"righteousness"* of God means that John the Baptist baptized Jesus in the Jordan. When He was baptized, He said to John, *"Permit it to be so now, for thus it is fitting for us to fulfill all righteousness" (Matthew 3:15)*. He bore the sins of the world in the most just and fair way when John the Baptist, the representative of all humankind, baptized him. Thus, John exclaimed on the very next day he baptized Jesus, *"Behold! The Lamb of God who takes away the sin of the world" (John 1:29).*

Then what does *"the sin of the world"* here mean? It represents all the sins of all the human beings from Adam and Eve, the first human beings on the earth, to the last person who will live in this world. The past people belonged to the world, the people of the present belong to the world, and those who will live in the future are also a part of the world. Jesus, the Alpha and the Omega, had offered one sacrifice for the sins of all time, bearing all the sins of the world once and for all through His baptism in the Jordan and dying on the Cross. And *'for thus'*, we have been sanctified.

The Bible clearly declares, *"By that will we have been sanctified through the offering of the body of Jesus Christ once for all" (Hebrews 10:10).* Note that this is written in the perfect present tense. We have been sanctified absolutely and sinless, from the very moment we believed in God until now and always will be. For the Lord is Almighty God, He has a bird's eye view of the beginning and the end of the world. Although it was about 2000 years ago when He was baptized, He took away all the sins that human beings commit from the beginning to the end of the world. Therefore, before He died on the Cross, He said, *"It is finished!" (John 19:30)* He took away all the sins of the world about 2000 years ago and died on the Cross in order to wash them away.

We still sin even after we're saved because our flesh is weak. However, Jesus has redeemed us from all the sins of the past, present and the future by bearing all the sins on His body through His baptism and being judged for them on the Cross.

This is the complete and righteous salvation of God.

If Jesus hadn't taken away with Him the sins that we will commit in the future, not a single human being could be redeemed from everyday sin, *"for the wages of sin is death"* *(Romans 6:23)*. When Jacob and Esau were still in their mother's womb, God separated them into two nations even before they did anything good or bad, and loved Jacob, but hated Esau, and said, *"The older shall serve the younger"* *(Genesis 25:23)*. This passage implies that the salvation of God has nothing to do with our own deeds, but is given to those who just believe in God's perfect salvation in His baptism and crucifixion.

We human beings are destined for hell as sinful beings from the moment we are born until the moment we die, but God foresaw our sins at first sight, and washed away all our sins once and for all by Jesus' baptism and the Cross because He loves us. We live in a blessed time. The prophet Isaiah said, *"Speak comport to Jerusalem, and cry out to her, that her warfare is ended, that her iniquity is pardoned; for she has received from the Lord's hand double for all her sins" (Isaiah 40:2)*. The time of our slavery to sin has ended through the gospel of Jesus' baptism and the Cross, therefore, anybody who believes in the gospel can be delivered from all his/her sins. *"'This is the covenant that I will make with them after whose days, says the Lord: I will put my laws into their hearts, and in their minds I will write them,' then He adds, 'Their sins and their lawless deeds I will remember no more.' Now where there is remission of these, there is no longer an offering for sin" (Hebrews 10:16-18)*.

God does not judge us for our daily sins anymore because He has already washed away all the sins of humankind and judged them through Jesus.

As a result, we can wait for the coming Lord and follow His Word, as the righteous without sin, even though we still commit sins in our lives.

Question 3: What is the baptism of repentance by John?

Answer: John the Baptist was a servant of God, who was born 6 months prior to Jesus, and was foretold in Malachi, would be the last Prophet in the Old Testament.

"Remember the Law of Moses, My servant, which I commanded him in Horeb for all Israel, with the statutes and judgments. Behold, I will send you Elijah the prophet before the coming of the great and dreadful day of the Lord. And he will turn the hearts of the children to their fathers, lest I come and strike the earth with a curse" (Malachi 4:4-6).

When Jesus was born, the people of Israel abandoned the words of God's Covenant and worshipped foreign gods. They offered the blind and blemished animals as sacrifices, and made the temple of God a place of business. Jesus Christ, too, is foretold in the Law of Moses and the Prophets. The Law gives humanity the knowledge of sin, showing how they are sinful (Romans 3:20). It is a sin not to abide by a single commandment written in the books of the Law.

In the Old Testament, a sinner who disobeyed any of the articles of the Law brought a sin offering in front of the tabernacle, put his hands on the head of the sin offering to pass his sin onto it, and killed the sin offering to be forgiven for the sin and be united with God again. Then, the priest took some of its blood and put it on the horns of the altar of burnt offering and poured out all the rest of its blood at the base of the altar.

However, the people of Israel couldn't be delivered from all their sins, regardless of their countless daily offerings. Therefore, God made a permanent statute for them, the Day of Atonement. It was at this time God would forgive their yearly sins on the tenth day of the seventh month. On that day Aaron, the High Priest, took two goats and cast lots for them; one for the Lord and the other for the scapegoat. Then, he laid his hands on the head of the goat for the Lord to lay all the yearly sins of the people of Israel on it. Aaron then slew it and took its blood to sprinkle it seven times on and in front of the mercy seat.

When he finished atoning for the Holy Place, he offered the other animal. He laid his hands on the head of the live goat and confessed over it all the yearly sins of the Israelites. By this method, all their yearly sins were passed onto it, and it was sent away into the wilderness by the hand of a suitable man. The Israelites were redeemed from their yearly sins in this way.

However, the sacrifice offered according to the Law of the Old Testament could not make those, who offered sacrifices continually year-by-year, perfect. It was merely a shadow of the good things (the righteous acts of Messiah) to come (Hebrews 10:1). People of Israel did not wait for Jesus Christ, the Savior. Instead, they worshipped the foreign gods of the sinful world, abandoning the words of the Prophets in the Old Testament.

Thus, God foretold that He would send John the Baptist in order to restore the hearts of the Israelites, to return them to Him, and to prepare their hearts to receive Jesus Christ. Before John the Baptist baptized Jesus, he gave the baptism of repentance to the people of Israel in the wilderness of Judea.

His purpose of baptizing them with water was to lead them to wait for and believe in Jesus. He taught that the Savior would be baptized by him in the way of the laying on of hands to take away all the sins of the world, and then crucified to save them from all their sins. He said that Jesus would come and take away the incomplete sacrifices of the past and offer the eternal sacrifice with His body; He would take all our sins through the baptism, just as the people of Israel were redeemed by bringing a sin offering without blemish, laying their hands on it, and slaying it according to the sacrificial system in the Old Testament.

Many Israelites confessed their sins, repented, and were baptized by him. "Repentance" means "to return one's mind to the Lord." Remembering the Law of the Old Testament, they came to John and confessed that they were hopeless sinners who could not but commit sins until they died. They also confessed that they could not enter the Kingdom of Heaven with their good deeds according to the Law, and returned their minds to Jesus Christ, who would blot out all their sins once and for all, opening the gate to the Kingdom of Heaven.

The baptism that John the Baptist gave to the people of Israel was the following. He let them confess how much they sinned in their lives, repented and looked for Jesus Christ, who would be baptized by him, the High Priest and representative of all humankind, and crucified to save them from all their sins, just as he baptized them. This is a true biblical repentance.

Therefore, John exclaimed to the people, *"I indeed baptize you with water unto repentance, but He who is coming after me is mightier than I, whose sandals I am not worthy to carry. He will baptize you with the Holy Spirit and fire"* *(Matthew 3:11).*

John the Baptist turned peoples' minds to Jesus, testified to them that Jesus would take away all the sins of the world (John 1:29) and die for them vicariously. Thus, Jesus Himself bore witness that John came to show us the way of righteousness (Matthew 21:32).

Question 4: Don't you think that understanding the baptism of Jesus as the must for salvation would nullify His death on the Cross in the gospel?

Answer: The baptism of Jesus and His death on the Cross are equally essential to our salvation. We cannot say that either one is more important than the other. However, the problem is that most Christians nowadays only know the blood of Jesus on the Cross. They believe that they have been forgiven because He died on the Cross, but it is not only the Cross with which Jesus took away the sins of the world. Since He was baptized by John the Baptist and bore all the sins of the world on His back, His death on the Cross could practically be the judgment for all our sins.

Believing only in the Cross without the baptism of Jesus is just like offering a sacrifice to the Lord without laying one's hands on it. Those who offered such offerings couldn't be redeemed for their sins because that kind of sacrifice was a lawless offering, which the Lord God couldn't accept. The Lord called to Moses and spoke to him from the tabernacle of meeting, saying *"If his offering is a burnt sacrifice of the herd, let him offer a male without blemish; he shall offer it of his own free will at the door of the tabernacle of meeting before the Lord. Then he shall put his hand on the head of the burnt offering, and it will be accepted on his behalf to make atonement for him" (Leviticus 1:3-4).*

The Lord is just and lawful. He has established the fair and just sacrificial system in order to wash away our sins.

When we offer a lawful sacrifice, the sacrifice is accepted by the Lord to make atonement for us. Without the laying on of hands, no sacrifice can be accepted to God. Likewise, if we omit the baptism of Jesus from our faith in Him, we cannot receive the remission of sins with that kind of faith.

One of the most common fallacies that today's Christians believe in is that they can be saved only by confessing Jesus to be their Savior, for the Lord is love. The Bible, of course, says, *"Whoever calls on the name of the Lord shall be saved" (Acts 2:21, Romans 10:13)*, whereas it also tells us that *"Not everyone who says to Me, 'Lord, Lord,' shall enter the kingdom of heaven, but he who does the will of My Father in Heaven" (Matthew 7:21).*

In order to confess that Jesus is the Savior, we should know the law of salvation that God has established. If we can be saved simply by believing in the name of Jesus, there would be no reason whatsoever for the Scriptures to be written about the sacrificial system of the Old Testament and about those who practice lawlessness in Matthew 7:21.

However, the amazing and perfect way of the Lord's salvation is clearly recorded in the Bible. Indeed, we can clearly see from Leviticus chapters 3 and 4 that a sinner had to lay his hands on the head of the sacrifice to pass his sins onto its head and then killed and sprinkled its blood when he offered sin and peace offerings. Offering a sacrifice without the laying on of hands or offering a sacrifice with blemish is too lawless to make atonement.

Both the words of the Old and New Testaments have their corresponding equivalents to each other (Isaiah 34:16). The baptism of Jesus in the Jordan is equal to the sinner's laying hands on the head of the sin offering in the Old Testament. When Jesus was baptized by John the Baptist in the Jordan, He said, *"Permit it to be so now, thus it is fitting for us to fulfill all righteousness" (Matthew 3:15).*

Here, *"all righteousness"* means "justice and fairness." This means that it is fitting for Jesus to become the sin offering for mankind through that method. It was also fitting for Him to be baptized by John the Baptist in the form of the laying on of hands to take away all the sins of the world in the fairest way, according to the sacrificial system, composed of the laying on of hands and blood, which God established in the Old Testament.

Believing only in the Cross means consequently that His death had nothing to do with our sins because our sins could have never been passed onto Him without the baptism of Jesus. It results in regarding His blood as unclean and incapable of washing them away (Hebrews 10:29).

Therefore, His blood would actually be effective in washing away the sins in the hearts of believers only if they believe that all their sins were laid on Him when John the Baptist baptized Him through the laying of his hands. Thus, the Apostle John testified that one who believes that Jesus is the Son of God, who came by water and blood, overcomes the world. Jesus came by water and blood, not only by water or by blood (1 John 5:4-6).

Jesus Christ explained to His disciples the things concerning Himself in all the Scriptures. Beginning with Moses and all the prophets, He showed that the sin offering in the Old Testament was Himself. David said in Psalms instead of Him, *"Behold, I come; in the scroll of the Book it is written of me—To do Your will, O God" (Psalms 40:7, Hebrews 10:7).*

As a result, His baptism does not nullify the Cross, but is actually the essential part of the Lord's gospel that completes and fulfills the meaning of the Cross. It also teaches us that we cannot have redemption unless there is the baptism and precious blood of Jesus Christ. What you mean by being saved is that you obtain the remission of sins by believing in the baptism of Jesus and His blood on the Cross and receive the gift of the Holy Spirit (1 John 5:8, Acts 2:38).

Question 5: **Could you give me an explanation of the Gospel of the water and the Spirit?**

Answer: If we had lost a needle somewhere outside, we would probably be looking for it in the area where we lost it. However, it sounds absolutely absurd to try to find it inside the house simply because it is brighter inside. I find some absurd people like that in today's churches. While they're easily involved in the midst of endless biblical controversies about the water baptism of believers, they never ask themselves this important question, "Why was Jesus baptized by John the Baptist?" Due to such a tendency, there happens to be a lot of denominations and sects in today's Christian community.

In order to put an end to these incessant controversies, we should get ourselves out of the chaotic village and get back to the place where we lost our needle. If we sincerely want to find the truth, we should get rid of the stereotype for we cannot find it in a village of religion. Why did the Apostles put so much emphasis on the baptism of Jesus Christ? The secret truth of the gospel of water and the Spirit that they received from Jesus was preached throughout the whole world.

Jesus said, *"Most assuredly, I say to you, unless one is born of water and the Spirit, he cannot enter the kingdom of God" (John 3:5).* The Bible tells us that Jesus came by water and blood in order to save us from all our sins (1 John 5:6).

352 Questions & Answers

The meaning of blood is His death on the Cross. Then, what do you mean by 'water'? Why did John the Baptist baptize Jesus? Why did He proclaim, *"Permit it to be so now, for thus it is fitting for us to fulfill all righteousness" (Matthew 3:15)* just before His baptism?

I sincerely hope you understand and believe in the gospel of the water and the Spirit, especially in the baptism of Jesus. Here are some brief explanations on the gospel of the water and the Spirit that He gave to His disciples. The Apostles put the greatest emphasis on the baptism of Jesus when they preached the gospel. The Apostle Paul said, *"For I delivered to you first of all that which I also received: that Christ died for our sins according to the Scriptures, and that He was buried, and that He rose again the third day according to the Scriptures" (1 Corinthians 15:3-4).*

What does it mean, *"Christ died for our sins according to the Scriptures"*? It means that His death atoned for all our sins according to the God-given method in the Old Testament. He died for us according to the revelation and covenant in the Old Testament. Hebrews 10:1 states, *"For the law, having a shadow of the good things to come."* Let us look at the typical sacrifice in Leviticus 1:3-5. A sinner should satisfy three conditions of the burnt offering for the atonement of his sins.

1) He brought an offering without blemish (Leviticus 1:3).

2) He had to put his hands on the head of the offering (Leviticus 1:4). Here, we should make clear of the law of God: Laying hands on the head of the offering was God's law to pass his sins onto it.

3) He had to kill it to atone for his sin (Leviticus 1:5).

On the Day of Atonement, Aaron laid both his hands on the head of a live goat, confessed over it all the iniquities and

Free book request www.nlmission.com

transgressions of the children of Israel, concerning all their sins, and put them on the head of the goat (Leviticus 16:21). At that time, Aaron was the representative of Israel. He alone put his hands on the head of the goat, but all the yearly sins of the people of Israel (about 2-3 millions) were passed onto it. The sacrifice of the Old Testament is a shadow of the good things to come. Jesus offered Himself by the will of God in order to sanctify us according to the Scriptures.

First of all, Jesus came in the flesh of a man to be the Lamb of God without blemish. He is the only begotten Son of God and *"the express image of His person" (Hebrews 1:3).* Thus, He is fitting as the sin offering for all of mankind.

Second, John the Baptist baptized Jesus in the Jordan. Baptism is given in the form of "laying on of hands," and John the Baptist is a descendant of Aaron and the representative of all mankind. When John put his hands on the head of Jesus Christ, all the sins of the world were passed onto Him according to the law God had established. Jesus said to John, *"Permit it to be so now, for thus it is fitting for us to fulfill all righteousness,"* and he baptized Him. All our sins had finally passed on Him. The very next day, John exclaimed, *"Behold! The Lamb of God who takes away the sin of the world" (John 1:29).*

Third, Jesus died on the Cross for the remission of all our sins, saying, *"It is finished!" (John 19:30)* He rose again from the dead in order to make us righteous in front of God. Remember that a sin offering was offered for the forgiveness of sins. A sinner had to put his hands on its head before he killed it. If he forgot one single step, in other words, if he omitted putting his hands on the head of the offering, he could not be redeemed due to his having practiced lawlessness. If a Christian doesn't have any idea what His baptism means, such a person must have had sins in his/her heart and cannot be saved simply by his/her own faith.

Most Christians know only half of His righteous act. The Apostle John makes clear the gospel in his first Epistle: *"This is who came by water and blood—Jesus Christ; not only by water, but by water and blood. And it is the Spirit who bears witness, because the Spirit is truth" (1 John 5:6).* There are a lot of passages in the Bible that support how essential His baptism is to complete His righteous act for our salvation. All Christians should return to the gospel of water and the Spirit.

Question 6: **What scriptures provide evidence that "the Apostles laid great emphasis on the Baptism of Jesus?"**

Answer: Most of all, we should discern the meaning of our baptism from that of the baptism of Jesus. We cannot be born again merely by receiving water baptism. We can be born again only by believing in Jesus Christ. Rituals such as baptism or circumcision are not indispensable conditions for the salvation of God. The Bible does not define the water baptism of believers as a must for their salvation. Rather, it puts great emphasis on the baptism that Jesus received from John the Baptist.

In fact, lots of Bible passages support that the baptism of Jesus is indispensable and essential for our salvation. First of all, His baptism is proclaimed as the prologue to His whole righteous act in each of the four Gospels. For example, the gospel according to Mark begins the gospel of Jesus Christ, exactly from the baptism of Jesus, and John wrote the gospel in date sequence, using terminologies such as *"the next day"*

(1:29) and *"the third day" (2:1)* starting from the day Jesus was baptized.

John the Baptist declared the Word of God on the very next day of Jesus' baptism, saying, *"Behold! The lamb of God who takes away the sin of the World" (John 1:29)*. This passage means that all the sins of the world were passed onto Jesus when John the Baptist baptized Him. And then, He died on the Cross for the atonement of our sins, saying, "It is finished!" (John 19:30), and rose again from the dead the third day.

The Apostle Paul also said, *"Christ died for our sins according to the Scriptures" (1 Corinthians 15:3)*. The Scriptures here refers to the Old Testament. How could a sinner offer a sacrifice to be forgiven in the Old Testament? He had to put his hands on the head of the sin offering before slaying it. If he had omitted the process of "putting hands on the head of the sin offering," he could not have been forgiven for having offered an illegal sacrifice.

The Apostle Paul said, *"Or do you now know that as many of us as were baptized into Christ Jesus were baptized into His Death?" (Romans 6:3)* Then, how can it be possible that we are baptized into Jesus? To be baptized into Christ Jesus is to believe in His baptism at the Jordan, not just our own water baptisms. When we believe in the fact that John the Baptist passed all our sins onto Him by laying his hands on Jesus' head, we can be baptized into Him.

"For as many of you as were baptized into Christ have put on Christ" (Galatians 3:27). Those who passed all their sins onto Jesus through John the Baptist by faith have become God's sinless children.

"In Him you were also circumcised with the circumcision made without hands, by putting off the body of the sins of the

flesh, by the circumcision of Christ" (Colossians 2:11). The way of being delivered from sin by putting off the body of the sins of the flesh is to be spiritually circumcised without hands *(Romans 2:29 states, "Circumcision is that of the heart.")*, that is, to believe in the baptism of Jesus, which cuts off the sins in our hearts, the Apostle Paul said.

"There is also an antitype which now saves us baptism (not the removal of the filth of the flesh, but the answer of a good conscience toward God,) through the resurrection of Jesus Christ" (1 Peter 3:21). Baptism is an antitype that saves us. As we already know, people perished in the days of Noah for not believing the water, and even today, there're still disobedient people who would perish even though they might believe in Jesus, because they don't believe in Jesus' baptism, which is the water.

The Apostle John revealed everything about the gospel in his first Epistle writing, *"This is He who came by water and blood Jesus Christ; not only by water, but by water and blood" (1 John 5:6)*. Jesus came to us both by His baptism and the Cross to save us from all our sins. John also said, *"And there are three who bear witness on earth: the Spirit, the water, and the blood; and these three agree as one" (1 John 5:8)*. This tells us that the baptism of Jesus, the Cross, and the Spirit all together compose one perfect salvation.

Jesus said to Nicodemus, *"Most assuredly, I say to you, unless one is born again of water and the Spirit, he cannot enter the kingdom of God" (John 3:5)*. We are born again of the water and the Spirit. The belief in His baptism of the water and the Cross is all you need in order to be redeemed and receive the Holy Spirit as a gift. This is what the Bible says about "being born again."

Thus, the Apostle Peter said, *"Repent, and let every one of you be baptized in the name of Jesus Christ for the remission of sins; and you shall receive the gift of the Holy Spirit" (Acts 2:38).* In order to receive the forgiveness of all sins and the gift of the Holy Spirit, you should have immutable faith in the baptism of Jesus with all your heart. What else can we possibly say? Don't deny the truth that so many passages support His baptism as an indispensable deed of His righteousness for our salvation. Christianity must return to the gospel of the water and the Spirit.

"Therefore, leaving the discussion of the elementary principles of Christ, let us go on to perfection, not laying again the foundation of repentance from dead works and of faith toward God, of the doctrine of baptisms, of laying on of hands, of resurrection of the dead, and of eternal judgment" (Hebrews 6:1-2). Here, we can get a clue to finding the original gospel of the Early Church. They taught the doctrine of baptisms, of the laying on of hands, of resurrecting from the dead, and of eternal judgment to those who just became Christians. We all should believe in our minds that Jesus took away all our sins through His baptism and died on the Cross in order to be judged for our sins according to the righteous law of God.

Question 7: **It is what I have already believed and taught unless you are simply adding emphasis to the often-ignored baptism of Jesus. What then is so different about the gospel of the water and the Spirit?**

Answer: "Being saved" means to receive the remission of all sins. It also means to be born again. When a sinner becomes a righteous person by believing in the gospel of life, we say, "he/she is born again of the water and the Spirit through Jesus' salvation". The Holy Spirit comes upon those who have been redeemed and born again and testifies that they God's children. Therefore, it is all the same after all; receiving the remission of sins, receiving the Holy Spirit, being redeemed, being born again, becoming a child of God, and becoming a righteous person.

Jesus said, *"I am the way, the truth, and the life. No one comes to the Father except through Me" (John 14:6),* which implies that only through Jesus, the only begotten Son of God, can we enter the Kingdom of God. Hence, we have to know how Jesus washed away all our sins and counted us as His people, who deserve to enter His Kingdom.

Nonetheless, most Christians still think that merely calling His name can save them. They believe in Jesus without ever opening the Bible, without knowing what He has done to save us from all our sins. God is the Spirit and the Holy One with whom there is no variation or shifting, but we live sinful lives. Entering the Kingdom of the Lord is possible only through Jesus, and we can believe in Him through the faith in *'the law of the Spirit of life in Christ Jesus' (Romans 8:1-2).*

A lot of people do not even know what Jesus did for salvation; rather, they blindly believe in Him in vain, saying, "Lord, Lord!" They also think they're saved, but they still have sins in their hearts. If you still have sin in your heart in spite of your faith in Jesus, from what have you been saved then? If someone asks, "How did Jesus wash away our sins?" the bulk of people reply, "He probably washed them away on the Cross." Then, for another question, "Do you have sin in your heart?" they say, "Certainly. Who can be absolutely free from sin on this earth?"

The name of Jesus means *"the Savior who saves His people from their sins" (Matthew 1:21).* We believe in Jesus in order to be saved from sin.

However, if we still have sin in our hearts, although we believe in Jesus, we are still sinners sold into bondage to sin and will be judged accordingly. The Apostle Paul said, *"There is therefore now no condemnation to those who are in Christ Jesus" (Romans 8:1).* It is thus certain that someone who still has sin in his/her heart is not yet one with Christ Jesus. Why do they remain as a sinner who is not redeemed and fallen away from salvation even though they still believe in Jesus? It is because they believe only in the blood of the Cross, without laying their sins on Him by the baptism of Jesus. Therefore, they still have sin in their hearts, whereas Jesus died on the Cross regardless of their sins.

There is a significant difference for Christians who believe in the baptism of Jesus and those who don't believe in it; some have redemption and become righteous by having faith in the baptism of Jesus, while the others still remain as sinners without faith in it. The Holy Spirit does not come upon a sinner. He only comes upon the righteous, who have been born again by the water and the Spirit.

Thus, the Apostle Paul said, *"Or do you not know that as many of us as were baptized into Christ Jesus were baptized into His death?" (Romans 6:3)* Many people believe that Jesus took away our sins on the Cross, but we can never confess that we have sinless hearts if we don't believe in the baptism of Jesus. If we do, we're guilty of telling a lie to God, which goes against our own consciences.

We surely still have sin in our hearts if we haven't passed all our sins onto Jesus by believing in His baptism. For those who don't believe the gospel of the baptism of Jesus and the Cross, they are prone to fall into legalism and be grave sinners. Therefore, no matter what they do, like praying in the deep mountains or praying earnestly for forgiveness during prayer meetings, they still find sins left in their hearts.

Jesus said, *"Not everyone who says to Me, 'Lord, Lord,' shall enter the kingdom of heaven, but he who does the will of My Father in heaven. Many will say to Me in that day, 'Lord, Lord, have we not prophesied in Your name, cast out demons in Your name, and done many wonders in Your name?' And then I will declare to them, 'I never knew you; depart from Me, you who practice lawlessness!"* (Matthew 7:21-23)

Who does *"those who practice lawlessness"* refer to? It refers to those who haven't received the perfect redemption in their hearts for having believed only in the Cross. That's an arbitrary faith, not from God. We're practicing lawlessness if we don't believe in the fact that Jesus has saved us through His baptism and the Cross. We cannot say we have the right faith before we know and believe in both the baptism of Jesus and the Cross.

Jesus said that if people want to be born again, it is possible only through the water and the Spirit. Just as people could have only been delivered from the waters of the flood if they had been in Noah's ark, you can receive the remission of all your sins and live a true faithful life only if you believe in the gospel of the water and the Spirit. Without the gospel of the water and the Spirit, you can neither receive the forgiveness of sins nor become God's children.

Question 8: **I was sure that believing in Jesus has saved me. I had been at peace with the convictions in my heart. But now I am confused by your messages. Should I believe in His baptism along with His cross to be saved?**

Answer: If you don't believe in Jesus' baptism, it is for sure that you have sin in your heart. The Apostle John said, *"If we say that we have no sin, we deceive ourselves, and the truth is not in us" (1 John 1:8).* If you say that you have no sin, even though you actually have sin because you don't believe in the baptism of Jesus, it is an act of deceiving your own conscience and is evidence that the truth is not in you. The conviction of salvation emerges in our hearts when we receive the remission of sins and the Holy Spirit as a gift by believing both in Jesus' baptism and the Cross.

The Apostle Paul said, *". . . a different gospel, which is not another . . ." (Galatians 1:7).* Nothing but the gospel of the water and the Spirit, which the Apostles received from Jesus and preached to people, can save us from all our sins. If we don't believe in the gospel of the water and the Spirit that the Apostles preached, we certainly still have sin in us.

How could we live with the conviction of salvation when we still have sin in us? When Christians, who are not yet born again, behave well in front of God, they're sure of their salvations in full joy and conviction; however, they lack conviction and are afraid because of the burden of sin in their hearts when they commit some serious sins. It is a pseudo-salvation based on their own thoughts and emotions, not from God. They are prone to offer prayers of repentance everyday to become gradually sanctified and to keep their easily shakable salvations.

Those who believe in this false salvation think that they'll at last be perfectly saved someday, if they maintain holy lives, asking God for forgiveness everyday and keeping the law by deeds. Nevertheless, they're still sinners if they haven't laid their sins on Jesus through the faith in His baptism.

The salvation that God has made is a perfect salvation, which tells us that Jesus took away all the sins of the world through His baptism by John in the Jordan and blotted them out on the Cross.

Thus, the Apostle John said, *"If we confess our sins, He is faithful and just to forgive us our sins and to cleanse us from all unrighteousness" (1 John 1:9).* If all our sins hadn't been forgiven through the gospel of the water and the Spirit for not knowing it, we have to confess in front of the Lord that we're still sinners, although we believe in Him and know that we are destined to go to hell for our sins. This is a true confession of sin. Sin cannot be washed away without the gospel of the water and the Spirit, no matter how slight the sin is. When we confess in this manner, the gospel of the water and the Spirit washes away all our sins at once and makes us righteous.

Now is an acceptable time (2 Corinthians 6:2). Anyone who hears and believes in the gospel of Jesus' baptism and the Cross is saved from all his/her sins, becomes righteous, and has a strong faith that he/she is always ready to enter the Kingdom of Heaven whenever the Lord may come. Any faith in doctrines and theologies, other than the true gospel, cannot save us from all our sins. Those are simply cunning tricks that the devil has put into the thoughts of human beings. We should get back to the gospel of the water and the Spirit and receive the true salvation from sins in our hearts. This is to love Him and His work.

Question 9: **If your understanding of "water and the Spirit" were correct, then salvation would not have been possible for the thief on the cross. If the thief on the Cross were considered as an exception to the rule, then God would not be just, because He broke His own rule of entering into the Kingdom. How can you explain the salvation of the thief on the cross?**

Answer: At that time, all Jews were waiting for the prophesied Messiah. Therefore, they knew well about "the Law and the sacrificial system," which God had given through Moses, more than any other people. They believed that the Messiah would come according to the atoning law of God, and would free them from all their sins.

However, they did not believe that the baptism of Jesus by John the Baptist was from God and was supposed to put all the sins of the world onto Jesus (Mark 11:27-33), but rather, they considered Him as a man who led the people astray and thus, crucified Him.

Since Romans were protected from being scourged or crucified according to Roman law (Acts 22:25-29, 23:27), we know that the thieves on the Cross were not Romans, but Jews. We also know that the thief was a Jew who feared God from his words, saying, *"Lord, remember me when You come into Your kingdom" (Luke 23:42).* The Jewish thief already knew the Law and the sacrificial system, which God gave to Moses. So he believed that the Messiah would come according to the atoning law of God.

Those who come to God must confess that they are sinners, destined to go to hell for their sins. The thief confessed his sins, saying, *"And we indeed justly, for we receive the due reward of our deeds" (Luke 23:41).* We can also know that the thief feared God and his hope was to enter the Kingdom of Heaven from his words, saying, *"Lord, remember me when You come into Your kingdom" (Luke 23:42)*.

He said, *"But this Man has done nothing wrong" (Luke 23:41)*. What did the thief know about what Jesus did? He believed that Jesus was conceived by the Holy Spirit, was born of the Virgin Mary, was baptized by John the Baptist, the representative of all mankind, took away all the sins of the world, and was crucified. He was a Jew who believed what Jesus did for all the people, including him, even though he was crucified to receive the due reward of his deeds on earth.

Those who confessed their sins through the baptism of John acknowledged God's righteousness when they heard all their sins would be passed onto Jesus through His baptism. However, those who didn't receive John's baptism of repentance rejected the will of God because they didn't believe in Jesus' baptism, either (Luke 7:28-30).

On the contrary, the thief who was saved confessed that everything Jesus did was correct and righteous, while the other Jews did not. He may have been one of the Jews who had heard all those things, which have been fulfilled among them (Luke 1:1). He could at last say that Jesus was righteous and the prophesied Messiah because he finally came to believe on the Cross that Jesus took away all his sins through His baptism. Accordingly, he was saved. He was also saved by believing in the gospel of the water and the Spirit. Because God is just, He justifies those who believe in the baptism of Jesus and the Cross according to His law of the Spirit of life.

Question 10: **Since God is gracious and compassionate, wouldn't He consider us righteous, although we have sin in our hearts if we just believe in Jesus?**

Answer: God is Love and also just. Hence, He judges sin uprightly no matter what. *"The wages of sin is death" (Romans 6:23).* This means that a sinner is destined to hell after being judged. He separates the righteous from sinners, just as He did the light from the darkness. God calls those, who have no sin by believing that Jesus washed away all their sins through His baptism and crucifixion, to be righteous.

However, those who still have sin in them, for not believing in the baptism of Jesus, are sinners in the presence of God. They are the ones who don't believe in the water, in other words, the baptism of Jesus, just as the people of the days of Noah didn't. If God considers sinners, who still have sin in them, righteous and sinless, then He must be lying and therefore cannot judge or reign all His creations.

He said, *"I will not justify the wicked" (Exodus 23:7).* The wicked are those who follow and depend more on the tradition of people, setting aside the gospel of the water and the Spirit, with which God has redeemed us from all our sins in the most just and fair way. Jesus said, *"Of sin, because they do not believe in Me" (John 16:9).* The only sin left on earth now is to not believe in the fact that Jesus has taken away all our sins through His baptism and the Cross, and has become our Savior. This is the sin of blaspheming against the Holy Spirit, which can never be forgiven. There is no other way at all for those who blaspheme against the Holy Spirit to be saved because they don't believe that Jesus washed away all their sins.

The Apostle John said, *"Whoever commits sin also commits lawlessness, and sin is lawlessness. And you know that*

He was manifested to take away our sins, and in Him there is no sin. Whoever abides in Him does not sin. Whoever sins has neither seen Him nor known Him" (1 John 3:4-6). It is committing lawlessness not to believe in the fact that Jesus has taken away all our sins through His baptism and the Cross. He shall reject those who commit such lawlessness on the last day.

Those who abide in Him have no sin and are united with Jesus by being baptized into Him. Those who have laid all the sins of their whole lives onto Him through their faiths in His baptism have no sin, even though they still sin because of the weaknesses of the flesh.

God calls those who have laid their sins on Jesus and have become sanctified by the law of the Spirit of life, to be righteous. He gives them the Holy Spirit as a gift. The Holy Spirit never comes upon those who have sin in their hearts. David said in his Psalm, *"You are not a God who takes pleasure in wickedness, nor shall evil dwell with You" (Psalms 5:4).* The Holy Spirit of God never dwells in the hearts of those who have sin in them. Even a sinner who doesn't have the Holy Spirit in him/her may say that he/she has been saved from sin, according to doctrines and his/her own thoughts. However, one can never say that one has no sin in his/her heart and is righteous with faith because his/her conscience smites him/her.

Therefore, such a person says that he/she is a sinner in the sight of other people, but actually thinks that he/she is a righteous person in the sight of God. But God never calls a sinner righteous. A sinner is the subject of His judgment and the sinner must believe in the gospel of the water and the Spirit to be saved.

Question 11: **If we say that Jesus has already eliminated all our sins of the past, the present and the future according to your assertion, how would the future of a person turn out if he continuously committed sin by thinking about the fact that he has already had his sins pardoned by believing in Jesus' baptism and the Cross? Even if this person kills another person, he will know that he has been atoned for even this kind of sin through Jesus on the Cross. Therefore, he will continue to sin without any hesitation just by believing that Jesus has already eliminated even the sins he will commit in the future. Please explain to me about these things.**

Answer: First of all, I thank you for raising questions about the gospel of the water and the Spirit. The questions you have made are the ones that many Christians have asked before they are born again. I know that you are worrying that the born again would continuously commit sin being relieved by the perfect gospel. However, I want to tell you that people who believe in the gospel of the water and the Spirit are not prone to live such a life you are worrying about, but rather lead a righteous life instead.

You should first think about this. If the Holy Spirit is truly within you, then you will bear holy fruits even if you don't wish to do so. On the other hand, if the Holy Spirit does not dwell within you, you will not be able to produce any of the fruits of the Spirit, no matter how hard you may try. How can a person possibly bear fruits of the Spirit if he/she does not have the Holy Spirit in his/her heart, even if he/she believes in Jesus somehow? This is impossible. The Lord said that a bad tree could never bear good fruits (Matthew 7:17-18).

I now want to ask you this question and also give an

answer to it. You do believe in Jesus, but are you truly leading your life while having triumphed over worldly sins? Are you living as a righteous servant of God overcoming worldly sins; serving the Lord more and letting others be saved from all their sins by delivering the gospel of the water and the Spirit to them? Have you truly become a righteous person who does not possess even the slightest amount of sin after having believed in Jesus? The only faith and gospel that lets you answer yes to this question is the gospel of the water and the Spirit, which the Lord has born witness to in the Old and New Testaments.

We continue to sin in the world even after we believe in Jesus. However, our Lord was baptized by John and shed His blood on the Cross to save us from all the sins of the world. Therefore, the Lord has done a righteous deed for us and we have been saved from our sins through faith in God's righteousness, the Lord's baptism and blood by which He has eliminated our sins.

I want to ask you some questions again. Are you free from the sins of your conscience? Were you not a sinner even after you believed in Jesus, just like you were before you believed in Him? If this is true, it is probably because you did not know about the gospel of the water and the Spirit. Therefore, you have fallen into the problems and distractions inherent in the flesh because you don't possess the Spirit in your heart. No matter how faithful of a believer you may be, you can only escape the thoughts of the flesh by emptying your heart and taking in the gospel of the water and the Spirit. You should discard your carnal thoughts and return to the written words of God in order to understand the fact that the gospel of the water and the Spirit is the truth.

There are many people in this world who change the law of salvation that the Lord has established in any way they wish, even though they confess to the Lord with their lips. If you are one of these kinds of people, the Lord will abandon you on the last day. I hope that this will not happen to anyone in this world. I pray that you are not a person who believes that Jesus' blood on the Cross is the only thing that can save you, and that you have asked questions out of the desire to live the remaining time of your life apart from sin.

However, your thoughts are thoughts of the flesh that are *"not subject to the law of God, nor indeed can be"(Romans 8:7)*. Paul says, *"Those who are in the flesh cannot please God" (Romans 8:8)*. If you truly wish to have the faith that pleases God, you should believe in the remarkable work of the Lord, in which He came to this world through the Virgin Mary, took over the sins of humankind through the baptism received by John the Baptist at the Jordan River, and thereby fulfilling all the righteousness of God.

Who do you think can carry out God's righteous work, a righteous person or a sinner? A sinner is still in the midst of sin because he/she has not received the remission of sins before God. Therefore, the only thing awaiting such a person is the judgment for his/her sins. God cannot let sinners enter His Kingdom because *"God is not someone who takes pleasure in wickedness" (Psalms 5:4)*. God said that if a sinner came out to Him and asked something from Him, He would not listen to the prayers of the sinner because their *"iniquities have separated them from God" (Isaiah 59:1-2)*. A sinner will definitely fall into hell since the wages of sin is death.

Only righteous people who have become holy and therefore possess no sin in their hearts can do righteous works. In addition, the Holy Spirit dwells inside the hearts of the righteous, who possess no sin after believing in Jesus' baptism and the Cross. The Apostle Peter said on the day of Pentecost,

"Repent, and let every one of you be baptized in the name of Jesus Christ for the remission of sins; and you shall receive the gift of the Holy Spirit" (Acts 2:38).

What this passage is saying is that if you want to have true faith and receive the remission of all your sins by faith, then you should believe both in Jesus' baptism and His death on the Cross. Such faith can let you *"be baptized in the name of Jesus,"* that is to say, you can receive the remission of your sins by having faith in His righteous deeds. Of course, the disciples of Jesus also ministered the ritual of baptism to the born-again believers, who had faith in His baptism and the Cross. Jesus commanded His disciples to baptize everyone in the name of the Father and of the Son and of the Holy Spirit (Matthew 28:19).

Furthermore, the Apostle Paul said, *"Anyone who does not have the Spirit of Christ is not a person of Christ" (Romans 8:9).* God gives the Holy Spirit to the righteous in order to seal them as His children. The Holy Spirit can never dwell inside sinners because they possess sin. The Holy Spirit does not like sin; instead, it prefers holiness (becoming apart from sin). The Spirit also guides righteous people along the righteous way and leads them to follow the will of the Father. Then, what is this will of the Father? It is to spread the gospel of the water and the Spirit to the people of every nation and to baptize them according to the Great Commission.

The flesh of the righteous and sinners commit sin until they die. However, the Lord has done the righteous deed of eliminating all the sins people commit with their flesh and hearts by His baptism and blood. This is the righteousness of God Jesus has fulfilled. Therefore, it is written in the Bible, *"For in it* (the true gospel) *the righteousness of God is revealed from faith to faith; as it is written, 'The just shall live by faith'"*

(Romans 1:17). A person who has received the remission of sins by believing in God's righteousness will win over *'the law of sin and death'* and follow His righteousness instead. This is only possible through the Holy Spirit, who comes on and dwells in those who believe in the gospel of the water and the Spirit.

All the sins of the past, the present and the future of a righteous person have been passed over to Jesus at the time He was baptized by John the Baptist. The flesh of the righteous have also died together with Jesus. When a person believes in this, he/she unites together with Jesus and in the likeness of His death. This becomes the judgment for all his/her sins (Romans chapter 6).

Therefore, even though the flesh of a righteous person also commit sins continuously throughout all his/her life, the Holy Spirit dwelling in his/her heart guides him/her so that he/she can follow the Spirit. A righteous person follows the Holy Spirit and does God's work because the Holy Spirit dwells within him/her.

Even at the time of the Apostles, many people used to unreasonably blame the born-again because they had the cheek to worry over the lives of the born-again people, who were ruled by the Holy Spirit. However, these kinds of people misunderstood the true gospel of the water and the Spirit the Apostles preached, as the instinctive thoughts of the flesh. Therefore, the Apostle Paul said to these people, *"What shall we say then? Shall we continue in sin that grace may abound? Certainly not! How shall we who died to sin live any longer in it?"(Romans 6:1-2)* He added, *"I thank God—through Jesus Christ our Lord! So then, with the mind I myself serve the law of God, but with the flesh the law of sin" (Romans 7:25).*

In conclusion, the flesh of the righteous is still insufficient and has no other choice but to continuously sin, but they still follow the Holy Spirit, preaching the gospel to the whole world. The righteous walk in the Spirit because their hearts rest under grace. *"What then? Shall we sin because we are not under law but under grace? Certainly not! Do you not know that to whom you present yourselves slaves to obey, you are that ones slaves whom you obey, whether of sin leading to death, or of obedience leading to righteousness?" (Romans 6:15-16)*

Just like real flowers are far different from artificial flowers, the master inside the heart of a righteous person and a sinner are different from each other. Since the master inside the heart of a righteous person is the Holy Spirit, the person is able to walk in the Spirit and follow the righteous truth in his/her life, which pleases God. On the other hand, a sinner has no other choice but to follow sin because the master inside him/her is sin itself. A sinner is unable to lead a holy life because he/she does not possess the Spirit, due to his/her many iniquities.

The assumption that believers in the gospel of the water and the Spirit are not able to lead holy lives is just a fallacy arising from the instinctive thoughts of the flesh. God warns them saying, *"But these speak evil of whatever they do not know; and whatever they know naturally, like brute beasts, in these things they corrupt themselves" (Jude 1:10).* Many people nowadays do not understand the lives of the righteous, even though they acknowledge the gospel of the water and the Spirit as the true gospel, because they don't fully know it and haven't received it in their hearts.

What do you think about the righteous works of the born-again saints? They have offered all their precious things, even themselves as the living sacrifices, for the good works of spreading the gospel to the whole world. According to your own thoughts, why do you think that the believers in the gospel of the water and the Spirit would purposely commit a sin on the pretext of the gospel?

The righteous do good works by faith in the midst of the light of truth and God's righteousness. Those who practice the righteousness of God have been born of God. We just hope that all sinners will return to the gospel in which Jesus has washed away all their sins by His baptism and blood.

Yes, our earnest wish is that you will receive the remission of sins by believing in the gospel of the water and the Spirit truly with your hearts, and wait for the Lord until the last day without sin. ✉

HAVE YOU TRULY BEEN BORN AGAIN OF WATER AND THE SPIRIT?

HAVE YOU TRULY BEEN BORN AGAIN OF WATER AND THE SPIRIT?

PAUL C. JONG

Among many Christian books written about being born again, this is the first book of our time to preach the gospel of the water and the Spirit in strict accordance with the Scriptures. Man can't enter the Kingdom of Heaven without being born again of water and the Spirit. To be born again means that a sinner is saved from all his lifelong sins by believing in the baptism of Jesus and His blood of the Cross. Let's believe in the gospel of the water and the Spirit and enter the Kingdom of Heaven as the righteous who have no sin.

RETURN TO THE GOSPEL OF THE WATER AND THE SPIRIT

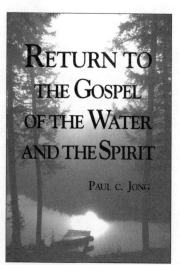

RETURN TO THE GOSPEL OF THE WATER AND THE SPIRIT

PAUL C. JONG

Let's return to the gospel of the water and the Spirit. Theology and doctrines themselves can't save us. However, many Christians still follow them, and consequently have not been born again yet. This book clearly tells us what mistakes theology and doctrines have made and how to believe in Jesus in the most proper way.

The Fail-safe Way for You to Receive the Holy Spirit

In Christianity, the most significantly discussed issue is salvation from sins and the indwelling of the Holy Spirit. However, few people have the exact knowledge of these two topics. Nevertheless, in reality people say that they believe in Jesus Christ while they are ignorant of true redemption and the Holy Spirit.

Do you know the true gospel that makes you receive the Holy Spirit? If you want to ask God for the indwelling of the Holy Spirit, then you must first know the gospel of the water and the Spirit and have faith in it. This book will certainly lead all Christians worldwide to receive the Holy Spirit through the remission of all their sins.

Our LORD Who Becomes the Righteousness of God (I) & (II)

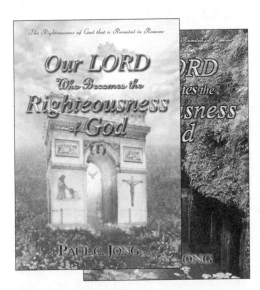

The teachings in these books will satisfy the thirst in your heart. Today's Christians continue to live while not knowing the true solution to the personal sins that they are committing daily. Do you know what God's righteousness is? The author hopes that you will ask yourself this question and believe in God's righteousness, which is dealt in detail in these books.

The Doctrines of Predestination, Justification, and Incremental Sanctification are the major Christian doctrines, which brought only confusion and emptiness into the souls of believers. But, dear Christians, now is the time when you must continue in the Truth which you have learned and been assured of.

These books will provide your soul with a great understanding and lead it to peace. The author wants you to possess the blessing of knowing God's righteousness.

IS THE AGE OF THE ANTICHRIST, MARTYRDOM, RAPTURE AND THE MILLENNIAL KINGDOM COMING? (I)

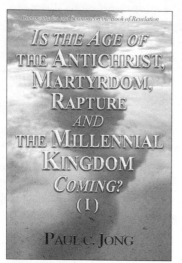

After the 9/11 terrorist attacks, traffic to "www.raptureready.com," an Internet site providing information on the end times, is reported to have increased to over 8 million hits, and according to a joint survey by CNN and TIME, over 59% of the Americans now believe in apocalyptic eschatology.

Responding to such demands of the time, the author provides a clear exposition of the key themes of the Book of Revelation, including the coming Antichrist, the martyrdom of the saints and their rapture, the Millennial Kingdom, and the New Heaven and Earth-all in the context of the whole Scripture and under the guidance of the Holy Spirit.

This book provides verse-by-verse commentaries on the Book of Revelation supplemented by the author's inspired sermons. Anyone who reads this book will come to grasp all the plans that God has in store for this world.

IS THE AGE OF THE ANTICHRIST, MARTYRDOM, RAPTURE AND THE MILLENNIAL KINGDOM COMING? (II)

Most Christians today believe in the theory of pre-tribulation rapture. Because they believe in this false doctrine teaching them that they would be lifted before the coming of the Great Tribulation of seven years, they are leading idle religious lives steeped in complacency.

But the rapture of the saints will occur only after the plagues of the seven trumpets run their course until the sixth plague is all poured-that is, the rapture will happen after the Antichrist emerges amidst global chaos and the born-again saints are martyred, and when the seventh trumpet is blown. It is at this time that Jesus would descend from Heaven, and the resurrection and rapture of the born-again saints would occur (1 Thessalonians 4:16-17).

The righteous who were born again by believing in "the gospel of the water and the Spirit" will be resurrected and take part in the Rapture, and thus become heirs to the Millennial Kingdom and the eternal Kingdom of Heaven, but the sinners who were unable to participate in this first resurrection will face the great punishment of the seven bowls poured by God and be cast into the eternal fire of hell.

The TABERNACLE: A Detailed Portrait of Jesus Christ (I)

How can we find out the truth hidden in the Tabernacle? Only by knowing the gospel of the water and the Spirit, the real substance of the Tabernacle, can we correctly understand and know the answer to this question.

In fact, the blue, purple, and scarlet thread and the fine woven linen manifested in the gate of the Tabernacle's court show us the works of Jesus Christ in the New Testament's time that have saved the mankind. In this way, the Old Testament's Word of the Tabernacle and the Word of the New Testament are closely and definitely related to each other, like fine woven linen. But, unfortunately, this truth has been hidden for a long time to every truth seeker in Christianity.

Coming to this earth, Jesus Christ was baptized by John and shed His blood on the Cross. Without understanding and believing in the gospel of the water and the Spirit, none of us can ever find out the truth revealed in the Tabernacle. We must now learn this truth of the Tabernacle and believe in it. We all need to realize and believe in the truth manifested in the blue, purple, and scarlet thread and the fine woven linen of the gate of the Tabernacle's court.

The TABERNACLE: A Detailed Portrait of Jesus Christ (II)

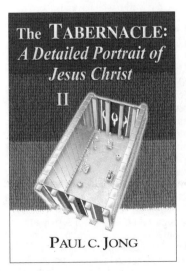

As God had commanded Moses to build the Tabernacle in the Old Testament, in the New Testament, God wants us to also build a Sanctuary in each of our hearts so that He may dwell in us. The material of faith with which we can build this Sanctuary in our hearts is the Word of the gospel of the water and the Spirit. With this gospel of the water and the Spirit, we must wash away all our sins and be cleansed. By telling us to build Him a Sanctuary, God is telling us to empty our hearts and believe in the gospel of the water and the Spirit. We must all cleanse our hearts by believing in the gospel of the water and the Spirit.

When we cleanse away all the sins of our hearts by believing in this gospel Truth, God then comes to dwell in them. It is by believing in this true gospel that you can build the holy Temples in your hearts. It is highly likely that until now, at least some of you have probably been offering your prayers of repentance to cleanse your hearts, trying to build the Temples by yourselves. But now is the time for you to abandon this false faith and be transformed by the renewing of your minds by believing in the gospel of the water and the Spirit.

The Elementary Principles of CHRIST

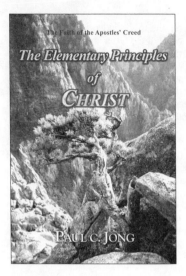

We must have the faith that the Apostles had and believe as they did, for their faith and beliefs came from the Holy Spirit. The Apostles believed in Jesus Christ, His Father, and the Holy Spirit as their God.

The Apostle Paul confessed that he died with Christ and was brought to new life with Him. He became an instrument of God by believing that he was baptized into Jesus Christ (Galatians 3:27). In God's gospel are found the baptism that Jesus received, the blood that He shed on the Cross, and the gift of the Holy Spirit that He has bestowed on everyone who believes in this true gospel of the water and the Spirit.

Do you know and believe in this original gospel? This is the very gospel that the Apostles had also believed. We, too, must therefore all believe in the gospel of the water and the Spirit.

The Gospel of Matthew (I), (II), (III), (IV), (V), (VI)

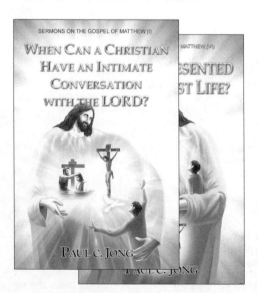

There are countless new Christians throughout the world, who have just been born again by believing in the gospel of the water and the Spirit that we have been spreading. We are indeed yearning to feed on the bread of life to them. But it is difficult for them to have fellowship with us in the true gospel, for they are all far away from us.

Therefore, to meet the spiritual needs of these people of Jesus Christ, the King of kings, The author proclaims that those who have received the remission of their sins by believing in the Word of Jesus Christ, must feed on His pure Word in order to defend their faith and sustain their spiritual lives. The sermons in these books have been prepared as new bread of life that will nourish the born-again to edify their spiritual growth.

Through His Church and servants, God will continue to provide you with this bread of life. May God's blessings be on all those who have been born again of water and the Spirit, who desires to have true spiritual fellowship with us in Jesus Christ.

The First Epistle of John (I) & (II)

He who believes that Jesus, who is God and the Savior, came by the gospel of the water and the Spirit to deliver all sinners from their sins, is saved from all his sins, and becomes a child of God the Father.

The First Epistle of John states that Jesus, who is God, came to us by the gospel of the water and the Spirit, and that He is the Son of God the Father. The Book, in other words, mostly emphasizes that Jesus is God (1 John 5:20), and concretely testifies the gospel of the water and the Spirit in chapter 5.

We must not hesitate to believe that Jesus Christ is God and to follow Him.

Sermons on Galatians: From Physical Circumcision to the Doctrine of Repentance (I) & (II)

Today's Christianity has turned into merely a world religion. Most Christians nowadays live in a situation of being sinners because they haven't been born again by spiritual faith. It is because they have only relied on Christian doctrines without being aware of the gospel of the water and the Spirit until now.

Therefore, now is the time for you to know the spiritual fallacies of the circumcisionists and keep distance from such faith. You have to know the contradictoriness of the prayers of repentance. Now is the time for you to stand firmer than ever on the gospel of the water and the Spirit.

If you haven't believed in this true gospel so far, you have to believe in our Savior who came to us by the gospel of the water and the Spirit even now. Now, you have to be complete Christians with the faith of believing in the gospel Truth of the water and the Spirit.

The Love of God Revealed through Jesus, The Only Begotten Son (I), (II), (III)

It is written, "No one has seen God at any time. The only begotten Son, who is in the bosom of the Father, He has declared Him" (John 1:18).

How perfectly did Jesus reveal the love of God to us! How perfectly did Jesus deliver us! What perfect Truth of salvation is the gospel of the water and the Spirit! We have never regretted receiving our salvation through our faith in Jesus, who came by water and blood (1 John 5:6).

Now, we have become His sinless people. Whoever believes in the gospel of the water and the Spirit can receive the eternal remission of sins and earn eternal life.

Eat My Flesh And Drink My Blood

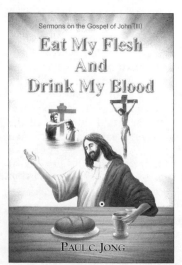

Until now, most Christians have not known the Truth, but only inherited religious acts. From the gospel to Holy Communion, today's Christianity maintains its orthodoxy not through the knowledge of the Truth, but by emphasizing only formal procedures and consecrated rites.

As a result, when today's Christians come across the bread and wine that signify the flesh and blood of Jesus during Communion, they are thankful only for the sacrifice of His blood, and they can't help but remain completely ignorant of the fact that Christ took upon Himself all their sins once and for all by being baptized by John the Baptist.

Therefore, I admonish all Christians throughout the whole world to learn, even from now on, what the flesh and blood of Jesus mean within the gospel of the water and the Spirit, to believe in it, and to thereby receive their salvation and also partake in Holy Communion with the right faith.

The Relationship Between the Ministry of JESUS and That of JOHN the BAPTIST Recorded in the Four Gospels

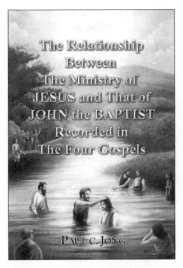

Do you perhaps think that it doesn't matter whether there needs to be the ministry of John the Baptist or not? You must believe according to the written Word of God. We must understand and believe in the ministry of John the Baptist within the frame of the ministry of Jesus Christ. John the Baptist in the New Testament was the prophet Elijah promised to be sent down to this earth according to the Book of Malachi chapter 4, verses 4-5. As the prophet Elijah to come, John the Baptist was born six months before Jesus, and he was the one who had pass on the sins of this world at once by giving Jesus the baptism at the Jordan River at the age of thirty. Thus, we must become the recipients of God's blessing by knowing the ministry of John the Baptist and accepting the ministry of Jesus Christ.

THE WILL OF THE HOLY TRINITY FOR HUMAN BEINGS

Through the Book of Genesis, God wants us to realize His good intentions toward us. Where is God's will for us revealed? It is revealed in the gospel Truth of the water and the Spirit that God accomplished through Jesus Christ. We must come into this good intention of God by faith, manifested in the gospel of the water and the Spirit. To do so, when we consider God's Word, we need to cast aside our existing carnal thoughts we have had, and believe in God's Word exactly as it is. All of us must throw away our mistaken knowledge accumulated until now, and open our spiritual eyes by placing our faith in the righteousness of God.

The Fall of Man and the Perfect Salvation of God

In the Book of Genesis, the purpose for which God created us is contained. When architects design a building or artists draw a painting, they first conceive the work that would be completed in their minds before they actually begin working on their project. Just like this, our God also had our salvation of mankind in His mind even before He created the heavens and the earth, and He made Adam and Eve with this purpose in mind. And God needed to explain to us the domain of Heaven, which is not seen by our eyes of the flesh, by drawing an analogy to the domain of the earth that we can all see and understand.

Even before the foundation of the world, God wanted to save mankind perfectly by giving the gospel of the water and the Spirit to everyone's heart. So although all human beings were made out of dust, they must learn and know the gospel Truth of the water and the Spirit to benefit their own souls. If people continue to live without knowing the dominion of Heaven, they will lose not only the things of the earth, but also everything that belongs to Heaven.

Heretics, Who Followed the Sins of Jeroboam (I) & (II)

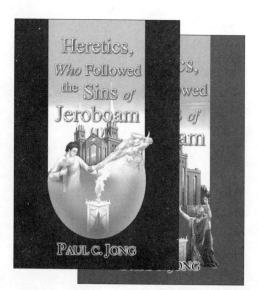

Christians today do not know what the gospel Truth of the water and the Spirit that the Lord has made and given us is. Thus, they continue to believe in the doctrines of Christianity and not the gospel of the water and the Spirit. For that reason, the fact of the matter is that despite their claim of having faith in Jesus, they continue to believe in and follow golden calves.

We must discern those that worship golden calves as God within Christianity. And by coming back before God of the Truth, we must offer the sacrifices of righteousness to God. The sacrifice that God receives with rejoice is the sacrifice of righteousness that people offer by faith after having received the remission of sin by having faith in the gospel of the water and the Spirit. Before God, you must seriously think about whether or not you are offering the sacrifice of God-given righteousness by the faith of believing in the gospel of the water and the Spirit.

The Lord's Prayer : Misinterpretations and Truth

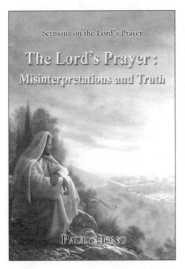

In order to interpret the Lord's Prayer correctly, we must first correctly understand the gospel of the water and the Spirit, which was spoken to us by the Lord. We have Truth in us when we not only know and understand the gospel of the water and the Spirit but also believe it with our hearts. The true gospel, which we believe in, has led us so far, so that we can lead truly faithful lives that the Lord wants from us in the Lord's Prayer.

Exegesis on the Book of ROMANS (I)

The righteousness of God is transparent. God's righteousness cannot be substituted by anything. That is because His righteousness is different from the righteousness of man. We need to know what God's righteousness is, and we need to believe in it.

God's righteousness is fundamentally different from human righteousness. The righteousness of mankind is like a filthy rag, but the righteousness of God is like a brilliant pearl shining forever. God's righteousness is the Truth that is absolutely needed by every sinner, transcending all ages.

HAVE YOU MET JESUS WITH THE GOSPEL OF THE WATER AND THE SPIRIT?

It is written, "No one has seen God at any time. The only begotten Son, who is in the bosom of the Father, He has declared Him" (John 1:18).

How perfectly did Jesus reveal the love of God to us! How perfectly did Jesus deliver us! What perfect Truth of salvation is the gospel of the water and the Spirit! We have never regretted receiving our salvation through our faith in Jesus, who came by water and blood (1 John 5:6).

Now, we have become His sinless people. Whoever believes in the gospel of the water and the Spirit can receive the eternal remission of sins and earn eternal life.

Sermons on the Gospel of Luke (I), (II), (III), (IV), (V), (VI), (VII)

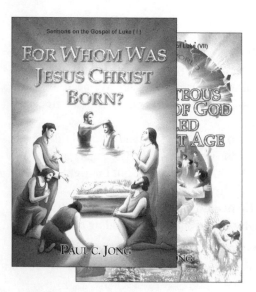

It is Jesus Christ who moves the entire history of this world. Our Lord came to this earth to save all humans from the sins of the world, and He has become the bread of new life for those of us who believe in the gospel of the water and the Spirit. In fact, it was to give this new life to us, who were all destined to hell for our sins that our Lord came looking for you and me.

No More Chaos, Void or Darkness Now (I) & (II)

Although we may be powerless and because the Word of God has power, when the Word falls to the ground it bears fruit without fail. Further, because the Word of God is alive we can see for ourselves that it is the same today and tomorrow, and forever unchanging. Unlike the words of man, God's Word never changes, for it is ever faithful. When God speaks, He fulfills exactly according to His Words.

For the Word of God has power, so when God said, "Let there be light," there was light, and when He said, "Let there be a greater light and a lesser light," it was fulfilled just as He had commanded.

THE DIFFERENCE BETWEEN ABEL'S FAITH AND CAIN'S FAITH

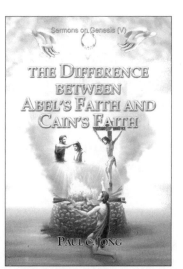

Whenever we stand before the presence of God to glorify Him, we should not approach Him through some religious rituals, but instead we have to approach Him by trusting in what He has done for us and thanking Him for His love. Only then does God accept our worship and pour the Holy Spirit on us abundantly.

FOR THE LOST SHEEP (I) & (II)

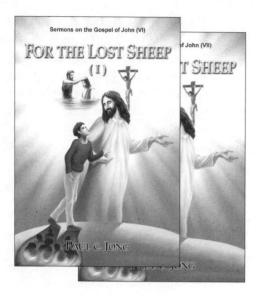

What God wants to do is to make us into His children by making us born again through the gospel of the water and the Spirit.

We humans are born as God's creations first, but if we receive the remission of sins by believing in the gospel of the water and the Spirit, we are born again as the children of God. This means that, after the Lord came and remitted all our sins, we who were blind could now obtain our sight.

WISDOM OF THE PRIMITIVE GOSPEL

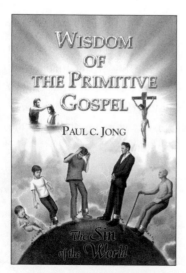

The primitive gospel is the Truth of salvation that's absolutely indispensable to everyone. Transcending all denominations, this primitive gospel will clearly teach every Christian how God's blessings could be bestowed on them. This true gospel will now fill your heart with God's overflowing love. And it will be the most precious gift to all your loved ones.

BE A GOSPEL WITNESS WHO SAVES
THE HUMAN RACE FROM DESTRUCTION

Mankind, who had eaten the fruit of the knowledge of good and evil, came to have the different standard for good and evil from God's. Then, which is correct, God's Word or our judgment? Our standard is always relative and selfish. Therefore we should cast away our own ideas and simply trust and follow God's Word focusing on "What does the Word of God say?" Ignoring God's Word and seeking self-righteousness is Cain's faith and religious belief. Abel put his faith in the Word of God he heard from his father, Adam, and offered the firstborn of his flock and of their fat. But self-conceited Cain brought an offering of the fruit of the ground to the Lord. God accepted Abel's offering but refused Cain's offering. It is God's lesson that faith in man-made religions cannot bring salvation.

THOSE WHO POSSESS ABRAHAM'S FAITH

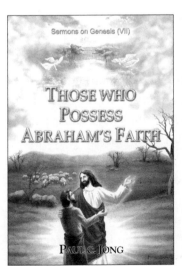

There are two kinds of righteousness in this world which are constantly in conflict and struggle with each another; these are the righteousness of God and the righteousness of man. Although God's righteousness faces many obstacles, it always prevails over the righteousness of man and leads us to the victorious way. That's because the Word of God is almighty. Because God's almighty power is with us, we are able to taste His blessings, for the Word of God has the power to reach our hearts, thoughts and souls, and brings all His blessings to us.

WHAT SHOULD WE STRIVE TO BELIEVE AND PREACH?

The Gospel of Mark testifies that Jesus Christ is the Son of God and God Himself. And it also testifies that He is our Savior. So we can see the writer of the Gospel of Mark bearing witness of Jesus forcefully, testifying that He is the very God and our Savior. This is why I would like to bear witness of this Jesus Christ who is manifested in the Gospel of Mark as much as possible based on the gospel of the water and the Spirit. What is obvious is that the core Truth of Christianity is found in the gospel of the water and the Spirit. Jesus said to Nicodemus, "Most assuredly, I say to you, unless one is born of water and the Spirit, he cannot enter the kingdom of God" (John 3:5).

FROM THIS CORRUPTED WORLD TO HEAVEN ABOVE

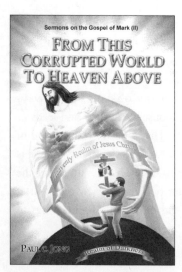

We must open our spiritual eyes and clearly see the wonders and beauty of this world. This is possible only when we escape from darkness through the Lord and live out our faith with the conviction that we have no sin. When you are born again through the gospel of the water and the Spirit and open your spiritual eyes, your life in this world will be more enjoyable than anyone else's life. So you must escape from darkness and dwell in the light, taking and enjoying everything the Lord has given you in your life, for the Word of God says, *"Let the hearts of those rejoice who seek the LORD!" (Psalm 105:3).*

THE BLESSING OF FAITH RECEIVED WITH THE HEART

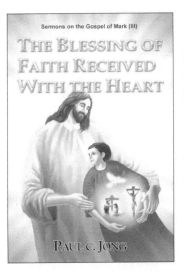

This special day of amnesty, when the remission of sins and the blessings of faith are received by believing in the gospel of the water and the Spirit with the heart, is found in no country in this world, but it is the greatest holiday that can be celebrated together with people from any country in the world. Today is the day you can receive the remission of sins, and it is the only common holiday celebrated together with God's people from all over the world.

The TABERNACLE (III): A Prefiguration of The Gospel of The Water and the Spirit

Every sinner must now believe in the genuine gospel. The God-given gospel of salvation is the gospel of the water and the Spirit that is manifested in the righteousness of God. The writer of the Book of Hebrews is trying to correct your misguided faith. Therefore, our faith needs to be deep rooted in the foundation of the gospel of the water and the Spirit. Those who are standing sure-footed on this absolute gospel Truth abide most certainly in the faith in the righteousness of Jesus Christ.

WHAT GOD IS SAYING TO US THROUGH
THE EPISTLE TO THE EPHESIANS

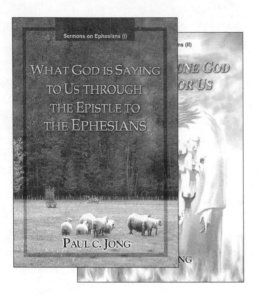

Today God has founded His Church on the faith of the believers in the gospel of the water and the Spirit. God's Church is the gathering of those who have been saved by believing in the gospel of the water and the Spirit. Therefore, if your hearts now have faith in the gospel of the water and the Spirit, you can then lead the true life of faith. Such a life of faith is possible only in God's Church. Furthermore, only such faith qualifies us to live forever in the Kingdom of the Lord. Through this faith we must receive the love of salvation and all the spiritual blessings of Heaven from God the Father, Jesus Christ and the Holy Spirit.

HOW CAN YOU STRENGTHEN YOUR FAITH?

Every sinner must now believe in the genuine gospel. The God-given gospel of salvation is the gospel of the water and the Spirit that is manifested in the righteousness of God. The writer of the Book of Hebrews is trying to correct your misguided faith. Therefore, our faith needs to be deep rooted in the foundation of the gospel of the water and the Spirit. Those who are standing sure-footed on this absolute gospel Truth abide most certainly in the faith in the righteousness of Jesus Christ.

SERMONS FOR THOSE WHO HAVE BECOME OUR COWORKERS

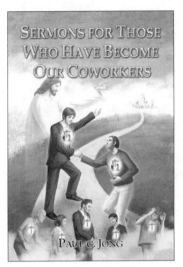

This book is a collection of sermons that have been written to direct our fellow coworkers and saints and to show them how to lead a life as a true servant of God. For this reason, this book is titled *"Sermons for Those Who Have Become Our Coworkers."*

The author earnestly desires to share fellowship with coworkers within the faith, those who believe wholeheartedly in the righteousness of Christ, excluding personal interests. He does really desire this because he has met them by faith in the Lord's righteousness and they are also preaching it now.

Paul C. Jong's Christian books have been translated into 65 major languages at this point: Afrikaans, Albanian, Arabic, Bengali, Bulgarian, Burmese, Cebuano, Chichewa, Chin, Chinese, Croatian, Czech, Danish, Dioula, Dutch, English, French, Georgian, German, Greek, Gujarati, Hebrew, Hindi, Hungarian, Indonesian, Iranian, Italian, Japanese, Javanese, Kannada, Khmer, Kirghiz, Kirundi, Latvian, Luganda, Luo, Madi, Malagasy, Malayalam, Marathi, Mindat, Mizo, Mongolian, Nepali, Polish, Portuguese, Romanian, Russian, Serbian, Shona, Slovak, Slovene, Spanish, Swahili, Swedish, Tagalog, Taiwanese, Tamil, Telugu, Thai, Turkish, Ukrainian, Urdu, Vietnamese, and Zou. They are also available now through our free e-book service.

E-book is digital book designed for you to feel a printed book on screen. You can read it easily on your PC monitor in your native language after downloading the viewer software and a text file. Feel free to visit our web site at http://www.nlmission.com or http://www.bjnewlife.org to download our e-books, and you will get the most remarkable Christian e-books absolutely for free.

And, would you like to take part in having our free Christian books known to more people worldwide? We would be very thankful if you link your website to ours so that many people get an opportunity to meet Jesus Christ through our inspired Christian books. Please visit our site at http://www.bjnewlife.org/english/about/take_banners.php to take our banners to your website. In addition, we would be also very thankful if you introduce our website to the webmasters around you for adding our link.

The New Life Mission
Contact: John Shin, General Secretary
E-mail: newlife@bjnewlife.org

The Official Website of The New Life Mission
www.nlmission.com *or*
www.bjnewlife.org

*W*orldwide websites of

The New Life Mission

Please find your vernacular websites below.
You can download Christian e-books and request Christian books for free.
Feel free to visit our websites below right now!

A
www.nlmafghanistan.com
www.nlmafrikaans.com
www.nlmalbania.com
www.nlmamharic.com
www.nlmangola.com
www.nlmarabemirates.com
www.nlmarabic.com
www.nlmargentina.com
www.nlmarmenia.com
www.nlmaruba.com
www.nlmaustralia.com
www.nlmaustria.com

B
www.nlmbahamas.com
www.nlmbahrain.com
www.nlmbangladesh.com
www.nlmbelarus.com
www.nlmbelgium.com
www.nlmbengali.com
www.nlmbenin.com
www.nlmbhutan.com
www.nlmbolivia.com
www.nlmbotswana.com
www.nlmbrasil.com
www.nlmbriton.com
www.nlmbrunei.com
www.nlmbulgalia.com
www.nlmburkinafaso.com
www.nlmburundi.com

C
www.nlmcameroon.com
www.nlmcanada.com
www.nlmcebuano.com
www.nlmchichewa.com
www.nlmchile.com
www.nlmchin.com

www.nlmchina.com
www.nlmcolombia.com
www.nlmcongo.com
www.nlmcostarica.com
www.nlmcotedivoire.com
www.nlmcroatia.com
www.nlmczech.com

D
www.nlmdenmark.com
www.nlmdioula.com
www.nlmdominica.com
www.nlmdutch.com

E
www.nlmecuador.com
www.nlmegypt.com
www.nlmelsalvador.com
www.nlmequatorialguinea.com
www.nlmethiopia.com

F
www.nlmfinland.com
www.nlmfrance.com
www.nlmfrench.com

G
www.nlmgabon.com
www.nlmgeorgian.com
www.nlmgerman.com
www.nlmgermany.com
www.nlmghana.com
www.nlmgreek.com
www.nlmgrenada.com
www.nlmguatemala.com
www.nlmgujarati.com

H
www.nlmhaiti.com
www.nlmhindi.com
www.nlmholland.com
www.nlmhonduras.com
www.nlmhungary.com

Turn over

© Some of these websites may not work because they are still under construction.

Worldwide websites of

 The New Life Mission

I
- www.nlm-india.com
- www.nlmindonesia.com
- www.nlmiran.com
- www.nlmiraq.com
- www.nlmisrael.com
- www.nlmitaly.com

J
- www.nlmjamaica.com
- www.nlmjapan.com
- www.nlmjavanese.com

K
- www.nlmkannada.com
- www.nlmkazakhstan.com
- www.nlmkenya.com
- www.nlmkhmer.com
- www.nlmkirghiz.com
- www.nlmkirundi.com
- www.nlmkorea.com

L
- www.nlmlatvia.com
- www.nlmluganda.com
- www.nlmluo.com

M
- www.nlmmadi.com
- www.nlmmalagasy.com
- www.nlmmalayalam.com
- www.nlmmalaysia.com
- www.nlmmarathi.com
- www.nlmmauritius.com
- www.nlmmexico.com
- www.nlmmindat.com
- www.nlmmizo.com
- www.nlmmoldova.com
- www.nlmmongolia.com
- www.nlmmyanmar.com

N
- www.nlmnepal.com
- www.nlmnewzealand.com
- www.nlmnigeria.com
- www.nlmnorthkorea.com
- www.nlmnorway.com

P
- www.nlmpakistan.com
- www.nlmpanama.com
- www.nlmperu.com
- www.nlmphilippines.com
- www.nlmpoland.com
- www.nlmportugal.com
- www.nlmportuguese.com
- www.nlmprcongo.com

Q
- www.nlmqatar.com

R
- www.nlmromania.com
- www.nlmrussia.com

S
- www.nlmsaudiarabia.com
- www.nlmserbian.com
- www.nlmshona.com
- www.nlmsingapore.com
- www.nlmslovakia.com
- www.nlmslovene.com
- www.nlmsolomon.com
- www.nlmsouthafrica.com
- www.nlmspain.com
- www.nlmspanish.com
- www.nlmsrilanka.com
- www.nlmsuriname.com
- www.nlmswahili.com
- www.nlmswaziland.com
- www.nlmsweden.com
- www.nlmswiss.com

T
- www.nlmtagalog.com
- www.nlmtaiwan.com
- www.nlmtamil.com
- www.nlmtanzania.com
- www.nlmtelugu.com
- www.nlmthailand.com
- www.nlmtogo.com
- www.nlmtonga.com
- www.nlmturkey.com

U
- www.nlmuganda.com
- www.nlmukraine.com
- www.nlmurdu.com
- www.nlmusa.com

V
- www.nlmvenezuela.com
- www.nlmvietnam.com

Z
- www.nlmzambia.com
- www.nlmzimbabwe.com
- www.nlmzou.com